Library of
Davidson College

Archaeology and the Religions of Canaan and Israel

ASOR Books Volume 7

Victor Matthews, editor

Billie Jean Collins
ASOR Director of Publications

ARCHAEOLOGY AND THE RELIGIONS
OF CANAAN AND ISRAEL

by

Beth Alpert Nakhai

American Schools of Oriental Research • Boston, MA

ARCHAEOLOGY AND THE RELIGIONS OF CANAAN AND ISRAEL

Copyright © 2001
The American Schools of Oriental Research

Cover illustration: Reconstruction of the contents of the 13th century sanctuary at Hazor. Photo courtesy of David Harris.

Library of Congress Cataloging-in-Publication Data

Nakhai, Beth Alpert, 1951-
 Archaeology and the religions of Canaan and Israel / by Beth Alpert Nakhai.
    p. cm. -- (ASOR books ; v. 7)
Includes bibliographical references and index.
  ISBN 0-89757-057-X
1. Palestine--Antiquities. 2. Temples--Palestine. 3. Excavations (Archaeology)--Palestine. 4. Sacrifice--Biblical teaching. 5. Bible. O.T.--Social scientific criticism. 6. Canaanites--Religion. 7. Bronze age--Palestine. I. Title. II. Series.
  DS111.7 .N35 2001
  933--dc21

Printed in the United States of America
on acid-free paper. ∞

Dedicated to Farzad and Mandana, with much love

CONTENTS

List of Maps	viii
Abbreviations	ix
Preface	x
Introduction	1
1 *Survey of Previous Scholarship*	5
2 *The Contribution of Social Sciences to the Study of Religion*	19
3 *The Textual Evidence*	39
4 *The Middle Bronze Age*	81
5 *The Late Bronze Age*	119
6 *Israelite Sacred Places of the Iron Age*	161
7 *Conclusions*	201
References	205
Index	253

LIST OF MAPS

Fig. 1 Map showing the location of Middle Bronze Age sites   85

Fig. 2 Detailed map showing the location of MBA sites   86

Fig. 3 Map showing the location of Late Bronze Age sites   120

Fig. 4 Map showing the location of Iron Age sites   169

ABBREVIATIONS

Dtn	Deut 12–26
DH	Deuteronomistic Historians (Deut, Josh, Judg, 1–2 Sam, 1–2 Kgs)
KK	1 Kgs 5:22–2 Kgs 25
J	Yahwist
E	Elohist
P	Priestly
D	Deuteronomistic
SSK 4	1 Sam, 2 Sam, 1 Kgs 1–4

PREFACE

Seven years have elapsed since this work was first accepted as a doctoral dissertation at the University of Arizona. Whether the number seven is as significant in modern times as it was in antiquity remains to be seen! That said, these seven years have been important ones for archaeologists and biblical scholars. Excavation in Israel and Jordan is taking place at a phenomenal pace. Had I ever imagined the work involved in updating my discussion of sites to accommodate the many new discoveries at well-known sites—and in adding newly discovered sanctuaries and shrines to an already extensive list—I would have struggled harder to meet my editor's initial publication deadline!

During these seven years, two critically important controversies have gripped our field, and the resolution of each will have important implications for our understanding of the Iron Age. "Revisionism" posits a date exilic or later for much of the biblical narrative, while the "Lower Chronology" moves much of what has been understood as United Monarchy into the Divided Monarchy. Since neither issue was pressing at the time I wrote my original text, I have given them scant attention here.

These seven years have been important for yet another reason, and that is the proliferation of critical new scholarly works. They include, but are not limited to, *The Anchor Bible Dictionary* (Freedman, ed. 1992); *The New Encyclopedia of Archaeological Excavation in the Holy Land* (Stern, ed. 1993); *A History of Israelite Religion in the Old Testament Period, Volume I: From the Beginnings to the End of the Monarchy* (Albertz 1994); *The Archaeology of Society in the Holy Land* (Levy, ed. 1995); *Civilizations of the Ancient Near East* (Sasson, ed. 1995); *Community, Identity, and Ideology: Social Sciences Approaches to the Hebrew Bible* (Carter and Meyers, eds. 1996); *The Oxford Encyclopedia of Archaeology in the Near East* (Meyers, ed. 1997); and *Gods, Goddesses, and Images of God in Ancient Israel* (Keel and Uehlinger 1998). I only regret that I was unable to more fully absorb each of their significant contributions.

There are many people whose help has been invaluable to me over the years. First, I would like to thank my one-time dissertation advisor, now a colleague and always a friend, William G. Dever. J. Edward Wright, Chair of the Committee on Judaic Studies, deserves special thanks for his support, encouragement and friendship.

Other faculty, not all still at the University of Arizona, have been most helpful, some while I was writing my dissertation and some in subsequent years. In particular, I would like to thank Albert Leonard, Jr., Shoshana Green, Leonard Dinnerstein, Susan Ackerman, Peter Machinist and Norman Yoffee.

Ruth Dickstein and her colleagues at the University of Arizona Library made it possible for me to complete my research in while in Tucson. Gary L. Christopherson, Director of the Center for Applied Spatial Analysis, and Marcy H. Rockman, Research Associate, created the four maps that appear in this book. Jeanne Davenport, Administrative Associate for the Committee on Judaic Studies transformed my typed manuscript into camera-ready copy. Without her skillful work, this volume would never have seen the light of day, and I am most grateful to her!

Others outside Tucson have provided me with much support and inspiration. My teachers at Harvard Divinity School helped broaden my horizons in many invaluable ways. Victor H. Matthews, ASOR Book Series Editor, and Albert Leonard, Jr., Chair, ASOR Committee on Publications, have guided this work to completion and I extend them my heartfelt gratitude. Thanks, too, to Billie Jean Collins, ASOR Director of Publications.

A number of archaeologists in Israel have encouraged me over the years. Many thanks are due to Seymour Gitin, Director of the W. F. Albright Institute of Archaeological Research in Jerusalem, who has shared with me much sage advice. I also want to thank Dr. Avraham Biran, Director of the Nelson Glueck School of Bibical Archaeology of the Hebrew Union College-Jewish Institute of Religion and Dalia Pakman, its curator. My thanks go as well to the staffs of the Albright Institute and Hebrew Union College, who always provide me with friendly homes in Jerusalem.

The encouragement and good humor of many dear friends made this endeavor possible and even pleasurable. I am thinking particularly of J. P. Dessel, Jennie R. Ebeling, Margaret O. Wilder, Susan M. Brooks and, last but never least, Norma Dever. Thanks all!

My debt to my family cannot be adequately expressed. Without the loving support of my parents, Esther Racoosin Alpert and Seymour Alpert, and my sisters Amy R. Alpert and Abbe F. Alpert, this project would never have come to fruition. The inspiration of my beloved grandmother, Rea Cohen Racoosin, is always with me. Two especially wonderful people, my husband Farzad and our daughter Mandana Lily, have lived with this effort daily. This book is dedicated to them, with much love.

Dissertation research was funded in part by the Dorot Foundation, the Memorial Foundation for Jewish Culture and the University of Arizona. The preparation of this volume was made possible by an American Association of University Women Educational Foundation Short-term Research Publication Grant. Early versions of Chapters 4, 5 and 6 were presented at the Annual Meetings of the American Schools of Oriental Research in 1990–1992. Travel to these conferences was funded in part by The University of Arizona's Committee on Judaic Studies, Department of Near Eastern Studies, Center for Middle Eastern Studies and Association of Women Faculty.

I am grateful to all for their advice and encouragement. Any errors are, of course, mine alone.

October 2000
Tucson, Arizona

INTRODUCTION

The religion of ancient Israel has fascinated participants and observers alike since the days when King David ruled in Jerusalem. Documentation of Israelite customs and beliefs may have begun as early as the tenth century B.C.E., soon after those groups that would become Israel first joined together to form a nation. The continuing—if somewhat disjointed—effort to record aspects of their social, political and religious history eventually resulted in a long and complicated document known variously as the Tanakh, Hebrew Bible or Old Testament. The chronological focus of this great work was the First Temple period, although some pieces may predate the Temple's construction and others derive from Second Temple times. Intertestamental literature, including the books of the Apocrypha and Pseudepigrapha and the Dead Sea Scrolls, relates to religious practices of the Jewish community during the Second Temple period, when Judah was under Persian, Greek and finally Roman rule. The New Testament is a useful source of information on early Judaism, and ancient historians such as Herodotus and Josephus have presented their own unique perspectives on the religion of Israel.

Many of these early texts themselves became the source for nearly two millennia of commentary by Jewish, Catholic and, eventually, Protestant theologians and scholars. At the same time, interest in the land of Palestine as the locus of the Bible cyclically waxed and waned. Byzantines under Constantine explored Christian and Jewish holy places and so did Europeans during the Crusades. Napoleon's explorations in Egypt triggered a renewed fascination with the antiquities of the biblical world and since then the amount of interest has increased exponentially. So, too, has interest in Israel's Near Eastern ancestors, the Canaanites and others.

In the nineteenth century, new fields such as sociology, anthropology and comparative religious studies, as well as new approaches to the study of the Bible, began to enrich our understanding of the religions of Canaan and Israel. At the same time, a growing interest in exploring Palestine—the land, its antiquities and its inhabitants, its ancient sites and modern villages—led to the development of the modern field of "biblical archaeology" (Dever 1985b; 1993a; and references therein).

For the most part, the impetus for these many explorations of ancient Israel was rooted in the religious convictions of modern explorers. Their motivation for investigating the religion of Israel's Canaanite ancestors was often their own deeply held religious beliefs. One consequence of this theological orientation has been that, despite advances in the field of archaeology, texts have traditionally provided the primary point of reference for studies of Canaanite and Israelite religions.

This book seeks to demonstrate that archaeological data provides a strong and independent witness to the religious practices of Canaanites and Israelites in the second to mid-first millennia B.C.E. Scholars have conventionally used archaeology to support—or in some cases to disprove—biblical narrative. However, as is shown here, the archaeological world, unbiased by the theological stance of its one-time inhabitants, provides independent data critical for reconstructing ancient religious practice and even belief.

Perhaps more significantly, these data stimulate discussions of the integral part played by religion in the social and political worlds of Canaan and Israel, discussions critical to a full understanding of the world of Canaanite and Israelite religion. Those of us raised with a constitutional commitment to the separation of church and state must remember that this modern societal construction bears no resemblance to ancient society. In antiquity, religion, economics and politics were all deeply embedded within the structure of society.

This book presents its critical evidence in seven chapters. Chapter One offers a history of scholarship in the field of Canaanite and Israelite religion. Advances in the study of ancient religion and society have been made particularly by those who have thought of religion as an element of society at-large, rather than as an isolated set of ritual behaviors. The chapter demonstrates that inadequate attention has been given to archaeological data, despite the importance of these data to the study of religion. In addition, it shows that archaeologists most commonly use material culture evidence from religious structures and installations to reconstruct ritual behaviors rather than to investigate socio-political relationships. Finally, it suggests the potential of studies that rely upon archaeological data and also incorporate the witness of contemporary texts.

Chapter Two discusses the contribution made by anthropological studies to understanding the role of religion in society. Since the nineteenth century, anthropologists have suggested that, together with their spiritual dimensions, religions in ancient societies had social and political dimensions. For example, sacrifice (known to have been the religious rite *par excellence* of Canaanites and Israelites) should be thought of as more than a set of arcane rituals. It reflected various dimensions of the socio-political structure of the worshipping community. For example, the sharing of sacral meals provided a multipurpose forum for the convening of kin or other social groups. One of the most stimulating contributions made by anthropologists has been their ethnographic studies of worshipping communities. Chapter Two discusses some of these studies and looks at archaeological analyses that have drawn upon the contributions made by ethnographic and other anthropological studies.

Chapter Three looks at the ritual texts from Ugarit and at pre-exilic portions of the Hebrew Bible. Like Chapter Two, this chapter focuses upon the ritual of sacrifice and demonstrates its central role in the religions of Canaan and Israel. Examination of the ritual texts from Ugarit demonstrates that overall, sacrifice was the primary ritual in Canaanite religion. In addition, the royal sharing of sacral meals is well documented. In consequence, sacrifice becomes particularly relevant for understanding the functioning of social and political elements in Canaanite society.

Turning to Israel, the study assesses the witness of various biblical authors including the Yahwist and the Elohist, ninth century prophets, Deuteronomistic Historians and Priestly writers. It documents the increased tendency toward control over sacrifice and other religious practices and suggests that the *bāmôt* (במות), excoriated by biblical writers, were in fact a centralizing institution for Israelite and Judaean monarchs. Control over religious practice was essential as royalty attempted to manage divergent clan and priestly groups.

In Chapter Four, the book turns to the evidence presented by archaeological data. Each of the next three chapters investigates the remains of sacred structures and installations, and of cultic paraphernalia. Emphasis is placed upon sites with representative or particularly significant architectural or artifactual assemblages. Chapter Four is concerned with the religion of Canaan in the Middle Bronze Age. It demonstrates that the development of religion in the first half of the second millennium was related to the slow growth of elite clan groups. For most of the MB II, religion was not a function of urban society. Rather, the locus of public worship was more often the rural cult center. By the MB IIC, however, the stimulus provided by the growing wealth and authority of religious professionals triggered the development of a new urban elite.

Chapter Five presents archaeological data for religion in the Late Bronze Age. As Canaan recovered from the devastating battles of the mid-second millennium, regional pilgrimage sanctuaries were set up in a number of locations. In the large cities, religion continued to reflect clan structure and political relationships. Over time, Egyptian control over the region increased and so did the number of Egypto-Canaanite temples designed to serve Egyptian imperial needs. Ultimately, Egypt exploited Canaanite ritual processes—and in particular the ritual of sacrifice—at the expense of the indigenous Canaanite population.

Chapter Six examines Israelite sacred sites from the beginning of the Iron Age until the destruction of the First Temple. The discussion focuses on the way in which the monarchs of Israel and Judah organized religion in support of the state, in particular through the increasing institutionalization of the regional *bāmôt*. At the same time, the efforts of some clan and priestly groups to resist these centralizing efforts are seen in alternate places of worship. These were constructed in semi-public town sanctuaries, or in workshop and domestic shrines. In all these locations, sacrifice of goods remained the primary religious ritual.

The concluding chapter stresses the continuing importance of attention given to the details of religious practice as seen through an examination of the archaeological record, and also to the integration of textual, anthropological and archaeological studies. It demonstrates that in Canaan and Israel, elite groups (clan groups and priestly guilds) accumulated status and wealth through their control over religion, as they benefited from the steady stream of offerings left for the gods. Over time, they (and sometimes outsiders) learned how to manipulate religion to serve multiple non-spiritual goals. Ultimately, the battle over political control in Israel would be couched in religious terms. The HB and the variety of sacred places in the Iron Age both attest to the reality of this struggle.

CHAPTER ONE
SURVEY OF PREVIOUS SCHOLARSHIP

In the past, discussions of Canaanite and Israelite religion have generally focussed on the theology and cult of the worshipping community, while devoting little attention to religion's socio-political components. One reason for this is the paucity of non-theological documents related to Canaan and Israel compared with those that come from surrounding lands. In those other regions, royal and temple archives filled with economic texts, correspondence, ritual incantations, legal documents and more are, by comparison, commonplace. Therefore, the economic, social and political elements of their societies are better known.

The Hebrew Bible, is, of course, the principle source for the study of Israelite faith, while the tablets from Ugarit provide a similar, although smaller, corpus of information about Canaanite beliefs. They, together with limited inscriptional material, provide much that is not accessible through anepigraphic sources. However, a brief review of previous scholarship demonstrates the pressing need for a reexamination of archaeology's ability to illuminate the ways in which religion functioned in Canaanite and Israelite society.[1]

A DEFINITION OF CANAANITE

First, however, the question of the relationship among the cultures of the Levant must be addressed. Particularly relevant are an understanding of the terms "Canaan" and "Canaanite" and an assessment of their application to the regions and peoples of Bronze Age Western Asia. That different scholars have used these terms in different ways has created confusion. Therefore it is important to delineate the boundaries of ancient Canaan and to clarify the definition of those people called Canaanite. The relationship between Israelite religion and the earlier religion(s) of Canaan must also be explored.

The problem in part is one of geography, exacerbated by the long history of political and religious conflicts within Western Asia. In consequence, a myriad of terms has been used to describe the region under study. Recently Ben-Tor commented upon the absence of scholarly consensus regarding the vocabulary of regional geography. He listed commonly used terms (including Israel, Land of Israel, Syria, Palestine, Syria-Palestine, Jordan, Lebanon, Transjordan, Holy Land, Canaan and southern Levant), suggested that chronological problems affect their overall applicability, and was able to offer no solution to this quandary (1992: 2–3).

The boundaries of ancient Canaan must be delineated, for in modern times the term Canaan has been used imprecisely. Inasmuch as Canaanites lived within well-defined regional territories or city-states with political and economic ties that drew them variously toward Syria, Mesopotamia or Egypt, geographic and cultural boundaries can be established. Overall, the territory of Canaan has been described as "the Levant's southern part, comprising Palestine, Lebanon, and southern Syria" (A. Mazar 1990a: 3) or "western Palestine (the area west of the Jordan River), whose northern boundary fluctuated between southern and central Lebanon" (Pitard 1998: 40). More specifically, "Canaan's boundaries began in the south at Wadi al-'Arish and reached north to the Lebanon and the Anti-Lebanon Mountain ranges. The western border was, of course, the Mediterranean, and the eastern was Transjordan (mostly the Bashan) and the Jordan River and Dead Sea farther south" (Hackett 1997a: 409).

Hackett's definition is derived from the parameters of usage in second millennium Egypt and Western Asia. It matches the area delineated in the eighteenth century Execration Texts from Saqarra; significantly, the first written reference to Canaan or Canaanite was found in a contemporary text from Mari. The term did not appear again until the late fifteenth century booty list of the Egyptian pharaoh Amenophis II. In later centuries, it appeared several times in the Amarna letters and in a text from Alalakh. It was also found in two texts from *ca.* the year 1200 B.C.E., a list of merchants discovered at Ugarit and the Egyptian Merneptah Stele (1997a: 408–9). Rainey (1996a) and Na'aman (1999), studying these and other documents, identified Canaan with the western Asiatic province administered by Egypt in the Late Bronze Age (Na'aman 1994a: 408; 1999: 36). They concluded (*contra* Lemche 1991) that Late Bronze Age peoples throughout the Near East were aware of an entity called Canaan, one with specific and well-known geographic boundaries (Rainey 1996a: fig. 1). "The phantom of the 'Great Canaan' should disappear from the scholarly literature" (Na'aman 1999: 36).

In the biblical imagination, Canaan was the Promised Land, its boundaries remembered in the Iron Age as indicated by Num 34:1–12 (and reiterated in Ezek 47:15–20, *inter alia*).[2] The northern border of Moses' Canaan, described in Num 34: 7–11, corresponded to the linguistic division between the northern (Akkadian) and southern (West Semitic) dialects of the Bronze Age (Rainey 1996a: 11–12). Additional passages further delineated the territory, which scribes also described by reference to the six, seven or ten pre-Israelite nations living within it. These included in somewhat varying combinations Hittites, Amorites, Canaanites, Perizzites, Hivites, Jebusites, Kenites, Kenizzites, Kadmonites, Rephaim and Girgashites (Gen 15:19–21; Ex 3:8; Deut 7:1; Josh 3:10; Josh 9:1–2; Judg 3:5, *inter alia*).[3] The different groupings can be understood by reference to three critical concepts: the land promised to Abraham, the land of Canaan to be taken by Israel and the land of Israel as known from the United Monarchy. The boundaries of the Promised Land were related to the territory that New Kingdom Egypt dominated in western Asia. That this Promised Land was greater than the land of Canaan reflects the fact that it included territory to be settled by Abraham's non-Israelite descendants as well. The repetitive delineation of territory in many biblical texts suggests its importance for Israelite historiography and for the Israelite scribal tradition (Kallai 1997).

The problem of defining Canaan is not limited to geographical issues; we must also grapple with the vocabulary of culture. In particular clarification of the ethnic marker "Canaanite" is important. Modern scholars often use Canaanite in a broad sense to describe the cultural continuum of third–second millennium peoples living in Syria-Palestine (western Syria, Lebanon, Jordan, Israel, and the Palestinian Entity), even though in antiquity this large area was never a single cultural or political unit (Pitard 1998: 40; Hackett 1997b: 411).

Modern scholars often identify Canaanites with the Amorites, originally semi-nomadic Semitic-speaking people who entered eastern Syria and northern Iraq in the late third and early second millennia (Knapp 1988: 130–31, 169). This "ethnolinguistic group" can most often be recognized in Middle Bronze Age texts when scribes affixed *MAR.TU* or *amurrû* to personal or tribal names, but sometimes these terms referred to westerners in general and not specifically to Amorites (Whiting 1995: 1231–32). Their move southwest through Syria and into Canaan sparked the cultural resurgence of its Canaanite MB II (Dever 1976b: 12; 1977: 84–87; see also Hackett 1997b: 409–10).[4] The Bible's claim for genealogical ties between Canaanites and Amorites (Gen 10:16) and its occasional identification of Amorites rather than Canaanites as the people who occupied the Promised Land (Gen 10:16; Judg 6:20) seem to support this claim of shared origins.

Texts demonstrate that the Canaanites were aware of their identity as Canaanites, and that peoples elsewhere in the ancient Near East shared this awareness (Hackett 1997b). Their self-identification indicates that they thought of themselves as separate from the people of Ugarit (Rainey 1996a: 5; 1996b: 71), creating challenges for those who use Ugaritic texts to discuss Canaanite religion. Even so, Ugaritic texts almost always provide the essential datum for describing Canaanite religion because, "while the Ugaritians distinguished themselves from Canaanites, Ugaritic religious literature has enough links with later biblical literature to place Ugarit on a cultural continuum with Canaan. The copious amounts of material from Ugarit may, then, suggest what LB Canaanite religion was like" (Hackett 1997b: 413; see also Schaeffer 1939: 57–60; Coogan 1978: 9–10; Day 1992: 831–32).[5]

Several issues thus require resolution. One is geographic: Canaan will be used to refer to the Bronze Age territory extending from central Lebanon to Israel's desert region, and from the Jordan Valley to the Mediterranean. Another is ethnic: Canaanite will be used to refer to those city-state residents who identified themselves with the appellation Canaanite. However, "citizenship" in the Bronze Age was claimed not only by reference to urban conglomerates but also to tribal or clan affiliation, and so Canaanite might not have been a meaningful term of self-identity for all people. The last is cultural: inasmuch as the residents of the city-states of Syria, including Ebla, Mari, Alalakh and Ugarit, shared elements of religion, architecture, language and material culture with those of Canaan, the term Syro-Canaanite will be used to describe this rather broad cultural continuum.[6]

A REVIEW OF PREVIOUS SCHOLARSHIP

To understand the importance of a study of Canaanite and Israelite religions that focuses upon their socio-political dimensions, it is necessary to review previous scholarly approaches. A brief survey of the literature demonstrates the critical need for a study that utilizes archaeological data as its basic resource, and that considers the place of religion in the social, political and economic world of ancient Canaan and Israel.

In the past, much archaeological work was motivated by an interest in biblical religion, and it viewed Israelite religion as a precursor for Christian faith.[7] While there have always been secularists within the scholarly community, the overall preoccupation has been with the theological components of pre-Christian religions.[8]

In general, questions about the archaeological corpus from the Bronze and Iron Ages have been limited to biblical issues. They have included establishing the historicity of the patriarchs as it might be known from studying the Middle Bronze Age, the exodus from Egypt and the desert wanderings as they might be known from studying Late Bronze Age sites in the Sinai and Negev Deserts and in Transjordan, the conquest of Canaan as it might be known from studying the destruction of Late Bronze Age Canaanite cities, the emergence of Israel through the study of purportedly Israelite settlements in the Iron Age I and the nature of the Israelite monarchy through the study of biblically identified Iron Age II sites.

Traditionally, studies of Canaanite and Israelite religions have been dictated by the biblical texts and they have commonly explored the relationship between them, the degree to which the latter developed out of the former, the point at which monotheism became a part of Israelite religion, and the prevalence of so-called syncretistic tendencies among the Israelite population. Conclusions were commonly based on textual evidence, sporadically supplemented by artifactual data. Scholarly biases are often apparent.[9] One result of this focus on biblical elements has been the perception of archaeology as a means of retrieving written documents while architectural and artifactual data have often been neglected. These factors, combined with the ever-growing body of archaeological data, make this study of Canaanite and Israelite religions and their place within society both timely and critical.

Scholarly approaches to the use of archaeology for the study of ancient Canaanite and Israelite religions were established in the late nineteenth and early twentieth centuries. Despite significant advances in the field of archaeology, the conventions established during this era shaped scholarship for much of the twentieth century.

A number of early scholars noted the potential of archaeology for illuminating the culture of the ancient Israelites (Kittel 1895; 1896; Driver 1909; Cook 1908; 1930). Particularly significant are ideas developed by subsequent researchers, including the description of the early roots of Israelite religion as grounded in Canaanite thought, the distinction between the popular and the so-called higher religion of the Israelite people and the increased awareness of Israelite culture as grounded in the cultures of surrounding peoples.

In this period, Handcock proffered the claim that archaeology did not alter the picture drawn by the Bible (1916). The assertion that archaeology only confirmed the validity of biblical texts, but was otherwise not helpful for studying ancient Israel was often repeated. Increasingly, scholars paid lip service to the value of archaeology while ignoring the contribution of its physical evidence.

Additional obstacles to the full utilization of archaeological data included the difficulty in accessing inadequately processed and reported excavation materials (Robinson 1932: vii) and the negative evaluation of these materials by some excavators.[10] In the light of such obstacles, it is not surprising that most scholars turned their attention to texts.

An important model that shaped the study of Canaanite and Israelite religions came from the developing field of comparative religious studies. Frazer used ethnographic studies of extant religions in his examination of ancient religious texts and employed an evolutionary model in which societies progressed from savagery to a high plane of moral and religious development. Over time, societies went through three phases, magic, religion and science, the last of which was considered superior (1919; 1925).

The growing importance of comparative religious studies and of studies in cultural patterning laid the groundwork for the "myth-and-ritual" approach to Near Eastern religions. Myths and rituals were understood to have been part of a widespread pattern of ancient Near Eastern religious thought and behavior (Hooke, ed. 1933; Hooke 1938). Mesopotamian, Egyptian, Canaanite and biblical texts were all used to reconstruct ancient religious rituals. The focus was on liturgy, worship, cult and ritual rather than on dogma or belief (Mowinckel 1946; Mowinckel in Sheehan 1981). Biblical folklore was considered the residue of what Israel had inherited from its neighbors, while Israel's customs and superstitions were understood as reinterpretations of those customs and superstitions popular among the neighboring nations (Gaster 1950; 1969).

While significant for exploring Canaanite and Israelite religions within a larger Near Eastern context, this cross-cultural approach employed generalization at the cost of specificity. With setting ignored, accuracy was undermined. The focus on text precluded an understanding of context. Questions relating to cultural specifics were not explored.

In *Elementary Forms of Religious Life*, Durkheim described religion as a social fact, a collective group experience. It was therefore not something determined by individual choice (1915). The sociologists' study of religion through the examination of the social group often utilized a linear, evolutionary approach, one that depicted the development of religion from a prelogical, primitive mentality to one more evolved, ethical, rational and individualistic (Causse in Kimbrough 1978).

While many scholars in the first part of the twentieth century did not seriously use archaeological data to study ancient Israelite religion, Graham and May (the latter a director of the Megiddo excavations) took a different approach. In *Culture and Conscience: An Archaeological Study of the New Religious Past in Ancient Palestine*, they sought to demonstrate that a careful study of material remains not only provided information concerning religious activities and rituals but also revealed insights into the spiritual dimensions of religion (1936). They examined religions from the Paleolithic through the Iron Age by reference to archaeological data and although restricted by their evolutionary approach, their utilization of archaeology to study ancient religions provided a scholarly balance and foreshadowed future developments.

Working similarly, Pritchard classified the known corpus of ceramic female figurines and used information from the Bible and other ancient texts to identify them by name (1943). In his opinion, archaeology provided "a vantage point that is completely independent of the written text for viewing the events and the cultic practices described in the many-stranded and often-revised tradition preserved finally in the biblical text" (1965: 323).

In the United States, the giant in archaeology and biblical studies for nearly half a century was W. F. Albright. In *From the Stone Age to Christianity: Monotheism and the Historical Process* (1940), Albright laid the foundations for much of his later work. This book described the evolutionary growth of man's idea of God. In it, paganism was part of the divine preparation for Christianity. While acknowledging that information about Canaanite religion was important for understanding that of Israel, Albright insisted that the earliest roots of Israelite religion were not West Semitic and, most importantly, that there was a decisive break between the Canaanite Late Bronze Age and the Israelite Iron Age I.

In later works, Albright reiterated his belief in the New Testament as fulfillment of the Old. It is therefore not surprising that his analysis placed biblical theology at a great distance from its putative pagan or "prelogical" roots. In addition, he further developed the theme that archaeology proves the historicity of the Bible (1942; 1954; 1960; 1963; 1968).

Albright's reliance on texts to the virtual exclusion of other material culture remains is surprising, because he had engaged in field research in Palestine since his arrival there late in 1919. Indeed, his excavation at Tell Beit Mirsim in the 1930's was a landmark project and his site report noteworthy for its inclusion of an innovative ceramic study (1943).

Albright's influence over his students and over the scholars with whom he had contact at the American School of Oriental Research in Jerusalem and elsewhere, was enormous. While European scholarship remained concerned with theoretical issues, in the United States excavation materials, when considered, were often used as proof of biblical accuracy. While scholars differed over the degree to which Israelite religion was indebted to that of the Canaanites, they generally accepted an evolutionary perspective. In this view, Canaanites had been engaged in primitive and pagan rites but, by the time of the prophets, Israelite religion had evolved into a morally and ethically superior faith. Thus, New Testament Christianity was shielded from the contaminants of a pagan past (Burrows 1941; McCown 1943).[11] Biblical scholars drawn from the ranks of the Protestant ministry increasingly dominated archaeology in the United States, a fact that contributed to the growth of this critical approach (Dever 1974).

G. E. Wright took issue with Albright's contention that archaeology functioned to prove the correctness of the biblical texts. He maintained instead that it provided the background for biblical studies (1960). "Archaeology in the biblical world covers virtually every ancient period. While in my judgment it is not an independent discipline, it is nevertheless a primary research arm of the historian of human culture and of human events" (1971: 167). Like those of Albright, Wright's analyses relied primarily on textual data.[12]

European archaeologists challenged the popular notion that Palestinian archaeology should be considered a branch of biblical studies. In Great Britain, Wheeler's insistence on scientific field work and analysis led him to describe Palestine as "that land of archaeological sin," the place "where more sins have probably been committed in the name of archaeology than on any commensurate portion of the earth's surface" (1954: 16, 84).

Dutch archaeologists Franken and Franken-Battershill suggested that archaeology in Palestine be considered a complementary and independent discipline and challenged archaeologists to accept the standards of the social sciences in their fieldwork and analysis. Echoing Graham and May's earlier work on religion and cult, they suggested that "though of necessity excavators deal with material rather than spiritual evidence, there is no reason why a minutely detailed study of certain material remains should not yield evidence of certain spiritual traits, practices or taboos" (1963: 143)

In the preface to *A Primer of Old Testament Archaeology*, K. Kenyon wrote,

> archaeology does not claim to be a discipline on its own. It is rather, today, a very highly specialised method of supplementing history in the very broadest sense. This widening of the term history concerns the periods for which there are none of the written records upon which history in the broadest sense depends, for which archaeology in effect writes the history; in a more exactly supplementary sense, archaeology provides a background for history in dealing with those periods for which some written records are available (1963: xv).

She reiterated the idea that "to the Bible the material remains revealed and interpreted by archaeology provide a background" (Kenyon 1978: 99; so too, Lapp 1969).

In *Ancient Israel: Its Life and Institutions*, the French archaeologist de Vaux wrote that "archaeology, in the strict sense, *i.e.*, the study of the material remains of the past, is only an auxiliary science, which helps us to reconstruct the actual setting in which the institutions functioned" (1961: viii; see also 1970). In this way, de Vaux emphasized

Israelite society and its various religious, political, legal and even familial institutions.

At the same time Americans, even those with archaeological field experience, continued to view archaeology as a sort of biblical corrective, confirming biblical narratives or enriching understanding of the biblical text (Glueck 1960; Freedman 1965; Callaway 1966). They had yet to view their subject as "Israel" and to see both Bible and archaeology as independent interpretive tools for investigating its culture, history and religion.

In Israel, the archaeological survey was becoming increasingly important (Aharoni 1957; 1970; Glueck 1960). Aharoni pioneered the regional archaeological survey as a tool for evaluating biblical narratives. He focussed on the problem of Israelite settlement in Canaan and he developed a research design that enabled him to collect archaeological data relevant to this particular question (1957; 1970). Overall, the questions in regional surveys and in contemporary excavation projects (see, e.g., Yadin 1958; 1972) remained biblical. Yeivin described a reciprocal relationship between the Bible and archaeology; each helped in interpreting the other (1966). His inclination was to assign secular functions to possibly sacred materials (1973), a corrective against those overly eager to find cultic explanations for virtually any object or building.

Several important works by anthropologists appeared at this time. In his article, "Religion as a Cultural System," Geertz suggested two stages for an anthropological analysis of religion (1969). The first required the analysis of systems of meanings as embodied in religious symbols while the second related these systems of meaning to social-structural and psychological processes. Archaeology has the potential to recover symbols, to advance from descriptive to systemic analysis and to correlate different types of systems and processes. The idea of using symbols to discover social structure was important, as was the idea of emphasizing process over stasis. Carefully constructed research designs (see Clarke 1968) can further these goals.

Beginning in the 1970s, Dever developed these ideas within the context of Syria-Palestine, stating that the goal of archaeology is to recover material culture, from which patterns of thought, belief and behavior can be reconstructed. Archaeological artifacts must be the primary sources for study; the Bible, secondary (1971; 1974).

In the same decade, a growing number of archaeologists used

architectural and artifactual data to study Canaanite and Israelite religions. Analyses centered on Canaanite religion (Negbi 1976; Herzog 1980; Tadmor 1982), on Bronze/Iron Age cultural continuity (Negbi 1976), and on the effect of external influences (or the lack thereof) on the formation and development of Israelite religion (Giveon 1978; Shiloh 1979; Tadmor 1982). Less frequent were discussions of Israelite cult (C. L. Meyers 1976) and of the relationship between the "official" Jerusalemite religion described in the Bible and the "folk" religion of other members of the Israelite population. Questions about theology and about socio-political aspects of religion were sometimes raised.

Site reports continued to include traditional descriptions of pottery, architecture, small finds and epigraphic materials. Now they also incorporated technical descriptions, comparative analyses and locational analyses, as well as data on ethnography, demography, settlement patterns, agriculture and faunal remains (Stern 1984; Finkelstein 1988).

Increasingly, explicit criteria were applied to archaeological studies of ancient religion. Renfrew developed a methodology for analyzing excavated materials from sacred sites and applied it to his excavation of the Late Bronze Age sanctuary at the Aegean site of Phylakopi (1985; and see chapter 4). Similarly, Dever demonstrated archaeology's potential for illuminating of the cult of ancient Israel (1983). Archaeologists could penetrate beyond literary traditions to retrieve information about Israelite religious practices by utilizing the methodology of the "New Archaeology"[13] and by emphasizing the independent, external value of artifactual data over and above the subjective witness of textual evidence. Analysis of this information increases the capacity for writing social and economic histories and thus for reconstructing the background for biblical accounts (Dever 1987a; 1991).

Holladay used archaeological data as the primary resource for his analysis of Israelite and Judaean religion. His discussion of these data assumed that religious activities are patterned and therefore apparent in the archaeological record. An " historically informed hypothetical model of religious organization in a typical Syro-Palestinian national state of the Iron II period" provided a conceptual framework for the many divergent facts (1987: 251). The collected data were evaluated in relationship to the proposed model.

D. N. Freedman wrote pessimistically about the potential for archaeology to contribute to biblical studies. He claimed that "the combination of the Bible and archaeology is somewhat artificial; the two have not really matched up very well" (1985: 6). Therefore, in his opinion, texts should provide the primary source of information about ancient religions (see also Haran 1978).

However, as will be demonstrated, an approach that integrates social science studies with archaeological and textual investigations can be most productive (see Meyers and Meyers 1989). Recent studies (including some mentioned above) have demonstrated the enormous potential that carefully controlled archaeological analysis and synthesis have for expanding our knowledge of religion in Canaan and Israel. That ancient religion was a reflection of politics, of economics and of social structure—and not just a matter of rituals and belief systems— makes recourse to archaeology all the more important.

SUMMARY

New questions designed to exploit the potential of archaeology must be raised. In the past, the agenda for studying ancient Near Eastern religions was set by reference to biblical texts. This approach was flawed because it denied the independent witness of material evidence and because it failed to acknowledge that this evidence was often much closer in time and in space to the peoples explored than are the generally late and purposefully biased texts which comprise the Hebrew Bible.

Most studies of ancient religion failed to incorporate the extremely diversified corpus of archaeological resources, although it contains information invaluable for reconstructing the religions of ancient Canaan and Israel. Inasmuch as the ancient texts represent only several of the many strands of religious behaviors and beliefs in Canaan and Israel, archaeology is indispensable for the study of Canaanite and Israelite religions from very important perspectives such as those of society, politics and economy.

NOTES

[1] Schiemann's comments are to the point:

> It is our contention that an archaeology based on rigorous recovery and recording procedures bears the greatest promise to provide new information related to an organismic view of the ancient West

Semitic religious life. Otherwise we seem to be stuck with a literary-dominated and therefore lopsided and static concept of this religious heritage, to which archaeology continues to add an example of this or that but essentially would not be missed if it were absent (1978: 136).

[2] In the HB, the earliest (although not the first) reference to Canaan is found in Judg 5: 19, in the description of Deborah and Barak's battle with the "kings of Canaan at Tanaach."
[3] The genealogy of Canaan, described in Gen 10:15–20, included additional groups among these descendants of Noah.
[4] At the same time, Canaanite culture of the Middle Bronze Age incorporated many indigenous and traditional elements, thus evincing continuity with its Early Bronze Age predecessor (Dever 1977: 82–84; A. Mazar 1990a: 104–5).
[5] Rainey cautioned that " Ugaritic tradition, Phoenician tradition and Israelite tradition, though sharing a common world of imagery, are not the same" (1996b: 71).
[6] The direct relevance of Ugaritic texts for the study of biblical religion must be questioned. The culture of Israel, religious and other, developed from Late Bronze Age traditions, and so Syro-Canaanite religion had an impact upon that of Iron Age Israel. However, while the religion of Ugarit illuminates Syro-Canaanite religious belief and practice, no explicit connection between LBA Ugarit and biblical authors can be documented. Studies of biblical poetry suggest some early parallels (Cross 1973: 112–44), but it may turn out that they would be better correlated with Canaanite city-states such as Hazor and Megiddo. It was, after all, these (and similar) city-states from which many Israelites originated. Excavators at these sites expect to uncover palace and temple archives, and when that happens, the transmission of Canaanite religious traditions to the people of Israel will be better understood (see, e.g., Ben-Tor 1997c: 124–26; 1999a: 2*–3*; see also Rainey 1965: 125).
[7] See, e.g., Albright 1940 and McCown 1943.
[8] See, e.g., Gray 1962; Fohrer 1972; Freedman 1985.
[9] See, e.g., Bright (1972: 116): "Canaanite religion ... presents us with no pretty picture. It was, in fact, an extraordinarily debasing form of paganism, specifically of the fertility cult."
[10] In *A Century of Excavation in Palestine*, R. A. S. Macalister, director of the large and prestigious excavation at Tel Gezer, described many types of archaeological evidence and incorporated studies of topography, political history, cultural history and ethnography (1925). While this might seem ideal, his negative and judgmental approach to the excavated data was discouraging.

For example, of the excavator working in Palestine Macalister wrote: "He must be content to turn over, month after month, the sordid relics of a sordid people, only occasionally striking a spark of excitement from them" (1925: 208). Regarding the excavated cultures: "It is no exaggeration to say that throughout these long centuries the native inhabitants of Palestine do not appear to have made a single contribution of any kind whatsoever to material civilisation. It was perhaps the most unprogressive country on the face of the earth. Its entire culture was derivative" (1925: 210).

[11] This perspective was not limited to Protestants. Y. Kaufmann, an Israeli Jewish scholar claimed that Israelite religion bore no relation to those of the surrounding cultures, despite vestigial pagan superstitions surviving in Israelite cult (1960).

[12] Rowley 1946; Gordon 1953; Orlinsky 1954; Pfeiffer 1961; Gray 1962; Habel 1964; Hahn 1966; Krauss 1966; Ringgren 1966; Segert 1967; Vriezen 1967; Orlinsky 1972.

[13] The "New Archaeology" movement of the 1980s, a movement developed by archaeologists in the United States, challenged excavators to: (1) consider social systems; (2) understand the processes behind the formation of archaeological remains; and (3) base their work upon commonly accepted scientific principles including the development of research designs prior to excavating (see Dever 1983; 1988; and references in both).

CHAPTER TWO
THE CONTRIBUTION OF SOCIAL SCIENCES TO THE STUDY OF RELIGION

As we saw in Chapter One, one of the weaknesses of most studies of the religions of Canaan and Israel has been their tendency to remained focussed within individual academic disciplines. Textual scholars have traditionally ignored the witness of the physical world and archaeologists have often resorted to texts only when challenged by conflicting material evidence. Advances in related fields (including prehistory, archaeology in Europe and the Americas, sociology and anthropology)[1] have been infrequently utilized, despite the fact that they can contribute positively to the study of religion in Canaan and Israel.

If we are to consider Canaanite religion as other than a series of arcane religious rites, if we are to consider Israelite religion as anything other than the precursor of contemporary faiths, and if we are ever to understand the fundamental roles played by these ancient religions within their own societies, then we must look beyond text-and-archaeology and explore the "outside world."

Possibilities abound. One is challenged by an awareness of the fundamental differences in critical method between social scientists and scholars of religion. According to F. Reynolds, these differences include: 1) the concentration of anthropologists on ethnographic studies of "non-literate," "tribal," "folk" or "village" traditions while scholars of religion focus on "classical" or "modern" forms of religion as expressed in literate traditions, and 2) the concentration of anthropologists on religion as an element of culture or society while scholars of religion focus on religion as religion (1984: 2–3).

Over the past century and more, the study of sacrifice has served anthropologists and sociologists as a conduit to the sacred world at large. Sacrificial rites, and teachings about them, have provided a means of discussing the social structure and the belief systems of those groups that engage in this ritual act. Analyses of sacrifice have become arenas in which theories of social behavior can be presented and tested. An increased awareness of how the study of sacrifice has promoted our understanding of other societies contributes to our task at hand: an exploration of the roles of religion in Canaan and Israel.[2] These two factors, the resources presented by ethnographies, and the insights into the relationship between sacrifice and social structure, enable a study of sacrifice based in anthropology and sociology to present a spectrum of insights not easily accessible through traditional textual and archaeological studies.

SOCIAL SCIENCES APPROACHES TO SACRIFICE

The origins of sacrifice are too couched in mystery to be clear to us in the modern world. However, several four-part schemata explaining its institutionalization have been proposed. One approaches sacrifice from a phenomenological stance:

> 1. Sacrifice as a gift which should be followed by a return gift ... 2. Sacrifice as parting with something of one's own for the benefit of another ... 3. Sacrifice as the repetition of a primordial event ... 4. Sacrifice as a form of symbolic sanctification ... (van Baaren 1964: 1–2).

An alternative schema summarizes anthropological contributions to the study of sacrifice. Sacrifice is understood "(1) to provide food for the god ...; (2) to assimilate the life force of the sacrificial animal ...; (3) to effect union with the deity ...; (4) a gift to induce the aid of the deity ..." (Milgrom 1981: 764). These concepts will be explored in the following review of approaches to sacrifice as a form of social behavior.

Frazer's multi-volume *The Golden Bough*, first published in 1919, is a comparative collection of folktales and mythologies. In his evolutionary scheme, primitive peoples depended upon magic until they realized that it was not a successful means of manipulating their environments. Religion then developed, in order to place the whimsicality of the world into the hands of others (i.e., gods). Science, like magic, was based upon the belief that the world could be successfully understood and manipulated (Anderson 1987: 6–7).

Sacrifice, in Frazer's opinion, developed from magical practices. The king or tribal chief was believed to have sacred or divine powers that assured the tribe's well-being. As the ruler aged, these powers diminished, thus jeopardizing tribal well-being. To forestall complete disaster, the king was made a scapegoat and sacrificed, thereby removing his weakness from the tribe. The subsequent installation of a new king rejuvenated both monarch and deity (1925; Faherty 1974: 129).

Nowadays, social scientists disregard elements of Frazer's work on account of its inaccurate and overly general comparisons and its use of now disfavored models. In its time however, Frazer's formulation of the death and rebirth of the divine king made a significant contribution to the study of ancient Near Eastern religions, particularly among Scandinavian and British "myth-and-ritual" scholars of the mid-twentieth century.

In his 1871 book entitled *Primitive Sacrifice*, E. B. Tylor developed the idea that sacrifice was a gift to the gods, intended to minimize hostility and to secure divine good favor. Over time, the concept of sacrifice developed into homage and finally into emotional self-sacrifice (Faherty 1974: 129). As used by Tylor and other anthropologists, the term "gift" carried with it an "element of exchange." An offering made to a god would be reciprocated by the granting of the god's good favors to the supplicant. This assumes a working relationship between deity and worshipper (Bourdillon 1980: 18). Many of Tylor's theories have been disproved, but his equating of sacrifice with gift has been of enduring significance.

G. Gray was a biblical scholar influenced by Tylor's definition of sacrifice. In his 1925 *Sacrifice in the Old Testament: Its Theory and Practice*, he analyzed cultic terminology in the Bible, identifying sacrifice as a gift or tribute. He suggested that, *inter alia*, עבודה (*ʿăvôdâ*), the basic term for religious worship, and מנחה (*minḥâ*), commonly translated as grain offering, derived from the vocabulary of vassaldom and treaty relations. From this Gray concluded that in the Bible, sacrifice was a gift intended to elicit life, sustenance and protection from the gods (Levine 1971: xxviii–xxxiii). B. Levine summarized Gray's contribution: "The terminology thus suggests the servant-lord relationship as that which underlies the sense of sacrifice as gift or tribute. It is the orientation of needs, relative to power, which explains the dynamics of cultic activity" (1971: xxx).

Levine, likewise concerned with cultic terminology and with the concept of biblical sacrifice, concurred with Tylor and Gray:

> The evidence is mounting in support of the gift theory. That is not to say that any unitary conception can account for all the phenomena, for the entire gamut of experiences that were embodied in Israelite ritual. What we are discussing is an organizing principle, on the basis of which we can accurately view all the diverse factors involved in cultic activity in their proper perspective. As an organizing principle, the proposition that the God of Israel desired the sacrifices of his people as a form of tribute to him as their sovereign, in return for which he would grant them the blessings of life, seems to convey the theory of Israelite sacrifice (1971c: xxxi–xxxli).

More recently, G. Anderson advocated the sacrifice-as-gift theory (1987). Like Gray, Anderson studied biblical terminology but his goal was to isolate vocabulary indicative of the social functions of the Israelite cult. For instance he compared the development of the words מנחה and שׁי (šay), both of which mean "gift" in the original Northwest Semitic. Within the context of local dialects, these secular words had come to have special cultic meanings. The cultic meaning which שׁי had in the Canaanite Late Bronze Age, as demonstrated by *ostraca* from Lachish, was never replicated in the HB. Alternately, מנחה developed a dual meaning in Hebrew, one in which the intersection of the political and cultic spheres of the Israelite world was illustrated. According to Anderson, this process of specialization and classification of religious vocabulary was typical to all cultic centers in the ancient Near East (1987: 53–54).

Beidelman cautioned that while sacrifice can be conceived of as gift, one must avoid a simplistic view of what was involved in reciprocity (1987: 547–48). In his analysis of the social and political dimensions of Israelite sacrifice, Anderson did not limit his presentation of sacrifice to the confines of the gift theory. Rather, he examined "those places where it [sacrifice] intersects with social and political history" (1987: 24; see also 1992b).

An interesting discussion of the distinction between gift and sacrifice is found in Georgoudi's ethnographic description of the modern Greek *kourbánia*. Although disavowed by high-ranking Greek Orthodox clergy, these animal sacrifices nonetheless receive the approbation of local religious authorities in a number of Greek villages. This is in part because distributing meat to the poor is seen as an exemplary act of Christian charity. Within the framework of sacrifice, this act acquits the devout of any debt to the saint to whom the sacrifice is made. Georgoudi concluded that "if church canons did not truly succeed in establishing a distinction between *gifts* offered to the church and clergy, which were permitted and even recommended, and *sacrifices,* which were constantly forbidden, it is undoubtedly because these things were organically linked in everyday practice" (1989: 201).

In *Lectures on the Religion of the Semites*, first published in 1889, Robertson Smith attempted to determine the nature of ancient Israelite sacrifice by studying the religious rituals of pre-Islamic Arabian tribes. He assumed that Israel was initially composed of kin-based tribes; their religion metamorphosed as they settled down within the urban world of Canaan. Although his ideas were based on many now-discounted theories, several of his "fundamental theoretical positions" are of enduring importance (Yoffee 1978: 309–10).

Among these is Robertson Smith's observation that sacred offerings were collected and distributed differently in tribal groups and in state polities (Anderson 1987: 23). Therefore, the form that religious rituals took in any society was to a great degree determined by that society's social structure. The enactment of sacrificial rituals must be connected with the social group practicing those rituals.[3] Religious practice was viewed from an ideational perspective as well as from a sociological one. Rituals symbolizing social organization were understood to express the organization's most fundamental beliefs (Hahn 1966: 49; see also Leach 1985; Douglas 1975).

Another of Robertson Smith's contributions was his idea that sacrifice was an act of communion, essential because it provided a forum in which clans joined together for sacral meals. Spiritual unification between a social group and its god was effected through the sharing of a sacred feast. In this, he was at odds with Tylor and others who thought the first purpose of sacrifice was as gift and tribute. He believed that gift and tribute sacrifices developed after the sacrifice for the commensal meal (Beidelman 1974: 54–56).

According to Robertson Smith, an additional dimension of sacrifice was piacular. Atonement for inappropriate acts was made through the enactment of sacrificial rituals that sought to reestablish harmony between a community and its god. The ingestion of the supernatural thus provided a forum for expiation as well as for renewed solidarity between deity and social group (de Vos and Suarez-Orozco 1987: 318).

Robertson Smith's discussion of sacrifice was based upon the theory of "survivals." This theory claimed that certain "functionless crude or superstitious elements of belief or custom ... found in civilized societies" were "fossilized remains, so to speak, of a time when the whole society had lived at the cruder level of culture suggested by these survivals" (Rogerson 1978: 23).[4]

Several of Robertson Smith's ideas have had a profound effect on the study of Israelite origins. These include his assumption of an analogous relationship between Arabian nomads and ancient Israelites, and his description of a two-phase process of Israelite development, during which tribes advanced from their original nomadic configuration to become settled urban dwellers.[5] However because his work was based upon theories of evolutionary development and of "survivals," theories no longer considered accurate ways of discussing social change (Beidelman 1974: 51),[6] Robertson Smith's conclusions have been called into question. For example in his study of the biblical vocabulary for non-Levitical sacrifice, Thompson argued that Robertson Smith incorrectly assessed the purpose of the commensal meal for pre-exilic Israel. Rather than a forum for joyous sharing, sacrifice was a time of solemnity best explained by notions of expiation and propitiation (1963: 249).

Recently however, some ethnographers examining modern-day sacrificial rituals have found evidence that supports at least some of Robertson Smith's earlier hypotheses. The Buid live in the mountains on the Philippine island of Mindoro. In the sacrifice called *fanurukan*, pigs are used to "establish a relationship of contiguity between the human and spirit worlds" (Gibson 1986: 182). As part of this ritual, the sharing of a sacral meal unites god and worshippers and binds members of the community in an act of fellowship (Gibson 1986: 183).

Among those Greek Orthodox villagers practicing *kourbánia*,

> the dominant element, which gives neo-Greek sacrifice its own physiognomy, is displayed ... in

> the communication among men established by the common meal, in the strong bonds created by the "common table" among the diners, whether they belong to one or several communities. Their equal sharing of the same blessed fleshly food makes all of them equally the beneficiaries of the boons requested in the prayers. The importance of this element emerges in the cooking of the meat and the ways it is distributed (Georgoudi 1989: 199).

It is clear that the creation of a sense of fellowship among worshippers must be considered a major component of the communal sacrificial meal.

In *Sacrifice: Its Nature and Function*, originally published in 1898, Hubert and Mauss described religion as a social phenomenon (1964). Its rites were designed to propitiate the gods and to further the interests of the social group. Unlike Tylor and Robertson Smith, Hubert and Mauss did not relate the various forms of sacrifice to an evolutionary model, but rather to a primitive, magical mode of thought designed to constrain the invisible powers (Hahn 1966: 61–62). Sacrifice created communion between the sacred and the profane.[7] "The gifts presented to the gods established a system of communication in which trust and reciprocity could be built" (de Vos and Suarez-Orozco 1987: 321). As such, sacrificial offerings mediated between men and gods.

Hubert and Mauss discussed rites of sacralization and desacralization, in which the worshipper sacrificed in order to enter into or exit from an especially potent state (1964). This conceptualization has been further refined:

1) Sacrifice to obtain or maintain closer contact with God or with other individual spirits.
2) Sacrifice to achieve some degree of separation from such spirits.
3) Sacrifice to acquire for the sacrificer (or for the person sacrificed for) an increase, or input, of non-personalized "power."
4) Sacrifice to achieve separation from, or the removal of, such diffuse force or power (Beattie 1980: 38–39).

A recent study of the biblical חטאת (*ḥaṭṭāt*), traditionally translated as "sin offering," capitalizes upon these insights. The חטאת, part of a system of rites of passage, was understood to separate the sacrificer from his previous condition. The עולה (*'olâ*) or burnt offering, on the other hand, aggregated the sacrificer to his new or renewed state. In a similar fashion, these rites of passage would "guarantee the regular alternation of times and seasons and, at the turn of the year ... regenerate the territory" (Marx 1989: 27), thereby re-establishing a once-lost *status quo* for an individual or for an entire community.

Although Durkheim did not specifically treat the ritual of sacrifice in *Elementary Forms of the Religious Life* (1915), his study of religion provided a foundation upon which many subsequent analyses were based. In his assertion that religion was a social "fact," Durkheim elaborated upon the best contribution of Robertson Smith, the idea that the structure of a society determined the form of its religious rituals.[8] Like Hubert and Mauss, Durkheim emphasized societal aspects of religion.

In equating religion with other social "facts" such as law, economy and the social group, Durkheim developed the idea that religious practice was part of a larger system and that the ways in which it functioned reflected the operation of the system as a whole. Religious practice was thought to always be a group experience. As such, it lacked meaning for the individual apart from his social unit (Hahn 1966: 60; Wilson 1984: 16).

Later anthropologists focussed upon these insights into the relationship between religion and social structure. Like Tylor and Frazer, Evans-Pritchard posited that religion derived as a response to basic questions about life (Morris 1987: 300). However, he avoided formulating laws by means of which all types of sacrifice could be classified but instead he " stressed the need to create a dialogue between anthropology and historical understanding" (Morris 1987: 188–89).

In *Nuer Religion*, Evans-Pritchard isolated two forms of sacrifice among the Nuer, a cattle herding Sudanese tribe. One was concerned primarily with social relations and the other with the moral and physical welfare of the individual. It was the latter sacrifice, the personal and the piacular, which concerned him (1956: 272). Evans-Pritchard related sacrifice to particular needs within the structure of Nuer society. He addressed the ways in which religious thought bore the general impressions of the social order while dismissing those such as Robertson Smith, Durkheim, Hubert and Mauss who related specific features of religion to social structure (Morris 1987: 198, 313).

According to Evans-Pritchard, the basic mechanism behind the piacular sacrifice of the Nuer was substitution, different elements of which were emphasized variously depending upon the circumstance. "According to the situation and particular purpose one element in this complex of meaning may be stressed in one rite and another element in another rite, or there are shifts in emphasis from one part of the sacrificial rite to another" (Morris 1987: 282). Therefore, a multiplicity of variables had to be considered in any discussion of religious rites or theological tenets. There are " rather different ways of thinking of the numinous at different levels of experience. We found these different ways of thinking reflected in the complex notions involved in sacrifice" (Morris 1987: 316). Religion, and especially sacrificial rites, must be understood as originating from within the structure of individual societies.

In his investigation of the way sacrifices were collected and used by the Israelite community, Anderson considers the ritual life of a society to be embedded within its social structure. Anderson's approach has benefited by an increasingly sophisticated understanding of Israelite origins, one that has challenged the traditional nomad-to-urbanite model. If there were no longer a sharp historical division between tribal and urban Israel, then the זבח (*zebaḥ*) could no longer be considered the sacrifice of nomads and the מנחה the sacrifice of the urban dweller. Rather, any interpretation of these sacrifices must accommodate new understandings of the ways in which ancient Israel was constituted (Anderson 1987: 23–24).

Detienne describes the inextricable connection between sacrifice and the socio-political order in classical Greece. He points to

> the first characteristic that justifies the central place of the blood sacrifice in Greek social and religious thought: the absolute coincidence of meat-eating and sacrificial practice .... But sacrifice derives its importance from another function, which reinforces the first: the necessary relationship between the exercise of social relatedness on all *political* levels within the system the Greeks call the city. Political power cannot be exercised without sacrificial practice (Detienne 1989: 3).

This, then, expresses "the solidarity between the domain of the political and that of the sacrificial" (Detienne 1989: 3). The link between classical Greek sacrifice and the socio-political order was demonstrated by the Pythagorean and Orphic schools, which adopted vegetarianism in order to protest the "dominant politico-religious system" and to orient themselves within mystical movements (Detienne 1989: 6). Alternately, one mark of the foreigner was that he was unable to sacrifice without the mediation of a *polis* citizen. Without the ability to sacrifice, the foreigner was denied political rights such as participation in prestigious contests and assemblies (Detienne 1989: 4).

Hartog elaborates upon this as he reflects on the differences between ancient Scythian nomads and Greek city dwellers. If sacrifice is linked to the political order of the *polis*, which it both supports and expresses, what can sacrifice be among nomads? Seen from this perspective, sacrificial practice thus becomes a way of inquiring into human groups, of marking distances and suggesting "otherness" (1989: 170).

In other words, those who participate in our sacrificial practices are *us*, foreigners who share in our sacrificial practices are *like us*, and those who sacrifice differently are *not us*. The implications of these investigations into classical Greek sacrificial practices are interesting. Inasmuch as sacrifice can be considered a mechanism by means of which self (or one's group) and other are defined and represented, it might serve as an effective means of discussing issues of ethnicity and group identification.

Douglas's study of Israelite—specifically Levitical—dietary codes is interesting. Like Durkheim and Evans-Pritchard, Douglas thought that "the properties of classification systems are derived from the social systems in which they are used. The symbolic universe reflects the social world" (Lang 1985: 10). Therefore,

> the Levitical insistence on the clear distinction between the polluting and the nonpolluting must be seen as a part of a larger pattern of social behavior. This society [Priestly Israel] uses clear, tight defining lines to distinguish between two classes of human beings, the Israelites and the rest. Since every outsider is considered a threat to society and religion, some parts of nature are singled out to represent an abominable intruder who breaches boundaries that should be kept intact (Lang 1985: 10)

Understood in this way, Priestly laws of sacrifice might be seen as a mechanism for separating Israelites from non-Israelites—and also for distinguishing between the Priestly group and others in Israel.

Many have found fault with Douglas' analysis of the Levitical codes in *Purity and Danger* (1969).[9] Douglas herself anticipates some of their criticisms in several essays collected in *Implicit Meanings* (1975). In "Deciphering a Meal," she links dietary codes with regulations for sacrificial animals, demonstrating that both derived from concepts of purity and impurity. Rules concerning pollution, and by extension diet and sacrifice, were thus related "to the way in which people conceptually and symbolically structure their environment" (Morris 1987: 213).

In a study that profited from Douglas' work, D. Davies also analyzes levitical sacrifice. In his opinion sacrifice was embedded within the covenant between Israel and God and was immediately concerned with transgressions by both parties to this covenantal agreement (1985: 155). Although it begs the question of when and for whom the sacrificial rules applied, Davies' statement that sacrifice was "an institutional way in which the social and religious life of the nation was both conceived and ordered" underscores the quintessential importance of that rite for ancient Israel (Davies 1985: 161). The essays by Douglas and Davies present a systemic way of looking at sacrifice, one formulated upon the presumption that levitical rules for sacrifice reflected a comprehensive world-view.

In effect, these rules stated: we are the people who express our ideas of self and other through our own special conceptualization of purity and impurity; those who are us share our ideas by sacrificing as we sacrifice and by eating as we eat. In this way, levitical regulations can be understood as a Priestly effort to provide cohesiveness to Judah, possibly even to present a programmatic means for retaining national identity in defiance of a threatened or actual loss of nationhood. Eventually, these regulations came to stand in lieu of actual geographical borders.

According to Neusner, the approach advocated by Douglas served "not only to decipher the facts of a given culture, but also to state the large issues of that culture as they are expressed through minute details of the way of life of those who stand within its frame" (1979: 33). Furthermore, "things which seem trivial are transformed into the very key to the structure of a culture and the order of a society" (Neusner 1979: 35).

From his study of the Mishnah's sacrificial system, Neusner concludes that it resulted from the needs of Jews faced with the loss of their sacred places and their sacral leadership in the centuries that followed the destruction of the Second Temple. In response to the threat of assimilation in the Diaspora, rabbinic leaders reformulated the now-useless Temple-centered rites of their past, rites that had been conserved in the Priestly codes of the Torah. What they created was a distinct (albeit strictly symbolic) body of ritual, one that defined "us" and "others," one that shifted emphasis from the Jerusalem Temple and its priesthood to the people themselves and one by means of which Israel could retain its national integrity despite its overwhelming spiritual and territorial losses (1979: 150–53).

Building upon these insights, it would seem that the choice of sacrificial objects in Canaan and Israel itself reflected concepts of "self" and "other." Most commonly, sacrificial animals were domestic and agricultural offerings were cultivated. At Ugarit, foodstuffs offered as sacrifice were products of the local agrarian economy (de Tarragon 1980: 43–44). The concept of sacrificial ritual as a way of demarcating "us" and "others" may aid in explaining this choice. Domesticated animals and cultivated crops became "us" and wild animals and plants "other." Inasmuch as the sacrificial object had been produced through the hard labor of the sacrificer, what was sacrificed was the self.[10]

In this context, the virtual absence of raw materials as offerings in Canaanite and Israelite sanctuaries is interesting.[11] Precious objects were presented only in worked form, perhaps because the means by which raw materials were procured were complex and impersonal. Those who mined, transported and worked gold, for example, were not those who finally owned it. On the other hand, offerings of precious objects such as jewelry or delicate stone vessels were the personal possessions of wealthy individuals for whom their presentation would have symbolized a presentation of self.

The Socio-economic Dimension of Sacrifice

In the mid-nineteenth century, Marx presented his view of history as "a series of interactions between different social groups, each having particular economic interests" (Wilson 1984: 14). He denied that religion could be understood on its own terms, but rather, "only by examining in specific historical circumstances the linkages between religion as a form of ideology and socioeconomic life" (Morris 1987: 42). A century elapsed before extensive research to better understand the socio-economic implications of sacrificial acts was conducted.[12]

Firth sought to explain the economic organization of sacrifice by focussing upon the ways in which ideas about controlling economic resources impact people's concepts of sacrifice. Two issues raised by Firth are of particular importance. First is the question of the allocation of resources. How are materials that are offered in sacrifice procured? In what ways does the choice of sacrificial offering reflect upon or place stress upon the economic well being of the individual and of the group? Second is the question of the implications of specific economic solutions for the ideology of sacrifice (1972: 326–27).

Firth cautions against adopting too materialistic an approach to the mechanisms involved in enacting sacrificial rites, since many sacrifices in any society are obligatory. Nonetheless, "there are enough examples of the prudent handling of resources to show that sacrifice does seem to be a matter of some economic calculation as well as ritual obligation" (1972: 327–28). In general, economic position affects the frequency and quality of sacrifice.

Bolle investigated the importance of economic priorities in dictating the choice of sacrificial animal. He studied the Khond of Orissa, India, a people believed to retain the recollection of human sacrifice that their ancestors practiced well into the nineteenth century C.E. Among the Khond, for an offering to be efficacious it had to represent an economic commitment. Human victims were acceptable only if they had been purchased and the act of purchase was stressed in formulas recited at the sacrifice: "We bought you with a price, and did not seize you. Now we sacrifice you according to custom, and no sin rests with us" (1983: 48). In the same way, when a Nuer substituted a wild cucumber for an animal victim, he stipulated that an animal later acquired could be offered as replacement for that sacrificed cucumber (Evans-Pritchard 1956: 203).

Firth distinguishes between sacrifices made by individuals and those made by groups. The decision to make sacrifices collective was, in his opinion, based upon two factors. One was ideological, as collective sacrifices reinforced group unity while the other was economic, as they also eased individual financial burdens. Although the sharing of costs and benefits may be related to the ideology of charity, "the emphasis upon the ritual unity of the sacrificing group may be a virtue which is closely allied to necessity" (1972: 330).

Gamble's analysis of faunal remains from the prehistoric sanctuary of Phylakopi on Melos, a Cycladic island, explores the economic implications of animal sacrifice from the perspective of a community that virtually forbade this rite. It did this not from ideological principles or theological concerns but rather from a pragmatic evaluation of local subsistence possibilities. That animal sacrifice was infrequent and involved few animals was underscored by the absence of large public spaces associated with the Phylakopi sanctuary (1985: 481).

The notion of substitution may be a mechanism to compensate for economic realities. One example of this is the Nuer, who

> themselves freely explain that it is not so much what is sacrificed that is important as the intentions of those who sacrifice. If a man is poor he will sacrifice a goat, or even a cucumber, in the place of an ox, and God will accept it. A man should give according to his circumstances, and the sacrifice is not less efficacious because it is a small thing (Evans-Pritchard 1956: 278-79).

Alternately, the Buid do not permit substitution because it is believed that predatory spirits desire human life and that animals are no substitute for humans (Gibson 1986: 179). Among the Greek Orthodox too, substitution of sacrificial victims cannot take place, even if the potential substitute is of equal or greater value than the promised victim (Georgoudi 1989: 202).

At the same time, Georgoudi's discussion of the neo-Greek *kourbánia* offers an interesting insight into the process of substitution. Domestic animals are considered "members of the family," and soon-to-be-sacrificed animals are cared for tenderly, called by names such as "my sons," "my boys," and "my brave ones" (Georgoudi 1989: 198). Likewise, the pigs sacrificed by the Buid in the *fanurakan* sacrifice were cared for specially in deference to their imminent sacred role. They were intimately associated with the household raising them, for they were born and raised in the home and fed with the same food humans ate (Gibson 1986: 183).

The ultimate in self-sacrifice might be that which takes place on a spiritual rather than material plane. Yet even this has economic ramifications. According to Firth,

> the greatest surrogate of all is the sacrifice of the mind and heart, the abnegation of individual judgement and desire in favour of devotion to more general moral ends .... This view is clearly compatible with our modern attitudes towards human personality, but one need not overlook entirely that removal of the notion of sacrifice from the material to the immaterial plane does away with an awkward problem of organization (1972: 331).

Still, economic calculations relating to sacrifice are not always of high priority. For Greek Orthodox villagers, the slaughtering of an ox and the distribution of its meat to the poor, within or even outside of the framework of the *kourbánia*, "is an exemplary act of Christian charity, an act so important that tradition naturally employs it to convey a man's progress toward holiness" (Georgoudi 1989: 200–201). Here, Leach's remarks are instructive.

> The material body of the sacrificial victim may well be a serious economic cost to the giver of the sacrifice, but, at the metaphysical level, economics is not the issue. What matters is the act of sacrifice as such, which is indeed a symbol of gift giving, but gift giving as an expression of reciprocal relationship rather than material exchange (1985: 139).

Evidence from the Nuer supports this statement. "The emphasis is not on the receiving but on the giving, on the sincerity of intention" (Evans-Pritchard 1956: 278–79). A similar observation has been made about classical Greek sacrifice. "The action itself, engaging the supernatural in human concerns, was paramount" (Jameson 1988: 962). Beidelman also warns against interpretations of ritual too rigidly linked to social structure. Ritual acts are ambiguous and will always retain mystical elements (1987: 548).

Although embedded in social relations, rituals are more than simply a paradigm for them. Whether they are performed to strengthen a relationship with supernatural powers, or whether they comprise an attempt to be rid of evil influence, religious sacrifices in some way express moral values. Even when a religious sacrifice is performed privately and for private ends, it reflects community values, including a common assessment of what can legitimately be given up for the end required. More commonly, however, sacrifices are public and serve to strengthen social ties as well as the beliefs and values of the community (Bourdillon 1980: 15).

Phenomenologically, these last cautionary notes are important athough pragmatically they are of little help in understanding sacrifice in antiquity through the study of its material remains. Detienne has even questioned whether sacrifice remains a legitimate topic for analysis.

> Today ... it seems important to say that the notion of sacrifice is indeed a category of the thought of yesterday, conceived of as arbitrarily as totemism ... both because it gathers into one artificial type elements taken from here and there in the symbolic fabric of societies and because it reveals the surprising power of annexation that Christianity still subtly exercises on the thought of those historians and sociologists who were convinced they were inventing a new science (1989: 20).

This may go too far. Still, the attempt to create an all-encompassing definition of sacrifice must be renounced. "Universal definitions of religion hinder ... because and to the extent that they aim at identifying essences when we should be trying to explore concrete sets of historical relations and processes" (Asad 1983: 252). Others, from differing perspectives, agree (see, e.g., de Heusch 1985: 23). In the absence of universal definitions, we must consider ways to explore the role of religion in specific contexts within specific ancient societies.

What is a fair goal for a study of religion? Douglas suggests that as we study religion, "we uncover a cogent set of conceptions and social events, which, when uncoded, tells us something important about ... how people cope with the dissonances and the recurrent and critical tensions of their collective existence" (Neusner 1979: 35). Georgoudi prefers to "see how the rite of popular worship interconnects with religious and social life ... and to comprehend, beyond its functionality, the values it carries for the culture in which it is alive" (1989: 203). Renfrew suggests that "the material record of human experience in different parts of the world and at different times contains information about the human mind" (1982: 26).

However before students of antiquity can explore spiritual complexities, they must illuminate religious behaviors within specific cultures. This goal can be furthered by the materials-oriented approach of archaeology. Physical *realia* (non-textual, textual and contextual) provide the primary data for archaeological analyses, and their study at individual sites and in discreet periods of time requires attention to details. At a synthetic level, the compiled data can be examined in relationship to other relevant assemblages and through these comparisons, issues of choice and decision-making processes can be better understood.

Assuming that "social systems maintain themselves for significant intervals of time in a steady state during which a high degree of cohesion and solidarity characterizes relationships among its members" (Harris 1968: 515), our most productive results come from examining the function of religion within individual, specific societies. Toward this goal, entities such as religious symbolism, the organization of rituals and the form and placement of religious and secular architecture provide a means for studying socio-political relations (S. G. Cole 1985: 49). The work of archaeologists thus becomes critical for investigating the contribution made by religion toward understanding not only the sacred but also the profane.

Anthropologically-based Studies of Sacred Sites

In his study of the Phylakopi sanctuary, Renfrew claims that religious beliefs form a "more or less coherent system or structure, to which the cult observances will relate" and that "structure in the belief system should engender pattern in cult practice, and it is this which we as archaeologists may hope to discern" (1985: 17). He therefore addresses those ritual features that he considered archaeologically identifiable. For Renfrew (1985: 25–26), the archaeological study of cult has the potential to illuminate three important aspects of religions: the behavioral (practice of cult), the societal (place of cult in religion and society) and the ideational (beliefs underlying cult). In his site report, he describes the material evidence for the Phylakopi cult, presented a model for understanding its ritual behaviors and suggested ways in which its study helped depict and interpret societal interactions on Melos and throughout the Aegean.

Alon and Levy used Renfrew's three aspects of religion as the foci for their investigation of religion at Chalcolithic Gilat in Israel's northern Negev Desert (1989: 170–71; see also Levy 1995 and references therein). They adapted Renfrew's list of criteria for identifying communal or public ritual acts in the archaeological record and devised a series of expectations to identify cultic activities at Gilat (including, with Renfrew, architecture and worship, ritual practices, religious experience, attention-focusing devises, cult images, repetition, and ceremonial centers and exchange; Alon and Levy 1989: 170–75).

Alon and Levy concluded that Gilat was a late fourth-early third millennium B.C.E. ceremonial center, one of the earliest known in the eastern Mediterranean. Trade centered in Gilat took place in a network of local, medium and long–range tiers. A sanctuary-affiliated elite traded religious services for material goods and especially for exotic cult objects. This process in turn fostered the growth of local elites (1989: 210–13)

SUMMARY

This review of the contributions of a century and more of sociologists and anthropologists to the study of religion concludes with words of cautious optimism for the potential that archaeology has for illuminating the role of religion in Canaanite and Israelite society. Despite their inability to reach overall consensus on the function and meaning of sacrifice, social scientists have been united in their insistence that religion in general, and sacrifice in particular, reflects various important aspects of society at-large. Investigations into ancient religion have many potential outcomes. They deepen our knowledge of social structure and further our understanding of ancient rituals and of the groups for whom these rituals reflected complex sacred and secular interactions.

As we saw in Chapter One, most scholars of ancient religion have paid little attention to religion's social, political and economic components. However, by capitalizing upon social science insights concerning the study of religion, and by applying these insights to textual, architectural and artifactual data, archaeologists can significantly enhance our awareness of the roles religion played in Canaanite and Israelite society.

NOTES

[1] See Carter and Meyers, eds. 1996 for a collection of classic and recent essays on the contribution of the social sciences to the study of the HB. See Carter 1996 for an overview of the subject.

[2] An excellent discussion of the private and personal dimensions of the sacrificial rite, including a review of the contributions of eminent psychoanalysts such as Freud and Piaget, is found in *Sacrifice and the Experience of Power* (de Vos and Suarez-Orozco 1987). My own study focuses upon the rite of sacrifice as it operates within the social group rather than for the individual.

[3] See, e.g., Anderson 1987. Anderson demonstrated that urban Canaanite royalty, pre-state Israel and monarchical Israel each had different modes of collecting tithes and redistributing accumulated agricultural goods (1987: 24, 77–90).

[4] In Israelite sacrifice, for example, the "survival" was a remnant of the totemic stage of social organization, during which time communion with the totem god was established as the totemic group ate its totemic object. The purpose of sacrifice, and particularly of sacrifice in which worshippers partook of the sacrificed animal, was to establish communion with the deity by ingesting it (Rogerson 1978: 26).

[5] See, *inter alia*, the works of A. Causse (Kimbrough 1978) and de Vaux (1964).

[6] For a rebuttal of the doctrine of "survivals," see Georgoudi 1989. She demonstrates that, contrary to accepted scholarly opinion, the neo-Greek *kourbánia* should not be viewed as a survival from ancient Greek sacrifice; rather, it should be understood within the context of Christian, and especially Orthodox, ideology.

[7] See also Georgoudi 1989: 199.

[8] For a discussion of Robertson Smith's influence on Durkheim, see Beidelman 1974: 58-61, 67.

[9] See, among others, Carrol 1985; Lang 1985: 9-10, n. 18; Morris 1987: 208-9.

[10] See, e.g., Beattie 1980: 30-31, in which he claims that domestic animals were sacrificed because they most closely symbolized home and thus the person on behalf of whom the sacrifice was being made.

[11] For further discussion of these sanctuaries, see chapters 4 through 6.

[12] For contemporary Marxist approaches to archaeology, see Gathercole 1984; Miller and Tilley 1984; Spriggs 1984; Spriggs, ed. 1984.

CHAPTER THREE
THE TEXTUAL EVIDENCE

As we saw in Chapter Two, sacrifice creates a forum in which various groups (religious, political, familial and clan-based) convene to participate in communal rites and to share in sacral meals while renewing ties and confirming group relationships. In addition, sacrifice provides a means of beseeching the deity, of offering thanks and of atoning for sin. The work of sociologists and anthropologists has demonstrated that the significance of sacrifice transcends individual rites and provides access to understanding society at-large. We now examine documentation for Canaanite and Israelite religions, to see what testimony the written texts provide. Relevant texts from Ugarit and from the HB provide the focus for this discussion, as these are the two critical corpora of written materials.

Sacrifice was the major rite of the religions of Western Asia, including those of Canaan and Israel. In Late Bronze Age Ugarit, the principal category of cultic vocabulary was that of sacrifice (de Tarragon 1980: 55–56). For Israel too, sacrifice provided the means through which the Israelite, whether royalty, clergy or commoner, worshipped Yahweh (or, occasionally, another deity). "According to biblical concepts, worship is tantamount to sacrificing" (Haran 1988: 23).[1]

As we know from the Ugaritic texts, Canaanite religion regarded the sacrificing to, and feeding of, the gods as a human responsibility.[2] For example, in the Kirta Epic, El told Kirta to "raise your hands to heaven, sacrifice to the Bull, your father El; serve Baal with your sacrifice, the son of Dagan with your provisions" (Coogan 1978: 59). At the beginning of the Aqhat Epic, its hero Danel "made an offering for the gods to eat, made an offering for the holy ones to drink" (Coogan 1978: 32). It is assumed that these sacrifices were at least partially consumed by ceremonial participants.

Israelite religion retained elements of an anthropomorphic conception of the divine being and so it too ensured the presence of Yahweh through the offering of foodstuffs. This was indicated through the use of such expressions as השלחן אשר לפני יהוה ("the table that stands before YHWH" in Ezek 41:22; see also Ezek 44:16), לחם אלהיו ("the bread of his God" in Lev 21:21–22; see also Lev 3:11; Num 28:2), and ריח הניחח ("the soothing odor" in Gen 8:21; see also Num 28:2). God's hunger and Israel's offerings as a means of alleviating it provided the critical language of Psalm 50:7–15 as well, although here the idea of sacrifice was turned on its head with the suggestion that God had no need of human offerings since he himself controlled all resources. Anderson notes that the idea that Yahweh required food was "*freely* introduced into *all genres* (cultic and epic narratives, psalms, and more) of Israel's literature in all periods" (1992b: 872).

In antiquity, offerings to the gods included vegetables and grains, oils, wine, honey, precious hand-made objects and, most importantly, animals. The act of slaughter and the sacrifice of live animals lay at the emotional core of many early religions.[3] Commenting on the power of animal sacrifice for its practitioners, Burkert wrote:

> The god is present at his place of sacrifice, a place distinguished by the heap of ashes left from "sacred" offerings burnt there over long periods of time, or by the horns and skulls of slaughtered rams and bulls, or by the altar-stone where the blood must be sprinkled. The worshipper experiences the god most powerfully not just in pious conduct or in prayer, song, and dance, but in the deadly blow of the axe, the gush of blood and the burning of thigh-pieces. The realm of the gods is sacred, but the "sacred" act done at the "sacred" place by the "consecrating" actor consists of slaughtering sacrificial animals (1983: 2).

According to some sources, ancient sacrifice originated from the need to sanctify the consumption of animal flesh, for the spilling of animal blood was an act of violence that required divine sanction (Hallo 1987: 3–11). For Israelites, according to the Priestly writers, slaughtering an animal for food alone constituted murder and thus ritual expiation in the form of the animal's blood upon the altar had to be made.[4] Therefore, the Priestly writers of Genesis 1 and of the Holiness Code of Leviticus 17–26 stressed that human beings were originally not meat-eaters (Milgrom 1971: 156). Perhaps it was for this reason that those

Israelite sacrificial rituals described in Leviticus were linked to the moral order (Rainey 1996b: 71). They were offered by the priesthood in a specific order, and for the purpose of expiation and propitiation, for consecration and for fellowship with God and with man.

THE TEXTS FROM UGARIT

Ugarit was an important Bronze Age city on the Syrian coast, the capital of a kingdom now well-known through excavations and textual studies. Its destruction in the late thirteenth century B.C.E. resulted in the preservation of an important archive, which illuminates many aspects of religion in the Late Bronze Age city.

The archive includes texts that document various elements of religion and of these, the poetic and the ritual texts are most useful. The poetic texts, both mythological and epic, have provided the basis for many studies of Canaanite religious practice. However, real-world description was not their intended purpose and the degree to which ritual acts attributed to deities or epic heroes reflected actual cultic praxis is uncertain. The corpus of ritual texts, although smaller than that of poetic texts, provides more detailed, if rather less picturesque, information about ritual activities.

Texts describing cultic practice, and in particular the descriptive ritual texts, should be dated to the last decades of the city of Ugarit (de Tarragon 1980: 183–84).[5] Levine suggests that the ritual texts "functionally speaking were quasi-canonical models, or manuals for the operation of the temple cults at Ugarit and vicinity" (1983: 473). Together with the poetic texts, the administrative records and the temple lists, they formed part of the temple archives.

The emphasis in these texts was on the major components of religious rites and particularly on animal sacrifice. The enumeration of secondary, non-sacrificial, rituals was not comprehensive (Levine 1983: 468). Levine enumerates the scope of the ritual texts found at Ugarit.

> In terms of content, the descriptive ritual records or describes a coherent rite, or more often, a complex of rites. It provides detailed information on the following subjects: 1) sacrificial offerings to specific deities, 2) dates, occasions, and sites where rites are performed, 3) ritual acts, such as purifications and processionals, which compose

overall celebrations, and 4) officiants, quite often the king, who had a significant role in the cult (1983: 467).

At Ugarit, the principle term for sacrifice, *dbḥ* referred to sacrifice or ritual offering (de Tarragon 1980: 55). In the title of a ritual text however, *dbḥ* also indicated a "sacral celebration" (Levine 1983: 473, n. 7). The most common type of sacrifice was *šlm*, variously translated as "peace" or "communion" offering.[6] It was almost always offered with *šrp*, a burnt offering. The word *ʿlm* also referred to a burnt offering, possibly one similar to the biblical *ʿolâ*.[7] *ʿly* referred to elevating something, possibly the statue of the god. *Šnpt* referred to offering a non-animal product, which was elevated for display to the deity (de Tarragon 1980: 59–65).

These descriptive ritual texts also specified the types of animals sacrificed during religious ceremonies. Levine describes four systems of animal classification: by class, by class and sex, by class and species (or *genus*) and by class, species (or *genus*) and sex (Levine 1963: 109). Oddly, the vocabulary for sacrificial rituals and sacrificial animals known in the ritual texts does not mirror that in the poetic texts (Levine 1963: 100; de Tarragon 1980: 33). This fluid terminology can be confusing at times. However, given the ample literary and archaeological data it need not hamper efforts to understand the role of sacrifice in these rituals.

In the seven rituals for the purification of the king (*yrṯḥṣ mlk brr*), the king's ritual acts were framed by offerings or sacrifices, the enumeration of which occupied the greatest part of the texts. Most common was the sacrifice of livestock, especially of sheep. Heifers were sacrificed twice as often as bulls. Specific organs such as the liver, lungs and nostrils were offered. In each instance, the limited number of animals stood in contrast to their variety (de Tarragon 1980: 17, 31–40).

Along with livestock, agricultural products, especially oils, vegetables and grains, were offered. While all were produced locally, some foodstuffs known to have been grown locally were not included among those offered in sacrifice. Units of measure for agricultural offerings, including *kt* and *ḍnt*, were specified.[8] Finally, precious metals were made into cult objects or were offered in the form of ingots and weights. Offerings of clothes and fabrics were also required (de Tarragon 1980: 43–49).

Another set of descriptive ritual texts described the process of clothing the divine statues and moving them to the *bt mlk*, the royal palace, or temple. The primary ritual, the transfer of the statues, was supplemented by the dressing of the statues and the presentation of offerings and sacrifices in conjunction with *dbḥ* or sacral meal. Seven *šlm* sacrifices took place. Food offerings included fish, oil, honey and wine. Precious metals were offered to the gods, as were the clothes and fabrics used for dressing the statues (de Tarragon 1980: 98–112).

The infrequency of the word *qdš* (holy) and its derivatives has led to the suggestion that religion at Ugarit was not concerned with issues of purity and of holiness. In striking contrast to Israelite ritual, at Ugarit there was no distinction between "pure" and "impure" animals. Rather, cultic vocabulary there was composed of technical terms related to sacrifice. In other words, religion (as we understand it) was informed by ritual practices rather than by theological concerns. The cult at Ugarit was also at one with its natural surroundings, its sacrifices being characteristic of the contemporary agrarian economy (de Tarragon 1980: 73–74).

An examination of the texts permits speculation about material remains from sacrificial rites that might be found in the excavation of Ugaritic temples. For example vessels in standardized sizes may indicate the use of measured quantities for agricultural offerings. Elegantly decorated vessels may have contained liquid libations and assemblages of tableware may reflect both ritual offerings and sacral meals. The sacrifice of animals required altars and knives, and animal bones themselves reflect the choice of animals and methods of sacrifice.

Statues of gods were found in temples at Ugarit and elsewhere. As we know from the ritual texts, jewelry and clothing were required to enact rituals for the dressing and moving of statues. Although clothing decomposes, fastenings and ornaments made of metals, bone, ivory or semi-precious stone might suggest the types of garments once used for dressing cultic participants and divine statues.

In summary, the thirteenth century B.C.E. texts from Ugarit, particularly the ritual texts, provide a great deal of information about West Semitic religious practice. As evidenced by the rituals for the purification of the king (in which each ritual act of the king was framed by sacrifices), the importance of sacrifice cannot be understated. Royal success required the complicity of the divine, which was asked for and acknowledged through the gesture of offering.

Seen from the perspective of the royal center in this Late Bronze Age capital city, sacrifice was not an act of individual piety but rather a function of the social group. Kings undertook the expense and the responsibility of sacrifice in order in promote their relationship with their patron gods, and to ensure that their city and its inhabitants were favored. The loss incurred by offering sacrifices was compensated for by the overall gain in societal well being.

SACRIFICE IN THE HEBREW BIBLE

Without the HB, one wonders whether the transition from Canaanite to Israelite faith would be apparent.[9] Were the shift perceptible, how accurately could archaeologists describe the beliefs of the new Israelite faith? The HB provides our primary tool for understanding its theological tenets and for relating this understanding to specific venues within Israel and Judah. To this end, texts concerning sacrificial practices are analyzed to determine cultic vocabulary and ritual acts and to establish the settings from which relevant texts originated. Perhaps not surprisingly, the fluidity of terms for sacrificial acts found in the Ugaritic texts is also found in the HB.

In general, the religious acts that defined the biblical repertoire consisted of making offerings and sacrifices and of erecting altars, *maṣṣebôt* (מצבות) and cairns. These acts were supplemented by fasting and by chanting liturgical compositions. It is important to emphasize their context by attributing them to specific periods and communities within the history of Israel. The practice of Israelite religion in the Iron I period (1200–1000 B.C.E.), prior to the monarchy, was more varied than it would become after decades and even centuries of regularization by the kings and their priesthood. Even then, worship in monarchical Israel and Judah remained far from uniform, despite the efforts of Deuteronomistic and Priestly writers and editors to present orderly pictures.[10] For them, the Temple and sacrifice there were central, and therefore these subjects occupy what perhaps seems to be a disproportionate amount of space in the HB.[11]

To examine biblical sacrifice, one must consider the textual sources of the descriptive material. In this way, social and historical contexts can be ascertained and changing concepts and ideologies can be investigated. What follows is a brief overview that highlights the setting of texts related to sacrifice in the HB, reviews relevant biblical "documents" and discusses the contribution of each document toward understanding this central religious ritual.

Biblical texts concerned with sacrifice can be divided into two categories. The first consists of non-programmatic descriptions of sacrifices and offerings. They are scattered throughout the narrative texts of the HB, in Genesis through 2 Kings, in certain of the prophetic and literary works, and in 1 and 2 Chronicles.

The second category consists of cultic calendars and of prescriptive and descriptive passages. These include descriptions of the *paschal* sacrifice (Exodus 12), the consecration of the Tabernacle (Exodus 29–31), offerings of animals and grains by members of the community (Leviticus 1–7), the initiation of priests (Leviticus 8–10), offerings relating to cleanliness and uncleanness (Leviticus 11–15), offerings on the Day of Atonement (Leviticus 16), offerings that are part of the Holiness Code (Leviticus 22, 24), offerings related to the centralization of worship (Deuteronomy 12) and so forth.

The HB is a composite document, comprising traditional oral narratives, administrative texts, legal codes, and written expositions.[12] The dating of the individual documents, and their composition and redaction, had been widely accepted, but more recently has been the subject of debate. The Yahwistic source, once placed in the royal court of the United Monarchy, and the Elohistic source, placed in Divided Monarchy Israel (see, e.g., von Rad 1966; Cross 1973: 293; Alter 1981: 131; Friedman 1987: 86–87) are now discussed as documents of the exilic and post-exilic eras (Van Seters 1975; 1983; Whybray 1987: 43–131). While some scholars present textually-based arguments for monarchic origins (Cross 1973; Friedman 1987; Jenks 1977; 1992; Peckham 1985; Cross 1998), others demur. Without external means for resolving such controversies, many scholars have altogether abandoned the effort to date the source documents within the Torah (see, e.g., Barton 1992; de Pury 1992). Refreshingly, others turn to recently excavated epigraphic materials to overcome these problems (Na'aman 1994b; Gnuse 2000).

While it may be impossible to resolve all discrepancies and to account for the origins of each biblical passage, the suggestion that the HB is primarily a post-Exilic document does an injustice to its many well-documented time-bound elements (see Dever 1998 and references therein). For example, Na'aman's recent analysis of Israelite and Judaean epigraphic material leads him to suggest that history writing (as opposed to administrative documentation) began in the eighth–seventh centuries (Na'aman 1994b: 230). While Na'aman's work focused upon the origins of Joshua, his conclusions support the pre-Exilic composition of other texts as well.

Deuteronomistic (D) and Priestly (P) texts in the Torah purport to describe acts of worship that took place as early as the era of the exodus from Egypt. While this event cannot be substantiated historically, the events of the LB II/Iron I transition provide a likely setting (Sarna 1988; Hoffmeier 1996 and references there). However as we will see, neither D nor P was composed prior to the late eighth century, and much of P dates to the exilic era. Fortunately, accounts of earlier religious practices can be found in texts that were composed somewhat earlier.

Classic models for the Documentary Hypothesis suggested that the Yahwistic document (J) was composed in the tenth century and the Elohist document (E) no later than the ninth. Both were said to contain materials that originated in earlier periods (Wellhausen 1957; Eissfeldt 1976; see Barton 1992 for a brief overview). They have been described as "variant forms in prose of an older, largely poetic Epic cycle of the era of the Judges" (Cross 1973: 293). As noted above, more recent studies suggest that they were composed later in the Divided Monarchy (Peckham 1985: 6, 18–19; Friedman 1987: 83–87; Gnuse 2000). Still, J and E remain the earliest narrative texts in the HB and so their depictions of sacrifice and other acts of worship provide insight into early visions of Israelite religious practice.

Each textual community had its own unique perspective, a lens through which actions in previous eras were viewed. The analysis here focuses on how the ancient Yahwistic and Elohistic writers themselves perceived changing ritual traditions. It does not assume that they necessarily described real historical events or actual people, although some passages may reflect actual occurrences.

It is intriguing to note the ways in which both these writing communities agreed in their descriptions of evolving ritual activities. Both described varied rituals and slow change and both were clear about how sacrifice and other rites were personal and intimate acts for Israelites living before the monarchy. Although neither J nor E communities were eyewitnesses to the early events they described, the confluence of their descriptions is so striking that it bears further examination.

Yahwistic Texts

The Yahwist was not much interested in ritual aspects of religion. Cultic acts in the J document that took place during the patriarchal period were limited to Gen 4:2–5 (Cain and Abel sacrificed to Yahweh), Gen 8:20–21 (Noah sacrificed to Yahweh), Gen 12:6–7 (Abram sacrificed to Yahweh at Shechem), Gen 12:8 (Abram sacrificed to Yahweh between Bethel and ʿAi), Gen 13:4 (Abram sacrificed to Yahweh between Bethel and ʿAi), Gen 13:18 (Abram sacrificed to Yahweh at Hebron), Gen 14:18–20 (Melchizedek presented a food offering),[13] Gen 15:8–12 (Abram halved and sacrificed animals to Yahweh),[14] and Gen 26:23–25 (Isaac sacrificed to Yahweh at Beersheba).

These sacrifices and other ritual acts took place at moments not regulated by any cultic calendar and at places not predetermined by any cultic authority. Some, such as the מנחה and בכרות (*bekōrôt*) of Cain and Abel (Gen 4:2–5) and Abraham's building an altar between Bethel and ʿAi (Gen 12:8) were spontaneously enacted. Others commemorated the making or fulfillment of promises: Noah's building an altar and offering עלת (*ʿōlōt*) upon reaching dry land (Gen 8:20–21), Abraham's building altars by terebinth trees near the Canaanite sanctuary at Shechem (Gen 12:6–7) and in Hebron (Gen 13:18) to commemorate Yahweh's appearance and promise to him, Abraham's unusual sacrificial ritual with halved animals and whole birds to attain assurance of Yahweh's promise to him (Gen 15:8–12),[15] and Isaac's building an altar at Beersheba to commemorate Yahweh's promise to him (Gen 26:23–25).

In the book of Exodus, J elaborated upon the importance of sacrifice as the appropriate way to worship Yahweh. The battle between Pharaoh and Yahweh was formulated in terms of Pharaoh's granting the Israelites permission to travel into the wilderness to worship Yahweh by making sacrifices (Exod 3:18; 5:3; 8:8). Ultimately he supplied the Israelites with animals for זבחים (*zebāḥim*) and עלת (Exod 10:24–26). The connection between sacrifice and worship was clearly established in Exod 4:23. It seems appropriate, then, that according to J, the first act Yahweh required of the incipient Israelite nation was the offering of the *paschal* sacrifice (Exod 12:21–23).

In summary, the cultic concerns of the Yahwist included making sacrifices, building altars and enacting blood rituals. Motivation included spontaneous impulse, commemoration of making or fulfilling promises, and obedience to divine command. Sacrifice attested to the sanctity of places where Yahweh revealed his name, witnessed pacts between man and God and was the instrument through which Yahweh's battle with Pharaoh was expressed. It was the sign of Israelite obedience to and worship of Yahweh.

Elohistic Texts

The Elohist's first references to religious rituals concerned Jacob/Israel: Gen 28:11b–12 (Jacob dreamed at Bethel), Gen 28:16–18 (Jacob anointed a מצבה [*maṣṣebâ*] at Bethel), Gen 28:20–22 (Jacob made a vow to Yahweh at Bethel), Gen 31:43–54 (Laban and Jacob exchanged vows, set up a גל [*gāl*; cairn] and a מצבה, sacrificed animals and shared in a sacred feast),[16] Gen 32:1–2 (Jacob was met by angels at Mahanaim), Gen 32:25–32 (Jacob wrestled with an angel and had a vision of God at Peniel), Gen 33:18–20 (Jacob set up an altar to God at El-Elohei-Israel near Shechem), Gen 35:1–7 (Jacob and his household erected an altar to God at Bethel) and Gen 46:1–4 (God made a vow to Jacob at Beersheba).[17]

At Bethel, cultic acts were related to visions of God (Gen 28:11b–12, 20–22; Gen 35:1–7). Two ritual sequences took place. The first, in Genesis 28, consisted of inducing a vision, erecting and anointing a sacred stone and making a vow concerning future temple building and tithing. The second, in Genesis 35, in obedience to a divine command, consisted of the purification of Jacob's household, the building of an altar and the naming of the place El-Bethel.

At Beersheba too, the offering of sacrifices preceded a vision (Gen 46:1–4). At Mahanaim, a visitation by angels resulted in the naming of the site (Gen 32:1–2) while at the Jabbok an extra-human visitation resulted in naming the site Peniel and giving Jacob the new name Israel (Gen 32:25–32). At Mizpah/Gal-ed/Jegar-sahadutha, the naming of the site, the erecting of sacred stones and the sharing of a sacrificial meal were related to the witnessing of a pact between kinsmen by marriage (Gen 31:43–54). No reason was given for the erecting and naming of the altar El-Elohei-Israel at Shechem (Gen 33:18–20).

Elohist passages describing the exodus from Egypt were similar. Moses built an altar and named it Yahweh-Nissi as witness to Yahweh's eternal battle with Amalek (Exod 17:15–16). Later, he built an altar, erected a מצבה for each of the twelve tribes, offered זבחים and שלמים

(*šelēmîm*) and engaged in blood rituals as witness to the written covenant between Yahweh and Israel (Exod 24:3–8). In Exodus 32, the story of the Golden Calf, an altar was built, an idol made, a חג (*ḥag*) to Yahweh declared and עלה and שלמים offered. Jethro offered an עלה וזבחים to Yahweh and shared a sacral meal with Aaron and the elders of Israel (Exod 18:12).

The Elohist's description of Jacob's reunion with Esau (Gen 33:1–11) presents a unique description of an offering ritual otherwise unattested in the HB. At the reunion between Jacob and Esau, Jacob bowed down (וישתחו) to his brother seven times (Gen 33:3)[18] and begged Esau to accept his offering (מנחתי), for he regarded Esau as a god (ראיתי פניך כראת פני אלהים) (Gen 33:10).

Exod 20:23–26 differs from other Elohistic passages on account of its prescriptive dimension. It forbade idol building and legislated the building of altars and the offering of עלה and שלמים (*šelēmîm*). It also associated the construction of altars with places chosen by Yahweh and with the blessing of the people. Although the passage has been attributed to the Elohist (so Friedman 1987: 251), it may have originally been an ordinance of an early, pro-high place community (Halpern 1983: 224–25), one that was subsequently incorporated into the Elohist document due to their mutual concerns.[19] As such, Exod 20:23–26 might be regarded as providing an independent witness to the religious practices of rural Israel.

According to the Elohist, sacrifice only had value within the relationship between people and the God of Israel. Exodus 21–23 (the Covenant Code) predated the Elohist but was later incorporated into the Elohistic text. Among other things, it ordered the death penalty for people sacrificing to gods other than Yahweh and presented some regulations regarding sacrificial rites. The Balaam story (Numbers 22–24) serves to illustrate the futility of building altars and offering sacrifices to other gods.

To summarize, sacred acts in the Elohist text were often somewhat complicated. The process of erecting altars and sacred stones was complex and could incorporate taking vows (Gen 28:20–22; Gen 31:43–54), anointing altars (Gen 28:16–18) and naming the places at which the altars or *maṣṣebôt* were erected (Gen 33:20; Gen 35:7; Exod 17:15–16). Naming places also took place in conjunction with divine visions and heavenly visitations (Gen 32:1–2, 30). A person was renamed, as well (Gen 32:27–28).

Covenant making, often associated with the erecting of altars or *maṣṣebôt* with the enacting of blood rites, with sacrifice and with the sharing of feasts and sacral meals, also occurred (Gen 31:43–54; Gen 33:1–11; Exod 18:11–12; Exod 24:3–8; Exod 32:5–6). Additional Elohistic cultic concerns included prohibitions against false worship, false sacrifice and idol making and prescriptions detailing festal celebrations and proper altar construction and location (Exod 20:23–26; Exod 21–23; Num 22–24).

Summary: Yahwistic and Elohist Sacrificial Practice

What can be said of the practice of Israelite religion described in the Yahwistic and Elohistic documents? Both depicted worship in the pre-monarchical period as spontaneous and unregulated. It seems that they faithfully presented traditional materials known within their own communities. In this way, they depicted Israel's ancestors as people who had worshipped in ways significantly different than those condoned in their own times. This is particularly interesting since both J and E composed their texts when, according to the HB, obedience to centralized religious authority was promoted over and against religious eclecticism.[20] Overall, their documents would have had to promote monarchical or priestly aims or they would not have been conserved and included in the canonized text.

Given this, both J and E might have chosen to promulgate the ideal of cultic centralization. Had they wished, they could have incorporated alternative descriptions of early worship practices, suggesting that Israel's ancestors were aware of the centralizing ideal from its earliest days. They might have made didactic use of the eclectic practices of Israel's forebears, using them as examples of religious behaviors that, while once permitted, needed to be foresworn in contemporary times.[21] However, this was not what they did, and the result is the rich mix of religious traditions that we see portrayed in their material.

The *bāmâ* was a cultic installation during the Iron II period, the time of the monarchy (see chapter 6; Nakhai 1994). Although it was vilified by Deuteronomistic writers as an early and pagan element within the Israelite community, the *bāmâ* had no place in the world of either J or E. Both were careful not use the term anachronistically when they described the pre-monarchical period. This interest in historic accuracy suggests that other of their descriptions might also be reliable.

Among the religious rites that J and E attributed to Israel's ancestors, the offering of sacrifices, especially animal sacrifices, stands out. Earlier, this had been the ritual act *par excellence* of the Canaanites. In contrast to the texts from Ugarit, which had described a royal, urban cult, the J and E passages reported on a decidedly rural world. Even so, it is evident that the vocabulary of sacrifice used by J and E (עֹלָה ,שְׁלָמִים) was adopted from their Canaanite progenitors.

It has traditionally been assumed (following the persuasive polemics of the Deuteronomistic and Priestly schools) that, subsequent to the construction of the Solomonic Temple, Jerusalem was considered the only legitimate center for the worship of Yahweh. The sanctuaries built by Jeroboam for the northern Israelites were considered renegade and the *bāmôt* of the towns and the countryside completely unacceptable. However J and E not only accepted, but even sanctioned, non-centralized worship, as they depicted it being undertaken by persons of no lesser stature than Israel's forebears.

This leads to speculation about the degree of religious centralization in Israel and Judah at the time in which J and E wrote, for it is hard to imagine that they would have lauded abhorrent religious practices. It is harder to imagine that their works would have been included in the canonized HB if they had depicted Israel's ancestors revering customs that had been abominated for half a millennium and more. In the end, Abraham was never shown sacrificing Isaac.

The varied cultic practices described by the Yahwist and the Elohist can be attributed to the different customs of those many groups that had over time joined together to form the nation of Israel. Presenting diversity in ritual practice was an efficacious means of warding off fragmentation in an often-divided nation. It is this political astuteness that was reflected in the eclectic and non-programmatic texts of the Yahwist and the Elohist.

The Book of Judges

The oral composition of the stories in Judges may be traced to an early stage in the history of Israel. Scholars disagree about the date of its literary roots, but agreement concerning the early and authentic nature of the stories themselves is common.[22]

> Old Israel's narrative art survives in its purest form
> in the Book of Judges, where theological updating

across the centuries was confined almost exclusively to the connectives between units; rarely did it invade their essential contents. This means that the stories stemming from the early days were fixed in all their essentials before they were ever employed in telling the authoritative story of Israel's life in Canaan (Boling 1975: 29).

These stories of Israel's early days in the land were later subjected to Josianic and post-Josianic Deuteronomistic editing (Boling 1992b).[23] Inasmuch as the Judges stories bear ancient recollections, their accounts of sacrifice and other rituals might accurately describe religious practices in Israel's pre-monarchical period.

Ritual acts described in Judges incorporate a number of different elements. Rites including naming places and people and sacrificing to Yahweh were often enacted in the presence of a divine messenger. The naming of Bokim and the sacrifice there following the speech of one such messenger reflectes the commitment of renewed obedience to Yahweh (Judg 2:1–5). Manoah used a rock upon which to offer Yahweh an עולה and a מנחה in the presence of another divine messenger.

At Ophrah-of-the-Abiezrites, Gideon prepared a meal of boiled kid, unleavened cakes and broth for Yahweh. Following the instructions of a divine messenger, he put the cakes and meat on a rock and poured out the broth. All were consumed by fire. Gideon then built an altar to Yahweh and named it "Yahweh Shalom" (Judg 6:17–24). He destroyed his father's baalistic אשרה (*ʾašērâ*) and altar and in its place built an altar to Yahweh, sacrificing a bull (עולה) upon it. This time, Gideon and not the altar received the new name (Judg 6:25–32).

The stories of sacrifice and festival in Judges 21 depicted rituals of a different sort. In v 4, the Israelites built an altar and offered עלה and שלמים. This was evidently the first step in an intertribal process of conflict resolution. In vv 19–23, the celebration of an annual pilgrimage in honor of YHWH (חג יהוה בשלו מימים ימימה) provided a means for recruiting wives for the Benjaminites. That this may have been a fall vineyard festival is suggested by vv 21 and 23, in which the daughters of Shiloh danced in the vineyards in accordance with tradition.[24]

Not surprisingly, given the date of their composition, redaction and compilation, many of the ritual acts in Judges were similar to those described in the Elohistic and Yahwistic documents. Among other things, they shared a concern for the immediate presence of Yahweh, for the change that his presence brought to a person or a place (signified by naming or renaming) and for the construction of a permanent marker to signify this event. The construction of altars and the offering of sacrifices were part of tribal relationships and of covenant making.

1 Samuel, 2 Samuel, 1 Kings 1–4

The many instances of sacrifice in 1 and 2 Samuel and in the pre-Temple passages in 1 Kings (1 Kings 1–4) depict a richly variegated cult in Israel's late pre-monarchical and early monarchical periods. They are particularly important since some sources within it, the Ark Narrative, the Saul Cycle and the History of David's Rise had roots early in the history of the monarchy.[25] At the same time, the editorial hand of the Deuteronomists is apparent (Flanagan 1992: 959–61; Brueggemann 1992: 966).

Certain of the ritual and sacrificial acts that were part of the pre-Temple vision of J, E and Judges are also found in 1 Samuel, 2 Samuel and 1 Kings 1–4 (SSK4). The most interesting ritual was the annual sacrifice, which included the celebration of the autumn vineyard חג. In Judges, the annual sacrifice was part of the story about obtaining wives for the Benjaminites (Judg 21:19–23). This same festival (מימים ימימה) probably provided the setting for the story of Hannah's entreaty to Yahweh at Shiloh (1 Sam 1). Descriptions of these festivals provide glimpses of regular religious activities that did not survive later cultic centralization. In addition, the story of Hannah at Shiloh incorporated descriptions of private worship. They included prostrating oneself, sacrificing, sharing a sacral meal and making vows. As expected of a vineyard festival, excessive wine drinking took place, thus explaining the conversation between Eli and Hannah in 1 Samuel 1:12–17.[26]

Not every annual sacrifice took place during the celebration of an established pilgrimage festival. Haran identified three family holidays in 1 Samuel that were not included in the later law codes of the Torah (1969: 22). They were annual sacrifices, the זבח הימים (*zebaḥ hayyāmîm*) in 1 Sam 1:21; 2:19; 20:6, the זבח משפחה (*zebaḥ mišpaḥâ* in 1 Sam 20:29 [see also 1 Sam 20:6]) and the זבח לעם בבמה (*zebaḥ lā'ām babāmâ*) in 1 Sam 9:12. To celebrate them, one visited a sanctuary, prayed, made vows and prostrated oneself upon arriving and leaving (Haran 1969: 11–14).[27] A similar sacrifice may have been alluded to in 2 Sam 15:12 when Ahitophel, at home in Giloh on the eve of Absalom's revolt, offered הזבחים.

In SSK4, the appearance of Yahweh or of divine messengers at sacred places marked by sacrifice or altar building remained important. For example, in 2 Sam 2:16–25, part of the original story of the census plague (McCarter 1984: 517), it was an angel who indicated the location for the altar upon which David offered עלה and שלמים.

Vows made at sacrificial celebrations were an important element in the religious practice of SSK4, as they were for the Elohist. The story of Elkanah, Hannah and Peninnah's pilgrimage to Shiloh provides one such instance (1 Samuel 1). Following a sacrificial meal, Hannah beseeches Yahweh, in response to which Yahweh causes her to bear Samuel (vv 9–20). Two aspects of vow redemption are described. At the time of the זבח הימים, Elkanah brought his household to Shiloh to redeem an earlier vow (v 21). To redeem her vow that any son of hers would be dedicated to Yahweh (v 11), Hannah brings Samuel, together with flour, wine and a sacrificial bull to Yahweh's sanctuary at Shiloh (vv 22–28).

The sharing of sacral meals was a religious element common to both J and SSK4. The aformentioned זבח הימים at Shiloh, for example, was the forum for a sacral meal shared by family members, since Elkanah scrupulously apportions the sacrificial meat among his two wives and their offspring (1 Sam 1:4–5).[28] Samuel blessed the זבח at the *bāmâ* in Zuph so that the sacral meal could be shared (1 Sam 9:13, 22–24). McCarter compares the portion of meat given by Samuel to Saul at this meal with the "thigh of consecration" known in Priestly texts to have been reserved for priests (1980: 180). It is interesting that both 1 Samuel 1 and 1 Samuel 9 presumed regulations for the apportionment of food shared in sacral meals.

Sacrifice commemorating special events was another rite known by J and SSK4. When the Philistines returned the Ark to Beth Shemesh for example, both the cart carrying it and the cows that pulled the cart were offered as עלה on a nearby stone (1 Sam 6:14). Then the Ark itself was placed upon the stone and the event was celebrated by the offering of עלה and שלמים (1 Sam 6:15).

זבחים שלמים were offered at Saul's coronation in Gilgal, when the new king and his people may have joined together in a sacral meal (1 Sam 11:15). The importance of the shared sacrificial meal is indicated in the story of the Ark's long journey from Baalath-judah to Jerusalem (2 Sam 6:1–19). When the Ark was finally placed in its tent in the City of David, David offered עלה and שלמים and blessed the people in

Yahweh's name. His gift to them of bread, meat and raisin cakes may indicate the sharing of a sacral meal. "The parallels suggest that 2 Samuel 6 preserves the details of a historically unique cultic event of a well-known type; there is no reason to suppose that it has been reshaped by any practice dating to post-Davidic times" (McCarter 1984: 182; see also Miller and Roberts 1977: 74–75).[29]

An elaboration upon the sacral meal is seen in the introduction of the משתה (*mišteh*; royal banquet) as a form of post-sacrificial feast. At least once prior to the construction Jerusalem Temple, Solomon offered עלה and שלמים in front of the Ark in Jerusalem. Following this sacrificial act, his household shared in a משתה (1 Kgs 3:15). All these stories indicate the importance of meal sharing as an element of sacrifice, whether as part of family worship or as part of communal or royal celebration.

The many similarities between religious and particularly sacrificial rites in SSK4 and the texts of the Elohist, the Yahwist and Judges indicate a general sense of agreement. Their analysis also provides a basis for examining those special elements in Israelite religion first introduced in SSK4.

The אשם (*'āšām*; guilt offering), later so important to the Priestly writers, was initially employed by a non-Israelite group. In 1 Sam 6:1–18, the Philistines offered an אשם in order to prevent further punishment for having detained the Ark of Yahweh. This sacrifice included cows never previously harnessed, a new wooden cart and magical golden figures offered as indemnity. The אשם was considered complete when the Ark reached Beth Shemesh and the cart and cows transporting it were offered together with additional עלה and with זבחים. Only then could the Philistine princes return home.

Magical water rites were another new element, first mentioned in 2 Samuel. David's water libation (ויסך אתם ליהוה) was a substitution ritual in which water was "sacrificed" to prevent shedding the blood of his three heroes (2 Sam 23:13–17).

In contrast to the spontaneity of sacrifice in J, E and Judges, the ramifications of unauthorized or improper sacrifice in SSK4 were pronounced. Regulations stipulated the correct method of sacrifice; even the choice of cultic vessels was specified.[30] 1 Sam 2:12–17 discussed the improper priestly handling of sacrifices. This was among the transgressions which resulted in the death of Hophni and Phinehas, the sons of the Shilonite priest Eli (1 Sam 2:34). Here, the young priests were condemned for taking portions of sacrificial meat that should have been left for Yahweh.³¹ The anti-Shiloh sentiments in 1 Sam 2 may reflect later thinking, but its attestation to a nascent priesthood is significant. The antiquity of this passage and the authenticity of its ritual practices permit a glimpse of otherwise unknown religious customs at a pre-monarchical Yahwistic sanctuary McCarter 1980: 83, 93; 1984: 13) .

The concept of sanctity of person and object was important too. Not only the Ark but also items for sacrifice (such as לחם הפנים; *leḥem happānîm*) were holy. They could be touched only by Levites or by people in a temporary state of sanctification. This is demonstrated in two separate passages. In one, Samuel tells the elders of Bethlehem to hallow themselves (התקדשו) before sacrificing, while he himself hallows (ויקדש) Jesse and his sons (1 Sam 16:1–13). In the other, Ahimelech, the priest at Nob, offers David and his soldiers the לחם קדש (*leḥem qōdeš*)/לחם הפנים. This holy bread had just been taken from its place before Yahweh. To eat it, David's soldiers had to be in a sanctified state, having refrained from sexual relations with women (1 Sam 21:1–6).³²

The first biblical references to the *bāmâ* are found in 1 Sam 9:11–25 where religious rites at the *bāmâ* in the district of Zuph are mentioned. These rites included the blessing of the sacrifice and the sharing of a sacral meal. According to SSK4, prior to the construction of the Jerusalem Temple *bāmôt* were also located in Bethel (1 Sam 10:5), outside Jerusalem (1 Kgs 3:3) and in Gibeon (1 Kgs 3:4).

In the final biblical passages relating to sacrifice prior to the construction of the Temple, the people sacrificed at *bāmôt* (מזבחים בבמות in 1 Kgs 3:2). Solomon sacrificed (מזבח ומקטיר) at *bāmôt* outside Jerusalem (1 Kgs 3:3). He also went to the chief *bāmâ* at Gibeon to sacrifice (לזבח), and there he offered עלת (1 Kgs 3:4).³³ As we will see, the *bāmâ* would endure throughout most of the Monarchy as the official non-Temple location at which Israelites and Judaeans worshipped. Its existence in the era just before the Monarchy might be expected, as it signified the move toward more formalized religious practice by those people in the process of becoming the nation of Israel. Indeed the beginnings of institutionalized religion as indicated by the existence of *bāmôt* and their staffs of priests may have helped trigger the trajectory toward statehood in the incipient nation of the late Iron I period.

In summary, the era just prior to the construction of the Jerusalem

Temple was one of increasing cultic regulation. Religious rituals of the Patriarchal, Exodus and early Settlement periods continued to be practiced. They include the sharing of sacral meals, the appearance of Yahweh or of divine messengers at places of sacrifice or altar building, and the coming together of clans at annual festivals. Increasing regulation—over pilgrimage festivals, over sacrificial practices, over access to holiness and over places of worship—was a new element. Significantly, this was the era in which the Central Highland settlers became engaged in the process of creating a shared understanding of their past and a shared vision of their future. Their quest for nationhood would culminate in the creation of a monarchy and of a royal religious center. Given the intimate relationship between priests and kings in Israel and other Near Eastern states, it does not seem surprising to find this relationship already developing in the late pre-state days.

Sacrificial Practice in the First Temple Period

A number of biblical texts purport to describe religious practice in Israel and Judah in the centuries during which the First Temple stood in Jerusalem. These include the books of 1 Kings 5–22 through Second Kings 25 (KK) and the witness of pre-exilic prophets such as Elijah, Isaiah, Amos, Hosea and Jeremiah. Other significant passages including the Deuteronomic core (Dtn [Deut 12–26, so Friedman 1987: 118; Knight 1985: 283-85; or Deut 4:44–28:68, so Boling 1992a and Boling 1992b]), the work of the Deuteronomistic Historians and redactors (DH [Dtr[1] and Dtr[2]], so Cross 1973: 274–89) and the earlier of the Priestly writings (P) also illuminate religion in the First Temple period.

The Witness of 1 Kings 5–22 through 2 Kings 1–25. The investigation of religious practice as described in 1 Kings 5–22 through 2 Kings 1–25 focuses upon identifying sacrificial rituals typical to the Temple period of the United and Divided Monarchy. As was true of J, E and SSK4, this material derived from multiple sources and was compiled and edited in an era subsequent to many of the events that it described. It cannot be understood as eyewitness accounting and the editorial perspective of its Deuteronomistic redactors must be acknowledged (Holloway 1992). It also retained records from, and memories of, actual events.

According to DH, the Solomonic Temple was the only legitimate place for the worship of Yahweh. Thus the sins of the kings of Israel were triggered by Jeroboam I's construction of sanctuaries at Bethel and Dan and exacerbated by episodes of Baal worship. In the south, the prevalence of worship at *bāmôt* became the measure of the wrongdoing of the successive kings of Judah. In consequence, any discussion of Israelite and Judaean worship must consider DH's standards and ideals, and their editorial predilections.

The Rule of Solomon. Overall, the description of the sacrifices and festivities celebrating the dedication of the new temple to Yahweh in Jerusalem (1 Kgs 8) can been attributed to DH; it expresses beliefs from a much later era. However, the unusual timing of the opening festivities (1 Kgs 8:2) was Solomonic in origin and in this the monarch acted with political expediency. No longer would Israel's main festival (חג), the festival at which the covenant between Yahweh and the Israelites was renewed, be the Spring Festival of Unleavened Bread. In its place, Solomon instituted the traditional Canaanite Fall Festival of the New Year, conjoining a celebration of the establishment of Yahweh's kingship with that of the unconditional kingship of the House of David (Cross 1973: 238–39).

Following the dedication of the Temple, Solomon made thrice-yearly sacrifices of עלות, שלמים and incense (והקטיר) there (1 Kgs 9:25). While these may have been personal sacrifices similar to those popular in pre-Temple days, their regularity argues otherwise. Instead their calendrical regularization suggests an early effort toward official systematization, eventually culminating in three institutionalized annual pilgrimage festivals celebrated at the Temple under the watchful eye of king and priest.

Solomon is also said to have worshipped the gods of his foreign wives (1 Kgs 11: 4–6)[34] and to have built *bāmôt* for their gods and for the gods Chemosh of Moab and Molech of Ammon (1 Kgs 11:7–8). This condemnation of an otherwise revered king serves to explain the virtual destruction of David's empire barely a generation after his death (1 Kgs 11:9–13). However given the scant evidence for tenth century states in Moab and Ammon (Herr 1997b: 132, 148–51), the Deuteronomistic condemnation of Solomon for his construction of, and worship at, *bāmôt* dedicated to Transjordanian gods must be understood as anachronistic. Aware of later *bāmôt* worship in Transjordan[35] and struggling to understand the civil war that broke out at the end of Solomon's reign, the Deuteronomists here accused Israel's king of wrongs he could not actually have committed.

The Bāmôt. The briefly unified nation of Israel split into two parts late in the tenth century B.C.E. To avoid the potential loss of his constituency, Jeroboam I, the first king of the northern nation of Israel, moved quickly to establish control by manipulating his country's religious structure. Little is known of his residences in Shechem and Penuel (1 Kgs 12:25), but they probably included royal chapels, as were known from Jerusalem and as were typical for Near Eastern monarchs. In the ninth century, Omri established Samaria as Israel's permanent capital (1 Kgs 16:24). His successor Ahab was condemned for building a temple to Baal there (1 Kgs 16:32), but subsequent to Jehu's coup and purge of Baal worship (2 Kgs 10:28), Yahweh worship was established in Samaria (2 Kgs 10:30) as well.[36]

Jeroboam also established Bethel and Dan as sacred sites at which Yahweh could be worshipped (1 Kgs 12:25–30). These sites were chosen both because of their strategic locations on the northern and southern borders of the new nation and because they already contained sanctuaries officiated over by priesthoods with loyal constituents.[37]

Jeroboam inaugurated a royal cult at both these sites that included the observance of a pilgrimage festival (חג). In celebration of the חג, the king offered sacrifice (להקטיר, לזבח) at the altar (1 Kgs 12:32–33). This חג was similar to the fall festival celebrated in Judah in the seventh month (cf. 1 Kgs 8:2, and above), but in Israel it would be celebrated in the eighth month, a move designed to further the religious schism between north and south.

Evidently the establishment of the royal cult at Dan and Bethel neither adequately ensured Israelite loyalty to the new king nor guaranteed his control over his kingdom. Jeroboam thus constructed בית במות (*bêt bāmôt*) throughout Israel. A non-Levitical priestly group, drawn from all classes of society, was created to officiate at them (1 Kgs 12:31). The loyalty of these *bāmôt* priests was reinforced through their additional responsibility for service at the royal sanctuary in Bethel (1 Kgs 12:32) (Nakhai 1994: 227).

In this way a two-tiered religious system came into existence. A royal cult, similar to that in Judah, was established in Israel. In addition to possible chapels at Shechem and Penuel, major sanctuaries were constructed in Dan and Bethel. The royal cult was complemented by an officially sanctioned *bāmôt* system of regional sacred sites. Later, a similar resolution to issues of royal control over religion was implemented in Judah (2 Kgs 23:5; Nakhai 1994: 22).

The Ninth Century Prophet Elijah. The belief that sacrifice could invoke both Yahweh and Baal provided the basis for the mid-ninth century competition between Elijah and the priests of Baal (1 Kgs 18:17–40). In this passage, Yahweh responds to a combination of sacrificial rituals, including the repair of an old Yahwistic altar; the construction of a new altar from twelve stones, which represented the twelve tribes (cf. Exod 24:4), the presentation of a bull for an עלה sacrifice, a water libation, with water poured three times over the עלה from jars (כדים)[38] and the successful invoking of Yahweh's name at the time of the regular מנחה offering (1 Kgs 18:30–38).

This complex series of rites differed in some ways from those enacted by the priests of Baal (1 Kgs 18:25–29). They offered a bull to Baal, and invoked his name repeatedly, set up an altar and danced wildly (ויפסחו) around it. Finally, they gashed themselves (ויתגדדו) until they drew blood. These rituals continued until the hour of the מנחה sacrifice.[39]

The futility of Elijah's efforts to vanquish the priesthood of Baal and its followers was demonstrated by the need for further religious reforms in Israel in the years that followed (2 Kgs 10:18–28). The forum for Jehu's purge of the priests of Baal in Samaria was once again a major sacrificial event, a great sacrifice (זבח גדול) to Baal (v 19), in which זבחים and עלות were offered (v 24).

Judaean Royalty and the Temple Priesthood. Several passages in Second Kings present information concerning the financing of the Jerusalem Temple through the collection of sacrificial offerings. The financial reorganization of the Temple during the reign of Joash late in the ninth century was detailed in 2 Kgs 12:4–16. Like those of his later successors Hezekiah and Josiah, Joash's Temple renovations occurred during a period of intense military threat, in this instance from Hazael of Aram (2 Kgs 12:17–18). Presumably, for Joash as later for Hezekiah and Josiah, work undertaken to restore the Temple was part of an overall program designed to strengthen the state by promoting support of its central religious institution.

Consecrated silver originally reached the Temple coffers either through taxation or through voluntarily contributions. The priests also had a private source of income, culled from funds contributed by the people through the offering of אשם and חטאות sacrifices (2 Kgs 12:4–16).[40] These offerings, designated for the priests' own use, were not brought into the Temple.

Joash was raised under the tutelage of the priest Jehoiada, and this may have influenced the important changes in the regulations regarding sacrificial practice that now took place. A new collection box was placed in the entrance to the Temple, and contributions to the Temple were deposited in it (2 Kgs 12:9). The silver accumulated was used to finance Temple repairs, to purchase materials and to pay the artisans. Separate contributions of silver were used for crafting cultic paraphernalia, including ספות כסף מזמרות מזרקות חצצרות כל־כלי זהב וכלי ־כסף (2 Kgs 12:14).

The significance of this detailed description of changes in the rules regarding Temple offerings must be seen in relation to the passage that follows. To deflect Hazael's threat to Jerusalem, Joash sends the accumulated treasures of the Temple and palace to the Aramean king (2 Kgs 12:17–18). However the priests' own treasury remains untouched, thus enabling the Temple to remain functional in the financially difficult period that followed. The allocation of sacrificial income thus enables the king and his priesthood to ensure the continuity of the Temple even in the face of political and military adversity.

A veritable catalogue of Judaean sacrifice in the late eighth century appears in the story of King Ahaz of Judah (2 Kgs 16). According to DH, Ahaz sinned by sacrificing at *bāmôt*, on hilltops and under trees (ויזבח ויקטר בבמות ועל־הגבעות ותחת כל־עץ רענן) (v 4). It is ironic, then, that his submission to the Neo-Assyrian monarch Tiglath-pileser III was also described in the context of sacrifice, since Ahaz built a sacrificial altar like that of his Assyrian sovereign (vv 10–18). Ahaz offered the morning sacrifice (לבקר) on his old altar (v 15) and used the new altar for his personal offerings of עלתו and מנחתו, נסכו (*niskô*) and the blood of שלמים sacrifices (v 13). The new altar was also used by the people of Judah for the morning עלה, the evening מנחה, the עלה, מנחה and blood of the שלמים offerings, as well as for the royal עלה and מנחה (v 15). This chapter supplies many details concerning the regularization of worship in Jerusalem in the third quarter of the eighth century B.C.E.

As part of his effort to regain Judah's independence from Assyria late in the eighth century B.C.E., Hezekiah embarked on a program of religious reform (2 Kgs 18:3–8). Ultimately unable to achieve his political goal, he, like Joash before him, raided the Temple treasury and even dismantled part of the Temple itself in order to purchase Sennacherib's favor. After Hezekiah's death, his son Manasseh reestablished many of the worship practices that Hezekiah had so recently purged (2 Kgs 21:2–9). His ability to do this so quickly and efficiently may have been a consequence of the strength of the Temple priesthood, which again had not been adversely affected by the royal plundering of Temple riches.

During the reign of Josiah, Temple offerings continued to provide the means for Temple renovations. Monies deposited in the collection box were used to fund the repairs and to pay the artisans. The high priest Hilkiah oversaw the process (2 Kgs 22:3–7). Religious reform had political overtones, as it had during the earlier reigns of Joash and Hezekiah. In this instance, the shifting geopolitical situation among Judah's powerful neighbors, Egypt, Assyria and Babylon, provided the impetus for reform. Again the priesthood, the collector of Temple offerings, played a critical role.

Summary: Worship in 1 Kings 5–2 Kings 25. Despite its Deuteronomistic perspective, KK contains important information about religious practice in Israel and Judah in the First Temple period. Centralized organization of worship as a means of establishing royal control was the motivating force behind the sweeping changes in religious practice noted in KK. These changes took place in times of political and military tension, when it was imperative to create a more powerful and financially solvent monarchy. In the south, they included efforts to focus attention upon the Jerusalem Temple, especially through the physical renovation of this central religious structure. Financial reorganization of the Temple treasury to support reconstruction efforts required the reorganization of funding. Here, the mechanism for offering gifts to the Temple and the way in which the priests controlled these offerings were critical. Indeed, the Jerusalem priests are shown to have had access to funds sufficient to support themselves and to reinvigorate Temple worship in times of military crisis and financial insolvency.

The construction of royal sanctuaries in Jerusalem, Bethel and Dan permitted the royalty illusions of Canaanite-style grandeur and permanence, more convincing in the long-lived Judaean House of David than in the briefer dynasties of Israel. Amos clearly articulated the matter *viz à viz* the northern kingdom when, in the mid-eighth century, he described Bethel as a king's sanctuary and a royal palace (מקדש־מלך הוא ובית ממלכה הוא) (Amos 7:13).

With these royal sanctuaries, the kings and their priests forced a mechanism for centralized control over Israelite and Judaean worshippers. Concomitant with this, a system of sacrificial offerings was established, at least in Judah (cf. 2 Kgs 12:4–16; 22:3–10). Its goal was to provide the royal sanctuaries and their priesthoods with an independent source of income. Pilgrimage festivals, either adapted from the Canaanite or created anew, became a means of creating community and exercising political and economic control over the rural populations of Israel and Judah.

At the same time, networks of regional *bāmôt* were established early in the Divided Monarchy. Their goal was to provide the people of Israel and Judah with access to easily accessible religious centers and to neutralize otherwise disenfranchised clergy by presenting them with alternate positions of status. From the anti-*bāmôt* stance adopted by DH, one can see the tensions inherent in this dual-access approach to Yahwism.

Over time, the *bāmôt* priesthood seems to have grown increasingly independent of the royal clergy. To eliminate the threat to monarchical authority that they came to pose, Hezekiah (2 Kgs 18:4) and Josiah (2 Kgs 23:5) waged campaigns against the rural *bāmôt*, hoping to eradicate the *bāmôt* priesthood's power base and to create additional support for the Jerusalem Temple (Nakhai 1994: 29).

Despite these attempts at control, it remained possible for Israelites and Judaeans to worship Yahweh in places of their own choosing. In the mid-ninth century for example, Elijah's battle with the priests of Baal took place at a mountaintop site far from the nation's capital and religious centers (1 Kgs 18). Later Naaman carried earth from Israel to Aram in order to offer Yahweh עלה and זבחים on soil from Yahweh's homeland, albeit in a foreign country (2 Kgs 5:15–18).

Not surprisingly, the most common terms for worship in KK came from the vocabulary of sacrifice. The roots ז.ב.ח., ע.ל.ה. and ק.ט.ר. and the term שלמם, were the most popular among the sacrificial vocabulary. They were used to refer to the proper worship of Yahweh as well as to the worship of foreign gods by Israelites or others. Regular morning and evening sacrifices are described in the stories of Elijah (1 Kgs 18:29, 36), Elisha (2 Kgs 3:20) and Ahaz (2 Kgs 16:15). Animal sacrifice for the enactment of blood rites is known from the reign of Ahaz (2 Kgs 16:13, 15). Water rites, a form of substitution sacrifice, were carried out by the prophets Elijah (1 Kgs 18:34–39) and Elisha (2 Kgs 3:4–20). As in the premonarchical era, sacrifice was the religious rite *par excellence* in the First Temple period.

THE EIGHTH CENTURY PROPHETS: ISAIAH, AMOS AND HOSEA

The long-standing prophetic tradition of opposition to sacrificial rites began with Samuel (1 Sam 15:22–23).[41] In general, prophets cautioned against offering sacrifices to Yahweh in place of living righteously. It is ironic then that the prophets' critical statements provide an important source of information about sacrificial practices in Israel and Judah.

In Israel of the eighth century B.C.E., Amos protested against morning זבחים, tithes, unleavened תודה (tôdâ) and נדבות (nidāvot) (Amos 4:4–5). He denied that זבחים and the מנחה were part of the wilderness tradition or that Yahweh wanted חגים, festive assemblies (עצרתיכם), שלמים, עלות, songs and harp music (Amos 5:21–27). Hosea also phrased his complaints about Israel in the vocabulary of sacrifice that was, in his opinion, offered illegitimately (Hos 2:13; 4:13–15; 6:6; 8:11–15; 9:4; 11:2).

Some years later in Judah, Isaiah claims that Yahweh desired righteous actions rather than sacrifice (מנחה, עלות, זבחים and more) (Isa 1:10–17). שלמים, מנחה, זבח and vows would provide the means through which Egypt would acknowledge and serve Yahweh, at altar and at *maṣṣebâ* (Isa 19:21).

The statements of these three prophets illustrate the range of sacrificial rites that were part of Israelite and Judaean worship in the eighth century. They also indicate a diversity of thought about appropriate ways of worshipping Yahweh. Although sacrifice was widely accepted as *the* way to worship, there was a dissident tradition, one rooted in prophetic circles, which excoriated improper sacrifice or sacrifice at the expense of righteous actions.[42]

As demonstrated above, sacrifice was the critical element in the royal cultus. It was not only the traditional religious gesture for expressing loyalty to one's god, but was also the primary source for funding religious institutions. The manipulation of sacrifice for political and military purposes was accepted as a royal prerogative. At its highest level, the priesthood was complicit in these monarchical stratagems. Seen from this perspective, it is clear that the prophetic diatribe against illegitimate sacrifice represented more than a pious effort to reform Yahwism. It was no less than a full-fledged attack on the monarchy and on its priesthood.

THE DEUTERONOMISTIC LAW CODE AND THE WORK OF THE DEUTERONOMISTS

Deuteronomy 12–26 (Dtn; or perhaps, Deut 4:44–28:68; see above) is understood as the late eighth century legal code upon which later Deuteronomistic writers expanded. Some have suggested northern roots for the fledging Deuteronomic community, although its specific origins are a matter of some debate.[43] Others disagree, claiming Josianic (see below) or even exilic origins for the text.[44] Given the correspondence between Hezekiah's royal acts and provisions within Dtn, the latter's origin within Hezekiah's reign seems likely (Weinfeld 1992: 174). Later, during Josiah's reign, it was found again by the priest Hilkiah (2 Kgs 22:8) and served as the basis for the Josianic reforms, as well (2 Kgs 23:3).[45]

Nearly all the information in Deuteronomy 12–26 concerning sacrifice is contained in Deuteronomy 12. Moses, said to be giving God's word to Israel before it entered Canaan, orders the demolition of Canaanite sacred places and objects (Deut 12:2–3). He then instructs Israel to worship Yahweh only in the chosen place in which Yahweh would cause his name to dwell, the implied but unnamed city of Jerusalem (Deut 12:4–5, 11, 13–14). This prohibition against sacrifice enacted at multiple local sites stands in contrast to older cultic and legal norms (Exod 20:24).[46] It is interesting that, given Deuteronomy 12–26's insistence upon centralization through its focus upon worship at the "chosen place," regulations concerning communal sacrifice in that special place are conspicuously absent (Weinfeld 1992: 177).

Worship was to take the form of sacrifices and offerings, including עֹלָה, זְבָחִים, tithes, contributions, vow-offerings, free-will offerings and first-born cattle and sheep (Deut 12:6). These sacrifices were to be shared by families, eaten communally in the presence of Yahweh at the "chosen place" (Deut 12:7). The consumption of sacrifice was seen as a way of providing for one's dependents and for the poor.[47] Many passages adjured Israelite men to share their sacral meals with their sons and daughters, male and female slaves, and the orphans, widows, resident aliens and Levites living in their settlements (*inter alia*, Deut 12:12, 18; 16:14). The importance of the Levites and of Israel's responsibility for providing them with support is specially emphasized (Deut 18:1–8).

The sacrificial regulations in Dtn make no mention of the priesthood as the intermediary between God and Israelites who offered sacrifices, although this theme was critically important in the thinking of the Priestly writers (Lev 9:22–24, *inter alia*). Nor were priests needed to expiate sin, for this was done through confession and prayer (Deut 21:7–8) rather than through sacrifice (Weinfeld 1992: 177).[48] The Priestly concern for sacrifice as a means of provisioning priests (Lev 7:29–36, *inter alia*) likewise did not have its roots in the Deuteronomic law codes.

Other rules for proper sacrifice are explained in Deut 12:8–28. Important among them is the proscription against eating blood in sacrificial or other meat (Deut 12:16, 23–27), a rule also important in the Priestly texts (see Gen 9:4–5; Lev 19:26) and reflected in the story of Saul's altar at Michmash (1 Sam 14:31–35). However, Deuteronomy 12–26 sanctioned the consumption of meat for non-sacral purposes (Deut 12:15, 21–22).

Appropriate occasions for sacrifice are now linked to the observance of the three annual pilgrimage festivals, Pesach or Mazzot (Deut 16:1–8), Shavuoth (Deut 16:9–12) and Sukkoth (Deut 16:13–15). Instructions are given for bringing offerings to Yahweh in his chosen place during these pilgrimage holidays (Deut 16:16–17).

The discussion of "Canaanite" religious practices (Deut 12:2–3) that would provide the language for the Deuteronomistic excoriation of Israel, is significant. Moses cautioned Israel to destroy Canaanite sacred places (כל־המקמות אשר עבדו־שם הגוים), and their altars (מצבתם, מזבחתם, אשריהם), and idols (פסילי אלהיהם). In this way, Deuteronomy 12–26 moves to counteract two important elements of contemporary religious life. These were the tolerated diversity within religious practice and the proliferation of Yahwistic sanctuaries that had been established by the kings of Israel and Judah.

In this context, it is interesting to consider what Deuteronomy 12–26 (and, later, the Deuteronomistic Historians who utilized this material) may have known about actual Canaanite religious practice. Inasmuch as there were Canaanites still living among the Israelites of the north (Ezek 16:3),[49] the Deuteronomic condemnation of Canaanite religion might have reflected familiarity with their traditional cultic practices. However, the composition of Dtn occurred some five hundred years after the overall collapse of Canaanite society in the southern Levant. Some religious practices or institutions disparaged by the

Deuteronomists may not have had Canaanite precedents but, like the *bāmôt,* were uniquely Israelite religious developments. The Deuteronomic diatribe against Canaanite religion is best understood to reflect intense antipathy toward sanctioned Israelite religious practice, especially when viewed in light of the chronic animosity in the north between the royal court and its prophetic antagonists.[50] These factors would have facilitated the popularity of Dtn in Jerusalem. When the text criticized "Canaanites," knowledgeable Jerusalemites heard a condemnation of "Israelites," until recently their great enemy (see 2 Kgs 16: 5–8 for the Syro-Ephraimite War).[51] The message of Dtn was made all the more powerful since, soon after, Israel suffered the disastrous consequences of Assyrian conquest and domination.

During the reign of Josiah late in the seventh century, the Deuteronomistic Historians (DH) expanded upon the earlier text of Dtn, which had proved so critical in shaping Hezekiah's religious policy of centralization. They also compiled and edited those documents that now comprise the books of Joshua, Judges, 1 and 2 Samuel, 1 Kings, and 2 Kings 1–23:35, creating a narrative sequence extending from Deuteronomy through the destruction of the First Temple (Dtr[1]). A final version of this text (Dtr[2]) was made during the Exilic period (Cross 1973: 287–89).

DH describes Israelite and Judaean religion so as to suggest that many people participated in a richly variegated cult, as detailed in 2 Kgs 23:4–25.[52] They also attribute the various travails of the Israelites and Judaeans to their transgressions and to those of their rulers and their priests, according to their own special standards. They condemn ritual acts that were widely accepted as legitimate. The offering of עלה and שלמים for example, once a traditional way of commemorating special events,[53] become a Deuteronomistic device for explaining the condemnation of Saul and his dynasty (1 Sam 10:8; 13:8–14). Similarly, DH seizes upon the issue of worship at Bethel, making the altar there the focus of the denunciation of Jeroboam I (1 Kgs 13:1–10).

DH offers deviation from loyalty to Yahweh as the explanation for the division of the monarchy at the end of Solomon's reign (1 Kgs 11:9–13). The fall of the kingdom of Israel is attributed to similar apostasies (2 Kgs 17:10). The Deuteronomistically determined sins of the rulers and people of Israel and Judah are condemned in formulaic language. Prime among these sins are sacrifice at *bāmôt* sanctuaries (מזבחים ומקטרים בבמות; 1 Kgs 22:42–44; 2 Kgs 12:3; 14:14; 15:35;

17:10; 23:5) and sacrifice to Nehushtan, the bronze serpent said to have been made by Moses and kept in the Jerusalem Temple (2 Kgs 18:4).[54]

DH and Transitions in Cultic Observances

The writings of DH document a move away from traditional cultic observances and demonstrate a new understanding of ritual acts. This is apparent in a number of Deuteronomistic passages inserts into the narratives in Samuel and Kings. For example, DH inserted 1 Sam 7:2–17 into the text of 1 Samuel (Mayes 1983: 96, n. 41). In response to a speech by Samuel (vv 2–4), the Israelites assembled at Mizpah (vv 5–6) and offered water sacrifices (וישאבו־מים וישפכו לפני יהוה) intended to wash away their guilt (McCarter 1980: 144). These water sacrifices differ from the "substitution" water sacrifices that were offered in pre-DH texts by David, Elijah and Elisha. In addition, they fast (ויצומו) and confess their sins to Yahweh (ויאמרו שם חטאנו ליהוה) (v 6). While both fasting and confession were intended to purge the community of guilt, in this instance fasting provided a special way to call out for Yahweh's attention.[55] Samuel's subsequent offering of an עולה כליל (*'ôlâ kālil*) was followed by a prayer for divine intercession against the Philistines (v 9).

This passage is significant for its documentation of the transition between literal and figurative sacrifice. Fasting, confession and a purifying water sacrifice were necessary ritual components, but they were components that required little by way of true economic sacrifice. At the same time, traditional animal sacrifice remained part of an entreaty for divine intercession.

Solomon's dedication of the Jerusalem Temple (1 Kings 8) is also attributed to DH (Cross 1973: 275–76). Once the important male Israelites had assembled in celebration of the חג of the seventh month (v 2), the lengthy ceremony began. Sacrifice initiated (זבחים זבח לפני יהוה in v 5) and closed (המנחה, העלה, זבח השלמים and חלבי השלמים in vv 62–64) the celebration. Although the language of sacrifice was traditional, the enormity of the offerings ("sheep and oxen in numbers past counting or reckoning" in v 5; "twenty-two thousand oxen and a hundred and twenty thousand sheep" in v 63) suggests that opulence rather than piety was what was desired.

Most significantly, the greatest part of this complex ceremony comprised non-sacrificial rituals. They include the positioning of the

Ark within the Temple (vv 6–8), the blessing of the people by the king (vv 14–21, 55–61), the blessing of the king by the people (v 66) and the offering of prayer (vv 22–53).

The analysis of 1 Sam 7:2–17 indicated the Deuteronomistic transition from the offering of goods to substitution rituals and other forms of observance. The Deuteronomistic description of the Temple dedication in 1 Kings 8 likewise underscores the late seventh century transition to complex religious rites, among which sacrifice was no longer the single central component. Instead, the culmination of pious observance was now prayer and blessing. This understanding had originated earlier in Dtn, which indicated that Yahweh had no literal need for food. Instead, the food of offering was to be shared with those in need. Passages in the book of Deuteronomy also suggest that "spiritual purification and repentance—consisting of confession and prayer—and not sacrificial offerings expiate sin" (Weinfeld 1992: 177).

To summarize, late in the seventh century B.C.E., a group of people with access to the Judaean royal court advocated wide-ranging religious reforms. These reforms were based upon prophetic teachings and otherwise little known law codes. Traditional places of worship and time-honored religious rituals, in particular worship at *bāmôt* and the ritual of sacrifice, became the vehicle for criticizing Israelites past and present. Worship was to take place exclusively at the Jerusalem Temple. The long-legitimate *bāmôt* and the ancient sanctuary at Bethel were now viewed as symbols of Israel's wicked past.

There was also a growing emphasis on non-material modes of worship including atonement, prayer and blessing. This is significant because they gave Judaeans legitimate ways to worship Yahweh without contravening the newly articulated exclusivity of the Jerusalem Temple. Ultimately (see Fishbane 1998), they provided the means for early rabbis to construct an enduring segue from Temple sacrifice to Judaic worship.

THE PRIESTLY WRITERS

The Priestly texts, comprising most of Leviticus and significant passages in Genesis, Exodus and Numbers, were almost entirely devoted to instructions for enacting cultically correct religious acts, in order to create a holy relationship with God. Critical scholarship of the Priestly material acknowledges its composition from disparate documents.[56] In general, the lack of consensus concerning the origins of the Priestly text reflects the difficulties encountered when applying source critical tools to this non-narrative genre of biblical literature (Anderson 1992b: 876).

To assess the historicity of the Priestly document and to better understand the setting from which it emerged, efforts have been made to pinpoint passages that may have recorded actual events. For example, an analysis of Exodus 35–39, Leviticus 8–9 and Numbers 7 suggests that these passages describe the construction and consecration of the Ark and the Tabernacle, and the initiation rites of the priestly cult (Levine 1965: 307).[57] The inclusion of two types of sacrificial instruction, for both prescriptive and descriptive sacrifices (Levine 1965; Rainey 1970), likewise indicates a high degree of realism within the P material.

The Priestly work, and especially the Holiness Code, shares concerns with those expressed in Ezekiel 40–48 (Eissfeldt 1965: 238; Boadt 1992: 717–20), although the order in which these two texts were composed was not been firmly established. Even so, the similarity between these documents supports a claim of Priestly realism (Friedman 1981: 60–61, 100, 108). According to B. Levine, a study of the social and religious community reflected in Leviticus creates a profile that "suit[s] the life situation of the reconstructed Judean community in the period after the Return, in the late sixth century B.C.E. and thereafter." However, "it is probable that some of the cultic praxis described in Leviticus is of great antiquity and reflects preexilic patterns of worship. All the contents Leviticus need not not be assigned to a single period of biblical history" (1992: 320).

The highly developed sacrificial cult, with specialized language used to describe complex ritual behaviors, also signifies the "maturation and individuation of the biblical cult . Thus the development of the Priestly vocabulary is part of a larger movement to develop a specialized and unique cultic identity that one sees in other cultic centers in the Iron Age" (Anderson 1992b: 875). Given the likelihood that the roots of the Priestly material were located in pre-exilic Temple practice, it is instructive to see what information P contains that may be relevant to the study of Israelite sacrifice.

For the Priestly writers, the sacrificial system was "intimately connected with the impurity system" (Milgrom 1992: 457). Sacrifice was made in response to specific criteria and in accordance with specific regulations. No longer were altars to be erected and sacrifices offered dependent upon individual desires. Instead, the enactment of sacrificial rites took place in a single public venue, the Tabernacle/Tent of Meeting[58] (see, *inter alia*, Lev 1:1, 3; 3:13; 4:4). Spontaneity of worship was replaced by calendric regulation (Leviticus 34; Numbers 28–29). The אשם and the חטאת sacrifices, although not the exclusive province of the Priestly writers, were fully developed by them (Lev 4:1–6:8; 7:1–10).[59]

Most of the Priestly laws concerning sacrifice and offering are found in Leviticus 1–7 and in Numbers 15, 28 and 29. The Leviticus material presents general rules for performing sacrifices, while the material in Numbers often indicates specific applications of the general rules (Anderson 1992b: 877). Other passages also underscore P's concern with didactic recitations of correct ritual behaviors. For example, to the Yahwist's story of Noah, P appended the prohibition against eating the blood of animals (Gen 9:1–5), a regulation also found in the Holiness Code (Lev 17:10–14). The J story of the *paschal* sacrifice is concerned with haste, with safety, and with Yahweh's actions in Egypt (Exod 12:21–23). P adds to it numerous regulations explaining how to choose, apportion, prepare and eat the sacrificial animal (Exod 12:1–10).

The Priestly texts of Exodus, Leviticus and Numbers (like those of Ezekiel 40–48) describe an ornate cultic practice concerned with holiness, contamination and ritual purity. They claim that sacrifice, when properly made, helped to ensure the holy status of the individual and of the community by granting entry into the realm of the ritually pure.

Correct sacrificial acts removed advertent and inadvertent guilt, expiated individual and group sins, and ensured the proper observation of holidays and the contribution of tithes. For the individual, there was a transition from expiation to consecration, culminating in fellowship (Rainey 1970: 498). This concern for ethical issues was a critical element in the Priestly documents.

Equally important, sacrifice provided a means of ritually bonding the whole community of Israel. The Priestly writers demonstrate concern for the community of Israel, formulated in its tribal and priestly components (Numbers 7; 8:5–19). Concern for the poor was expressed through the inclusion of offerings such as birds and cereal (Milgrom 1992: 458). Purification offerings were matched to the social (Lev 4:1–23) and economic (Lev 5:1–13) standing of those individuals making offerings (Anderson 1992b: 875). These can be understood as ways of expressing concern for communal well being.

The absence of theological tenets such as holiness and purity in the

Late Bronze Age texts at Ugarit was noted earlier. Outside the work of the Priestly writers, biblical Israel too rarely expressed concern for such matters.[60] Gen 1:27 and Lev 19:2 are often cited as proof that P believed humankind holy because it was created in the image of its holy deity. However, Lev 20:7–8 suggests that for P, holiness meant being in a proper relationship with God, a relationship defined by obedience to Yahweh's many rules. Properly enacted sacrifice was an important way of expressing this obedience. In formulating and articulating complicated laws of cultic praxis and in linking them to the spiritual quality of holiness, P contributes an order and a rationale to Israelite religion that differs from those expressions of faith and from those worship practices that preceded it.

These Priestly texts provide an end-point for our examination of biblical sacrifice. In their insistence that adherence to strict ritual regulations creates a state of holiness linking individual to nation and to God, the Priestly texts differ significantly from the earlier texts of J, E, Judges, SSK4 and KK, stripped as much as possible of their Deuteronomistic interpolations. Dtn, DH and P, on the other hand, share many theological and cultic similarities, including their demand for the triumph of the Jerusalem Temple as Israel's sole sacred place, and their claim for the Temple clergy as its single legitimate priesthood.

SUMMARY

Enlightened by anthropological advances in the study of religion and society that suggest that sacrifice provides a witness to specific religious rituals and serves as a way of examining society at-large, this discussion of Canaanite and Israelite religion has focused on the rite of sacrifice. Not surprisingly, the testimony of the Ugaritic ritual texts and of the HB was to a multiplicity of worship experiences and to the importance of sacrifice as the primary means of ritual enactment.

For Canaanites and Israelites, sacrifice was *the* sacred rite, the primary focus of religious ritual and the means by which people defined their relationship to each other and to their deities. Monarchs defined their relationship to gods or God through the fulfillment of sacrificial responsibilities, and defined the responsibilities of their subjects in the same way. One important factor was social and political loyalty. Just as important, however, was the economic element, in which a subject provided his master, whether human or divine, with requisite provisions.

Offerings of livestock, agricultural goods and luxury items are all attested in the texts.

Sacrifice also provided the forum for the convening of the social group. Sacral meals were shared at one-time gatherings and at annual festivals. Kingship was proclaimed, and covenants ratified and ties between tribes or clans confirmed.

Neither the Ugaritic texts nor the HB can serve as a guidebook for the excavation of Canaanite and Israelite sacred sites. Insofar as they describe a wide variety of religious acts, however, they well support the evidence of archaeology, which, as we shall see, has consistently borne witness to the spiritual richness of Canaanite and Israelite cult.

NOTES

[1] Rituals other than sacrifice were also incorporated into Canaanite and Israelite religious ceremonies. Texts and archaeological remains indicate the reciting or chanting of liturgical compositions accompanied by music and, perhaps, by dance. Purification through ritual washing took place. The dressing of statues of the deities and their transfer from temple to palace are attested in Ugaritic ritual texts. Festivals such as the New Year and special occasions such as the coronation of a king required special cultic acts.

[2] Religion in Mesopotamia, too, involved the "feeding" of the gods, as sacrificial foods were placed in front of statues of the deities (see Heidel 1963: 46; Anderson 1987: 18–19).

[3] Animal sacrifice was practiced in the Mediterranean world, including Greece, Ugarit, Phoenicia and Israel. It was not, however, employed by either the Egyptians or the Mesopotamians (Rainey 1996b: 71).

[4] Olyan suggests that an important difference between Israelite sacrificial cult and the cults of other West Semitic religions was that the "manipulation of blood" played a central role in Israel, but not elsewhere (1997: 83).

[5] The poetic texts reflect archaic situations and attained their final form through a long process of scribal conservation (de Tarragon 1980: 183–84).

[6] The $\check{s}lmm$ offering in the Ugaritic and biblical texts has been described as a cultic offering in which sacrificial animals were consumed by worshippers at a festive meal (Anderson 1987: 36–37, 51).

[7] Anderson notes that in both Ugaritic and Priestly sacrifice, the offering of the עולה and the שלמים were paired. The former offered nourishment to the deity and the latter to the people (1992b: 879).

[8] A $d\underline{n}$ was a jar, a $k\underline{t}$ "a measure for foodstuffs" (Gordon 1965: 386, 424).

[9] Coogan suggests that Israelite religion (at least in its private and non-official

manifestations) was at one with Canaanite religions of the first millennium B.C.E. (1987a: 120).

[10] For a fuller discussion of the Deuteronomistic and Priestly writers, see below.

[11] For a reflection of the centrality of Temple sacrifice in biblical thought, see Fishbane 1998: 123–35. In this essay, he traces rabbinic substitutions for Temple sacrifice in the centuries after the Temple's final destruction in 70 C.E.

[12] For more on Source Criticism and the Documentary Hypothesis, see Knight and Tucker, eds. 1985 and articles therein; Friedman 1987; Barton 1992; and references therein.

[13] Friedman tentatively assigns Genesis 14 to J (1987: 247). According to von Rad, however, the story was "substantially, generically, and literarily completely isolated and was apparently first incorporated into its present context by a redactor" (von Rad 1972: 175).

[14] Friedman tentatively assigned Genesis 15 to J, but indicates that it may have been a composite text or one written by the final biblical redactor (1987: 247, 256). J. Ha, however, stresses the compositional unity of this passage and suggests that it was written by an official scribe or teacher (1989: 215–17).

[15] Other instances of "halving" related to covenant-making are found in Josh 8:30–35 (following a sacrifice to Yahweh, the people of Israel, divided in two, faced Mt. Gerizim and Mt. Ebal and listened to Joshua read the law) and Jer 34:18–20 (a threat and a reminder of Gen 15:10). Judg 19:22–30 (a man cut his concubine into pieces to rally Israelites to action) and 1 Sam 11:7 (Saul cut a pair of oxen into pieces to threaten the Israelites) also relate dismemberment to some sort of covenantal relationship among the Israelite tribes.

[16] The erecting of the cairn may be a J element within this story (Speiser 1964: 248). Alternately, the entire passage may be attributed to the Elohist writer (Friedman 1987: 248).

[17] Although the question of human sacrifice in the HB is an important one, it is not discussed here since it was not a part of regular Israelite worship. Consequently, the Elohist's description of Abraham's near-sacrifice of Isaac (Gen 22:1–19) is not among the ritual acts included in this discussion. For further discussion of child sacrifice in the HB, see Smith 1990: 132–38.

[18] The number seven had special qualities in the sacred world of Canaan and Israel.

[19] The enduring popularity of the prescribed altar is attested in Josh 8:30–31, where a late Deuteronomic editor (Mayes 1983: 56–57) claimed that Joshua built the Mt. Ebal altar according to these regulations.

[20] So, e.g., Cross 1973: 293.

[21] Genesis 14 may originally have been an independent composition. Had J incorporated it into the biblical text, then vv 18–20 might be construed as a Yahwistic allusion to the appropriateness of Jerusalem for Israelite worship.

However, the sharing of a sacral meal by Abraham and Melchizedek, the high priest of El Elyon in Salem, is far from a full-fledged endorsement of the centrality of Jerusalem for the worship of Yahweh.

[22] According to Boling, the core text should be dated to the time of the Yahwist, in the tenth century (1992a: 1114). However, if history writing did not begin until later (Na'aman 1994b: 227–30), then the date for the composition of the Judges material must be altered accordingly.

[23] The seventh-early sixth century compiling and editing of Deuteronomy, Joshua, Judges, 1–2 Samuel and 1–2 Kings is generally attributed to the Deuteronomistic Historians, although modifications to this idea have been suggested. For more on DH, see below and, *inter alia*, Cross 1973; Friedman 1981; Ginsberg 1982; Ackroyd 1985; Peckham 1985; Friedman 1987; Boling 1992a; Boling 1992b; McKenzie 1992; Weinfeld 1992; Albertz 1994; Cross 1998; and see McKenzie 1992 for an overview of scholarly research on the Deuteronomistic History.

[24] I would like to thank S. Ackerman for pointing this out, and for elaborating upon its relevance to the story of Hannah in 1 Samuel 1 (Ackerman 1998: 257–64).

[25] McCarter suggests a date as early as the pre-Temple period of the United Monarchy (1980: 23–30).

[26] See Ackerman 1998: 257–64.

[27] If the annual celebration in Judges 21 and in 1 Sam 1:3 was the fall vineyard festival, then the זבח הימים of 1 Sam 1:21 may have been the next annual occurrence of this fall festival. However, v 21 states that Elkanah intended not only to sacrifice but also to redeem his vow, a vow not mentioned in the story of previous trip to Shiloh. It may be, then, that two celebrations were referred to in 1 Samuel, one public and the other private.

[28] For a discussion of this festival within the context of the family cult, see Albertz 1994: 101–2.

[29] Psalm 132 also described the transfer of the Ark from the countryside to Jerusalem. It has been dated to the time of David (Cross 1973: 97).

[30] These cultic implements included a three-pronged fork (המזלג שלש־השנים) and four cooking pots (כיור, דוד, and קלחת; 1 Sam 2:13–14). McCarter prefers the reading of 4QSam[a], which mentioned only two cooking pots, the סיר and the פרור (1980: 79). According to Kelso, כיור referred to a copper vessel used in the Tabernacle or First Temple as a laver, but in the sanctuary at Shiloh as a cooking pot. The דוד, קלחת, פרור and סיר were all cooking pots, most commonly clay, but perhaps made of metal when used in the Shiloh sanctuary (1948: 18–31).

[31] It is difficult to describe the correct method of apportionment since vv 13–14 and vv 15–16 present two different ways of preparing the sacrificial offerings.

³² This story originated during David's reign (McCarter 1984: 13).

³³ Despite Deuteronomic interpolations in the 1 Kings 3 material, there is no reason to doubt its authenticity.

³⁴ In vv 7–8, Solomon is described as worshipping in ways generally associated with Israelite *bāmâ* worship. The verbs used to describe Solomon's worship at the "foreign" *bāmôt* (ז.ב.ח. and ק.ט.ר.) are otherwise used to describe Israelite *bāmâ* worship (Barrick 1980: 53).

³⁵ This is the first biblical mention of *bāmôt* being used for non-Israelite religious practice. The Mesha Stele is a Moabite text dated to the late ninth century (Pritchard, ed. 1969: 320–21; Graham 1989; Lemaire 1994; Pardee 1997). A century later, Isaiah also referred to Moabite *bāmôt* (Isa 15:2; 16:2). For more on the Mesha Stele, see chapter 6.

³⁶ The longevity of the Yahwistic shrines at Shechem, Shiloh and Samaria is suggested by a passage in Jeremiah. It is set in the period just following the Babylonian destruction of Jerusalem and the subsequent murder of Gedaliah, the governor who Nebuchadnezzar had appointed to oversee Judah. Upon learning of Gedaliah's murder, eighty men from these three towns shaved their beards, tore their clothes and cut themselves to indicate their intense mourning. They then hurried to Jerusalem, carrying offerings for the Temple (Jer 41:4–5). It is surely not coincidental that it was men from Shechem, Shiloh and Samaria who engaged in sacred and traditional rites at this time of great national crisis.

³⁷ Judges 17–18 describes the establishment of a premonarchical sanctuary at Dan, and the installation of a priesthood there. Bethel was a sacred place traditionally associated with the patriarchs and matriarchs (Gen 12:8; 13:3–4; 28:10–22; 35:7, 8, 13–15), with religious activities in the tribal era (20:18–28), and with the work of the prophets Deborah (Judg 4:4–5) and Samuel (1 Sam 7:15–16).

³⁸ The כד (*kad*) was a clay water jar (Kelso 1948: 19).

³⁹ The significance of the regular מנחה offering as an appropriate time for entreating Yahweh is also seen in 2 Kgs 3:20. There, Yahweh delivered the water promised by Elisha to the Judahite army in Moab in the morning at the time of the מנחה sacrifice (בבקר כעלות המנחה).

⁴⁰ The אשם, originally a Philistine guilt offering (see 1 Sam 6:4), was adopted by the Judaean priesthood and offered in conjunction with the חטאת sacrifice.

⁴¹ A similarly negative attitude toward Israelite sacrifice was also presented in Ps 50:7–14. Yahweh's worshippers were those who made their covenant with him through sacrifice (v 5). However, rather than sacrificial acts and the sharing of sacral meals (vv 8–13), Yahweh now demanded sacrifices of thanksgiving (זבח לאלהים תודה) and the redemption of vows (v 14).

⁴² Anderson (1992b: 882) and others (Toeg 1974; Fishbane 1985; Childs 1986)

have noted that a critique of the sacrificial system is also found in an unexpected location, ensconced within the Priestly writings. They point to Leviticus 26 and to Num 15:22–31 as evidence that the priests themselves had concerns about potential abuses, concerns that they expressed in language similar to that of Israel's prophets.

[43] Whether the earliest Deuteronomists were disenfranchised Levitical priests living in Shiloh (Friedman 1987: 122–23) or in northern sanctuaries in general (Boling 1992b: 1013), affiliated with northern prophetic circles (Nicholson 1967) or reliant upon the Elohistic text (Ginsberg 1982: 19–21, 90) is a matter of debate. In all these reconstructions, Dtn was then brought to Jerusalem by people fleeing from the disaster of the Assyrian destruction in 732–721 B.C.E. Once it was in Jerusalem, Hezekiah utilized it as the basis for his efforts at centralization and religious reform (see Boling 1982: 132–33).

[44] Others suggest that the Deuteronomistic work was post-exilic in its entirety (see Noth 1972 for the classic exposition of this theory; Peckham 1985; see McKenzie 1992 for a useful review of the history of scholarship).

[45] Alternatively, Cross dates the original composition of the book of Deuteronomy (Dtr[1]) to the Josianic era. It was later redacted in the Exilic era (Dtr[2]) (Cross 1973: 249, 287–89).

[46] Dtn insisted upon centralizing sacrifice (Deut 12:13–14) while intentionally employing language similar to that used in earlier codes which allowed for greater diversity of practice (Exod 20:24) (Levinson 2000: 281).

[47] Sacrifice as a means of providing for Yahweh, so important in the Priestly writings (see, e.g., Lev 8:21 and 28, which described "a food offering of soothing odor to Yahweh") had no place in the work of the Deuteronomists.

[48] This stands in contrast to the many rituals of expiation in Leviticus, in which priestly enactments were essential.

[49] Ezekiel's sixth century condemnation of Judah ("Canaan is the land of your ancestry and there you were born") is more likely to reflect Iron II realities than Iron I transitions, although this passage has often been taken to reflect Israel's Late Bronze Age origins.

[50] This animosity is well documented in the HB. The conflict between Elijah and Ahab (1 Kgs 17–18) was one of many such battles.

[51] Late in the eighth century, Rezin of Damascus and Pekah of Israel had joined together and attacked Ahaz of Judah. Judaean vassalage to Tiglath-pileser III was the outcome of this military onslaught. The memory of this Syro-Ephraimite War could not have been far from the minds of the Deuteronomists.

[52] For more on this, see Dever 1994.

[53] These same sacrifices were acceptable when offered by Joshua on Mt. Ebal (Josh 8:31), and they played a significant role in Solomon's dedication of the

Jerusalem Temple (1 Kgs 8:63–64).

[54] Illegitimate sacrifice was not the only means by which the successive kings of Israel and Judah were condemned. Alternate vocabulary for worship included וישתחו ... וילך ויעבד (1 Kgs 16:31). Accusations included the kings' having built *bāmôt*, *maṣṣebôt* and *ʾašerîm* and having engaged in other practices abominable to those within the Deuteronomistic tradition (see, e.g., 1 Kgs 14:22–24; 2 Kgs 23).

[55] Here and elsewhere, "fasting as a potent auxiliary of an intercession-prayer" has been identified as one of seven basic types of fasting found in biblical and post-biblical Israel (Brongers 1977: 3).

[56] Some understand P to have been an independent document, originating in the sanctuary in Shiloh (Milgrom 1992 and references therein). Others posit P's awareness of JE, suggesting that it was written to serve as a corrective and an alternative to the JE document (Friedman 1987: 188–89), or they indicate P's dependence upon a composite JE document, to which important Priestly lore was added (Cross 1973: 305–25). Ideas for dating its composition include the premonarchical era (Milgrom 1992: 460), the reign of Hezekiah (Friedman 1989: 214), the period between the Josianic reform and the destruction of the First Temple (Friedman 1981: 44), and the late exilic period (Cross 1973: 32–25). See, also, Peckham 1985: 69–71; he suggested that the Priestly text (his "Ps") was written as a commentary on the Deuteronomistic history.

While scholars acknowledge a distinction between the Holiness Code (Leviticus 17–26) and the rest of the Priestly material (Eissfeldt 1965: 233–39; Cross 1973: 314; Friedman 1987: 214–15; Anderson 1992b: 876; Milgrom 1992: 454), consensus about whether H was a separate document, and about whether H preceded or followed P, has been harder to achieve (Anderson 1992b: 876). Milgrom (1992) suggests a redaction of P, written in the late eighth century and identified by the *siglum* H ("Holiness"). Other investigations, such as those examining Priestly doublets, likewise indicate variant resources within the canonical text of P (Anderson 1992a; 1992b: 876 and sources therein).

[57] The Tabernacle, said to be housed in the Jerusalem Temple, was central to the Priestly sacrificial cult.

[58] After the reign of Solomon, of course, the Jerusalem Temple replaced the Tabernacle as the locus for priestly concerns and ritual enactment.

[59] The discovery of ritually destroyed pottery at sacred sites is common and may be explained in part by reference to a rule concerning the Priestly חטאת sacrifice. This rule required that pottery vessels (כלי־חרש) had to be smashed once חטאת sacrifices were boiled in them (Lev 6:21 [Hebrew]; Lev 6:28 [English]).

⁶⁰ References to personal holiness (ק.ד.ש.), which was required for one to appear before Yahweh or to touch sacred objects, are also found outside the Priestly material (1 Sam 16:5; 21:4–6). Purity laws that predate the Priestly writers are found in Leviticus 11–15 (W. Moran, cited in Friedman 1981: 102), a series of laws concerning dietary purity.

CHAPTER FOUR
THE MIDDLE BRONZE AGE

As we have seen, forms of religious practice are in no small measure dependent upon "secular" circumstances, and so our discussion of the sacred places of the Canaanite Bronze Age must take into account not only sanctuaries and their contents but also the socio-political structures within which they were embedded. Anthropological studies of religion have stressed the ways in which religious practice is both affected by, and explanatory of, social structure. Textual studies have likewise demonstrated the intricate relationship between religious practice—particularly sacrificial rituals—and society at-large. It should be expected that places of worship known from archaeological work would also reflect these many concerns.

However with the analysis of excavation results that follows, the emphasis of this study must change. Different genres of evidence lend themselves best to different sorts of inquiries. The concerns of priestly communities are evinced through their documentation of sacrificial practice, seen so clearly in the Ugaritic and biblical texts already discussed. Therefore, textual studies allow for focused investigations of sacrifice, of ritual, of meaning and of the place of sacrifice within the society of worshippers. Archaeological evidence offers different opportunities. While altars and sacrificial remains are often excavated, the most impressive corpus of sacred remains is architectural rather than artifactual. In some ways, this changes the orientation of our analysis, as our focus shifts from ritual to the built environment. In other ways, the focus remains constant, as we endeavor to understand how religion functioned in Canaanite and Israelite society. Sacred structures stand within deliberately conceived and purposefully constructed settings; their investigation in relationship to the contexts within which they were physically and socially embedded yields important information about religion and society.

This chapter analyzes archaeological evidence for Syro-Canaanite religious practice in the Middle Bronze Age and demonstrates that it reflected societal conditions and changes. In the largest cities, the complex social fabric created by the joining of various tribal and clan groups for the purpose of shared urban functions was mirrored by the multiplicity of their sacred structures. These were sited in central locations, in conjunction with royal palaces, by gateways and in residential areas. By projecting the relationship between religious structures and society, one can link these various sacred places to different groups within the city. The differences among religious structures, their cultic paraphernalia and their iconography are understood to represent meaningful differences among the various social groups living in the new Middle Bronze Age urban environment.

PRECEDENTS: THE CHALCOLITHIC AND EARLY BRONZE AGES

Through a brief examination of fourth through third-millennium Canaan, one can envision the roots of many aspects of Middle Bronze Age religion and social structure. Studies of material culture have led scholars to suggest that the Amorite population of Middle Bronze Age Canaan was not intrusive. Instead "the indigenous Middle Bronze Age population had *always* been West Semitic or 'Amorite'" (Dever 1980: 58). It may be possible, therefore, to trace some continuity in religious traditions between the Chalcolithic and the EB III to stable elements among the native residents of the region (Amiran 1981: 53; 1989: 32).

In a study of fifth and fourth millennium religion in the Negev and Sinai Deserts, Avner identifies three types of cultic sites, standing stone (*maṣṣebôt*) shrines, open-air sanctuaries and crenellations or cairn lines. In the standing stone shrines, *maṣṣebôt* representing individual deities were grouped in specific configurations. Open-air sanctuaries were commonly rectangular and included some combination of elongated holy-of-holies, altars, stone basins, standing stones and circular stone installations. They were often constructed in pairs.[1]

Crenellations or rows of cairns are found throughout the Sinai and Negev, in Transjordan and elsewhere. According to Avner, they were commemorative monuments, either tombs of venerated individuals or sites sacred for other reasons and were located near roadways to facilitate pilgrimage. Over time, elements of the religion of these desert cultures would be incorporated into that of the more urban population of the Early Bronze Age north (1984; 1990; 1993).

Elsewhere, permanent public sanctuaries of the Chalcolithic were constructed at Gilat, Tuleilat Ghassul and Ein Gedi. They were used for village and pilgrimage worship. Together with new, formal burial grounds, these sanctuaries reflect the emergence of chiefdoms in the mid-fifth to mid-fourth millennia (Levy 1995: 234–37). Developing religious sentiments emphasized the fertility of flocks and fields (Epstein 1985; Alon and Levy 1989: 190–93; Gonen 1992: 64–66 and references therein). Ritual gift-giving regulated by the new social elites was fundamental to the fabric of Chalcolithic religion (Alon and Levy 1989; Levy 1995).

Artifactual evidence for Chalcolithic worship concerns extends into the EB I–II, as well (Ben-Tor 1992: 92–93). With concerns for subsistence at the core of religious observance, the relationship between a developing religious hierarchy and an economic elite is evident. As Canaan became somewhat urbanized in the Early Bronze Age, religion was increasingly incorporated into the fabric of city life. In the EB II period, religion was characterized by "the larger trend of incorporating religious iconography into architecture, and then into sites …. What may well have been individual and independent traditions or mechanisms for religious and ritual behavior become increasingly part of the urban prerogative" (Joffe 1993: 83). The construction of temples and other public architecture was initiated by the ruling elites who exercised control over urban ritual activities in order to ensure their continuing social and economic dominance (Joffe 1993: 84; A. Mazar 1990a: 140).

Together with the urban elites that created and maintained the infrastructure of EB II and EB III cities were rural elites tied to the land by long-term crop investments. "The essential units of social organization, kin groups with a variety of extending strategies, were likely similar in both the urban and rural aspects of society" (Joffe 1993: 85; see also Marfoe 1979). The strength of Early Bronze Age religious institutions, whose members were drawn from both city and countryside populations, is best explained through reference to their function in uniting tribal or kin groups with varying subsistence strategies.

During the EB III period, "palace" and "temple" complexes (Megiddo Building 3177, Temples 5192, 5269, 4040) and specialized public structures (Beth Yerah granary) were constructed (Ben-Tor 1992). The confluence of social, religious and economic elites suggests the ways in which all these elements of society were inextricably bound. At the end of the period, late in the third millennium, the urban world collapsed and village and pastoral ways of life prevailed throughout the EB IV (Dever 1995). It was primarily the resilience of the indigenous social structure that facilitated the urban revival of the Middle Bronze Age several centuries later.

THE MIDDLE BRONZE AGE

The origins of the incipient urban culture of the MB IIA in Canaan have often been sought in those urban sites in Syria (such as Hama, Qatna and Ebla) that had thrived throughout the EB IV (Tubb 1983: 50; Kempinski 1992: 210). Still, it is worth noting that "[T]he MBIIA culture ... is not a 'new' culture brought from outside, but represents a development of the indigenous population" (Tubb 1983: 57). Somewhat later, the MB IIB must be considered a natural development of the MB IIA; the search for foreigner invaders and major upheavals should be abandoned (Kochavi, Beck and Gophna 1979: 164–65).[2]

The MB IIA was also a period of "interregional affinities" (D. Cole 1984: 96). Sites continuously occupied during that period were those located in naturally strategic locations or along the main military corridor between Egypt and Syria, and those protected by the terrain of the Central Highlands. It was not until the MB IIC that contacts between coastal and interior regions in Canaan, and between Syria and Canaan were reestablished (D. Cole 1984: 96–97).[3]

The Middle Bronze Age coincided with Egypt's Middle Kingdom and Second Intermediate Period. Over the years, numerous chronologies to explain this complex period of internal development and international relationships have been suggested. Dever's recent timeframe will be followed here (Dever 1992a: fig. 1). However, the terminology used will be Albright's more widely accepted MB IIA, MB IIB and MB IIC.[4]

The geographic range of Middle Bronze Age sites covered in this analysis is broad and includes sites in modern-day Israel, Jordan, Palestine, Lebanon and Syria (figs. 1–2). The nature of the relationship between Egypt, Canaan, the Syrian coastal cities, inland Syria and Mesopotamia is critical for understanding the events of the Middle Bronze Age. Inland Syrian sites, including Ebla, Mari and Alalakh, were within the Mesopotamian sphere of influence. Coastal sites such

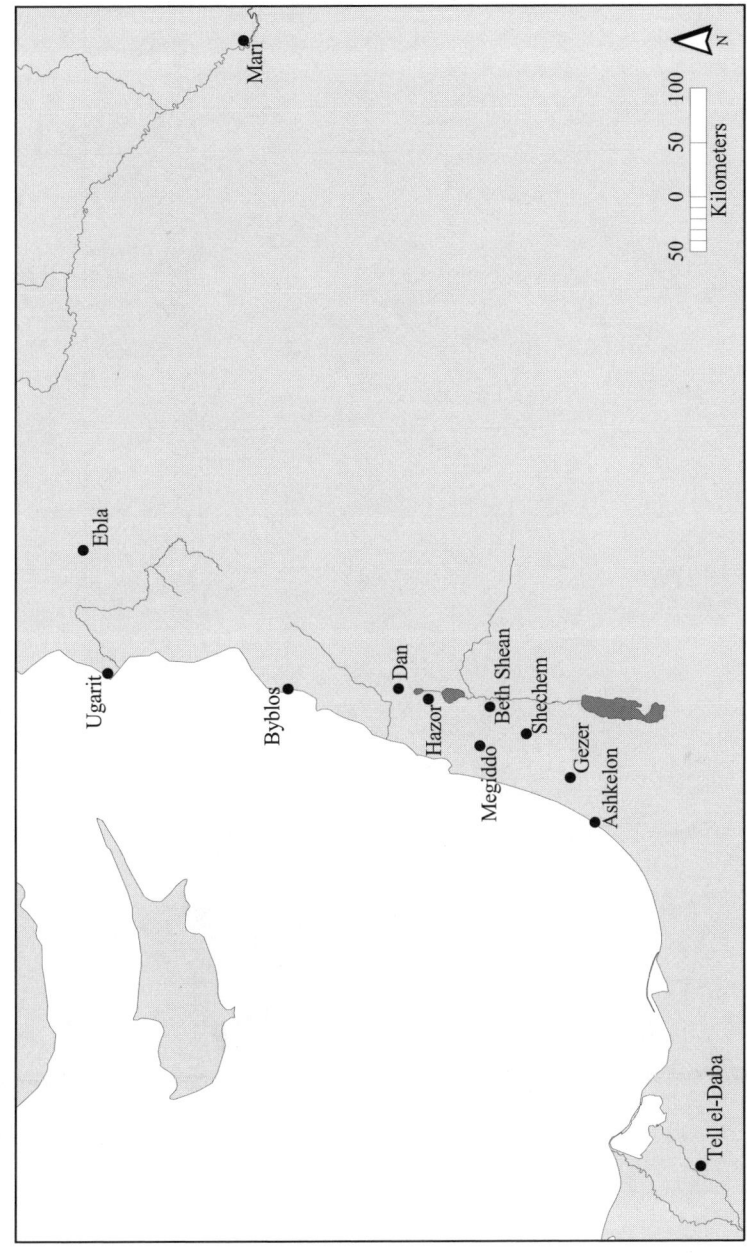

Fig. 1 Map showing the location of Middle Bronze Age sites. Map by Marcy H. Rockman.

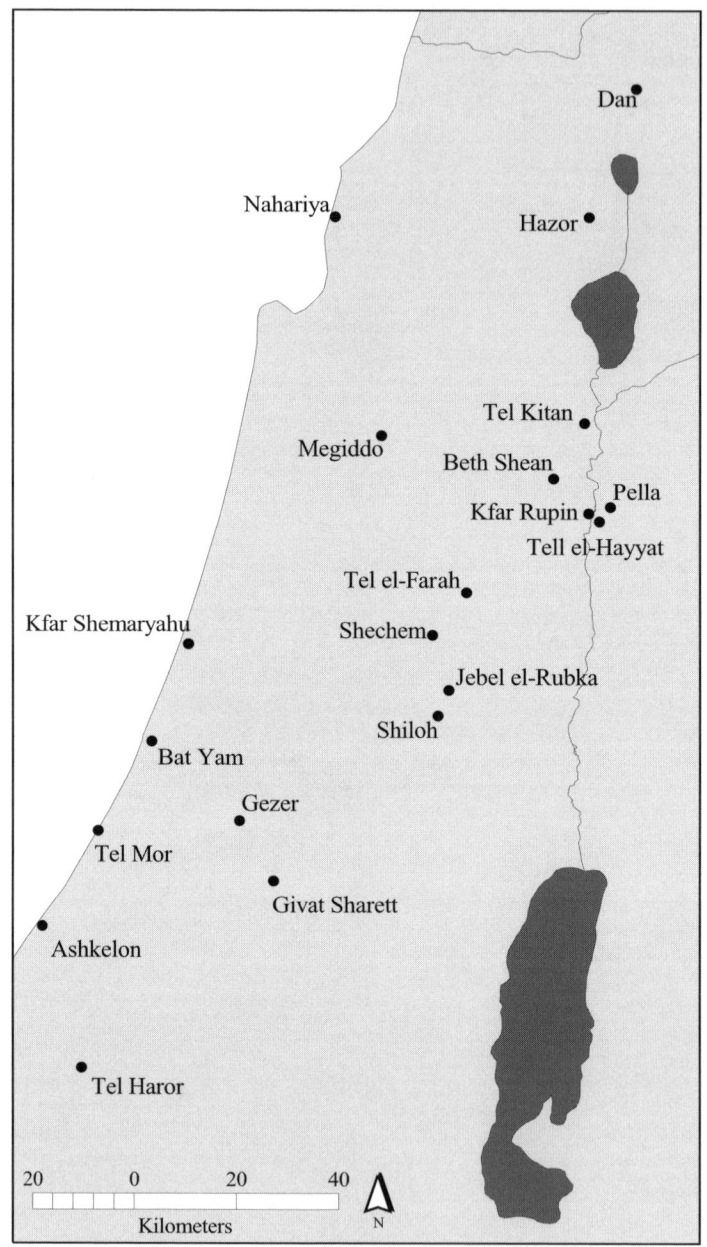

Fig. 2 Detailed map showing the location of MBA sites. Map by Marcy H. Rockman.

as Byblos and Ugarit, and those farther to the south in Canaan, felt the impact of Egyptian trade contacts (Ilan 1995: 308; Pitard 1998: 39–40). The complexity of these interrelationships is highlighted by the fact that while Canaanite Hazor displayed Syrian affinities, the Egyptian site of Tell el-Dabʿa revealed a commitment to Canaanite traditions. Given the cosmopolitan nature of the Middle Bronze Age and the international contacts attested by its archives and material culture, the importance of examining sacred places in wide-ranging geographic locations seems obvious.

The Middle Kingdom was a period of economic invigoration for Egypt. An extensive network of fortresses and trading centers was created. International trade flourished, providing the Egyptian elite with elegant imports, necessary supplies and markets for goods (Franke 1995: 739). Egypt resumed trading with the port cities of Byblos and Ugarit on the Syrian coast early in the 12th Dynasty (1991–1786 B.C.E.) and the relationship between Egypt and Byblos became particularly close (Gardiner 1964: 129–33; T. James 1979: 52–53). The leaders of the Syrian cities sought Egyptian royal and nomarchical patronage because of the prestige that accrued to urban centers involved with Egypt, and the associated economic well-being. Actual control by Egypt was not a factor (Teissier 1990: 70–71).

Excavations of cities in the Canaanite interior have uncovered numerous Egyptian artifacts that likewise attest to the resumption of commercial and even diplomatic relationships between these two regions (Dever 1987b: 171–72). According to some (see Yadin 1978 and references there), MB IIA Canaan was part of the 12th Dynasty Egyptian empire. Others (see Weinstein 1975 and references there; Bienkowski 1986: 131) suggest that this rather elusive relationship was defined by Egyptian commercial interests in Canaanite products.

SYRIAN SITES IN THE MIDDLE BRONZE AGE

The "monumental symmetrical" temple, new in Canaan in the MB IIA–C, derived from contemporary and even earlier sacred structures in late third–early second millennium Syria (A. Mazar 1992b: 166–69).[5] In Syria, monumental, and at times multiple, temples stood in a number of major cities including Ebla, Mari, Alalakh, Byblos and Ugarit.[6] These cities, while oriented toward different cultural spheres (the first three toward Mesopotamia and the last two toward Egypt), shared a number of important characteristics. Taken together, they provide critical documentation for the religion of Syria in the Middle Bronze Age.

Ebla

The sacred structures of MB IIA (Stratum IIA)–MB IIB (Stratum IIIB) Ebla preserved much of the earlier EB IV construction. They were clustered in two areas within the city. Temple D was located on the acropolis, along with Royal Palace E and various administrative buildings. The acropolis area was girded by at least six Lower City temples. Temples N, B1, B2, C and two others, described by their excavator as a "curious typology of tower-chapels," were constructed among the residential neighborhoods of the city (Matthiae 1980: 115–16, 123–24).

In the Upper City, the great Temple D was built over the ruins of an earlier sanctuary. It was massive by Canaanite standards, approximately 30 m long with walls 4–5 m thick. The floor plan was tripartite (Matthiae 1980: 114, fig. 30). A large basalt lion guarded the approach to the antechamber. At the rear of the innermost room, a cult niche held a limestone basin with carved sides. Nearby, a circular basalt basin stood on a decorated pedestal. Following the partial destruction of Temple D at the end of the MB IIB, the sanctity of the site was preserved by a small temple that was used for the rest of the Bronze Age (Matthiae 1980: 130–32).

Temple N, the largest temple in the Lower City, was a single chambered building with walls 3–4 m thick. A deep platform extended across the back of the building. An offering table composed of large basalt slabs (one of which was spouted) and a decorated limestone basin with two compartments lay nearby (Matthiae 1980: 125–26, fig. 27).

Temple B1 was similar to Temple N, but smaller. It was separated from Temple B2 to its north by an open space. Temple B2 was a multi-roomed structure with indirect access through an exterior courtyard. It had a mudbrick platform on the southern wall of its central chamber. In each of its several subsidiary rooms were cultic objects including altars and offering tables. One room also contained three engaged ornamental pillars. The discovery of these small but fully equipped sacred chambers led to the suggestion that Temple B2 was used for individualized cultic acts (Matthiae 1980: 126–31, figs. 28–29).

Subterranean tunnels with monumental carved lintels linked Temples B1 and B2.[7] Overall, their function is uncertain. Some served as shaft tombs and generally it seems that they were used in celebration of a funerary cult. Three other sacred structures were excavated in Ebla's Lower City. They include Temple C, Building Q(?) and a building located northeast of the acropolis (Matthiae 1980: 115, 130).

As was typical of Bronze Age cities, the Upper City at Ebla was the religious, administrative and residential center for the ruling elite while the Lower City was home to the majority of the population. Late third millennium texts note a separation between the Upper and Lower Cities. They also indicate that the Lower City was divided into four separate districts, each with its own gate and its own god. Temples dedicated to the four major gods of Ebla, Dagon, Rasap, Eshtar and Kamish are described and other chapels and temples are indicated (Matthiae 1980: 189; Bonfil 1997: 85–86).

In Middle Bronze Age Ebla, the many sanctuaries in the Lower City ringed the acropolis and provided the orientation for the city's major roadways. The only entrance to the Upper City was from the southwest side of the tel, allowing residents of the Lower City to control access. This suggests that the power of a ruling elite was not absolute for its ability to retain authority depended upon others.

Other than the main roads that linked the four city gates and the acropolis, few streets connected the residential zones in the Lower City. Each neighborhood, with its own sanctuary, was home to a different clan or kin group. While all city residents may have participated in periodic communal rites in the acropolis temple, local groups maintained their own indigenous religious institutions. The three fortress temples (Temples D, B1 and N) suggest the accumulation of great wealth and indicate that relationships were not always harmonious among residents of the city.

Mari

The Temple of Dagan at Mari was constructed on a traditionally sacred spot west of the vast royal palace. Built by Ishtup-ilum, the temple was originally dedicated to a god called "King of the Land" and later rededicated to Dagan (Amiet 1980: 486–87). Ishtup-ilum's military campaigns to the Mediterranean coast early in the nineteenth century may have presented an opportunity for the dissemination of religious ideas, since standing stones and obelisks, typical of Canaanite coastal sites and Syrian cult, stood in the courtyard of this sacred building.

Alalakh

At Alalakh, a sequence of sanctuaries was located on virtually the same spot throughout the second millennium, beginning in the MB IIA (Level XVI).[8] The early temples were characterized by rooms on a single axis although entry to some rooms was not direct (Woolley 1955: 33–35, figs. 19–22). The Level VII temple of the MB IIC is the best known in the sequence and was located adjacent to the palace of Yarim-lim. Entry into this bipartite building with 4 m thick walls, and to a small adjoining chamber, was through a courtyard area (Dever 1985a: 70, fig. 1; McClellan 1989: 183, fig. 26, 35).

Byblos

At Byblos, the sequence of sacred structures continued almost unbroken for some three millennia, resulting in the poor preservation of its many Middle Bronze Age temples (Dunand 1982). The Early Bronze Age occupation had ended in destruction, and the new sanctuaries of the Middle Bronze Age differed from their predecessors.[9] Byblos of the MB IIA period was a flourishing settlement, due in part to its close cultural and economic relationship with 12th Dynasty Egypt. Its wealth is demonstrated by the luxury items found in its royal tombs and by the many temple offerings. The richest finds, including gold figurines and ceremonial metal tools, were found in jars or under the floors of the open-air sanctuaries (Jidejian 1968: 25–29; Dunand 1982: 132). Little is known of Byblos during the MB IIB and MB IIC periods.

The sacred architecture of the MB IIA was characterized by worship in unroofed buildings and in courtyards filled with standing pillars or obelisks. The four Middle Bronze Age temples, located on the eastern side of the city near the gate, were grouped around the public area that had been created out of the Early Bronze Age Sacred Lake (Dunand 1982: 197). They comprise the Obelisk Temple, the Syrian Temple (*Bâtiment* II), the temple that covered the Early Bronze Age *Champs des Offrandes* and a small temple on the southeast slope of the tel.

The Obelisk Temple, located near the northeast city gate on the site of a previous sacred structure, was dedicated to the Canaanite god

Reshef (Dunand 1982: 195; Negbi 1976: 123). Its irregular and complex plan included a courtyard area, in which stood an open-air *cella* and nearly thirty obelisks, including one dedicated to an Egyptian god by a Byblian king.[10]

Furnishings included basins, offering tables and flat areas for presenting offerings. More than thirteen hundred votive offerings, including a large number of figurines,[11] were buried, sometimes in jars, under the floor of the courtyard. Several smaller rooms were situated around the courtyard area and additional votive offerings were found under their floors. A jewelry workshop was uncovered (Amiet 1980: 481, fig. 845; Jidejian 1968: 35–39; Negbi 1976: 123). The Obelisk Temple of the MB IIA derived from Egyptian prototypes[12] and also incorporated elements of the traditional Canaanite open-air *maṣṣebôt* sanctuary.

The poorly preserved Syrian Temple (*Bâtiment* II/Temple of Baalat Gebel) is recognized only by its fragmented foundations. It was tripartite, with narrow chambers along both long sides and walls 2 m thick. South of the building was the courtyard in which the Montet Jar, its offerings presumably dedicated to the goddess Baalat Gebel, was found (Matthiae 1975: 55, plan 4). A number of figurines were found in and near the temple (Negbi 1976: 122–23), and fragmentary remains of domestic architecture were excavated nearby.

A small obelisk stood among the fragmentary remains of the small temple on the southeast slope of the tel. Little is known of its plan and furnishings, or of those of the sacred structure constructed over the Early Bronze Age *Champs des Offrandes*.

The multiple temples at Byblos can be related to the various clan groups within the city. The temples were located on the eastern side of the tel, grouped around a central public area not far from the city gate. Although nothing of the MB IIA palace is known, royal dedicatory monuments and luxurious offerings clarify the connection between the Obelisk Temple and the Byblian ruling clan. Some badly disturbed domestic architecture uncovered near the Syrian Temple suggests its neighborhood setting. Byblos's great political importance and its pivotal geographic location ensured this city's important role in the transmission of culture, including religion, among the various urban centers and clan groups of MB IIA Egypt, Syria and Canaan.

Ugarit

It has long been assumed that the Late Bronze Age Temples of Baal and Dagan at Ugarit were originally constructed early in the second millennium (Yon 1984: 45). Dornemann has suggested parallels with the Alalakh temples but this remains speculative in the absence of published plans (1981: 62).

Summary: *Middle Bronze II Syrian Sites*

The large cities in MB II Syria were home to many often rather impressive sanctuaries. Ebla had a minimum of six, Byblos four and Ugarit two. In these cities, as in Mari and Alalakh (at least in the MB IIC), the location of the buildings suggests that some were for the royalty while others were used by kin groups residing in the cities' various neighborhoods. The exclusively urban setting for these sacred buildings may be due more to the vagaries of excavation than anything else, but the number and location of sanctuaries within the various cities highlight the way in which the organization of Middle Bronze Age religion was an outcome of the overall structure of society.

CANAAN IN THE MIDDLE BRONZE IIA PERIOD

In MB IIA Canaan, the situation was significantly different than in the north. Although the MB IIA was the longest period of uninterrupted development in the second millennium, it was a period typified by the establishment of small settlements that would only later develop into true cities (Dever 1992a: 2). Attestations to religious life in the first quarter of the second millennium are therefore limited to regional or village sanctuaries (Tell el-Hayyat, Nahariya, Bat Yam, Kfar Shemaryahu, Megiddo, Gezer[?], Dan[?]).

Megiddo

Megiddo, located on the Via Maris, had close ties to Egypt in the MB IIA period. On account of its vital position in controlling routes between Egypt and important centers to its north and east, Egypt may have deployed a garrison there (Harif 1978: 31). Alternatively, the relationship might better be defined as strictly economic (Weinstein 1975: 13–14). Broken Egyptian stone statuettes found embedded in the later Stratum VIIB Temple, including one of a high-ranking official named Thuthotep, probably originated in the temple in this period (Ussishkin 1997b: 462). Whatever the relationship between Egypt and Megiddo, Egyptian contacts were a factor in the development of religion there.

The earliest temples in the Megiddo sacred precinct (Area BB) date to the Early Bronze Age. Later, cultic installations were constructed in the new MB IIA (Stratum XIII) village. These include the small Cult Room 4040c and High Place "D" (later, "F"), composed of an altar and a number of meter-high *stelae*. This installation resembled that at the center of the Byblian Obelisk Temple (Kempinski 1989a: 178–80).

Seven-cup offering vessels are similar to those from other sanctuaries of the period. A silver crescent and five female figurines were found at High Place "D." Figurines from "F" were also female, and many were posed in militant postures. The Megiddo figurines have parallels at Byblos, Ugarit and Nahariya and suggest that a goddess was the primary deity worshipped at these MB IIA sites (Negbi 1976: 131; Kempinski 1989a: 178).

Gradually, the fortified village of MB IIA Megiddo grew. A palace and private houses were constructed near the sacred center, access to which was now restricted. This area provided the central focus of the new city. Even when the Stratum XII city was destroyed, the sacred area remained unchanged (Kempinski 1989a: 46–47).

Later, in the MB IIB period (Stratum XI), a royal complex including Palace 5059 and subsidiary buildings was constructed west of the sacred area. It was enclosed within a wall and associated with the gateway area. Construction was also begun on a system of fortifications. Evidence from the palace and tombs likewise suggests a growing dynastic family (Kempinski 1989a: 57–58).

In summary, MB IIA Megiddo was a village which, like others in Canaan, underwent a slow process of expansion. Given its small size, a complex social structure should not be anticipated. However the development of a palace complex linked to the Megiddo's traditional sacred area suggests that the stimulus provided by growing religious authority enabled one local group to gain a position of status and authority over others.

Cooperation among these clan groups must also have existed, for the small village was gradually transformed into a large walled city. The MB IIB period at Megiddo would be one in which the ruling clan that had emerged in the MB IIA would establish its dominant position over an increasingly complex site.

Nahariya

In the MB IIA period, Nahariya was a regional cultic center somewhat removed from any contemporary settlement.[13] The first sanctuary (Stratum V) consisted of a small square room, outside of which stood a circular stone altar (M. Dothan 1957: 122). Cultic objects found on the altar include pots filled with small scraps of silver and bronze and miniature vessels (especially seven-spouted lamps). Cooking pots and the ashes and bones of small animals, cattle and sheep were also found (M. Dothan 1981: 74–75).

Later in the MB IIA period (Stratum IV), the earlier cult room was incorporated into a circular platform 14 m in diameter. A stone altar stood nearby and a residential building for cultic staff stood to its north. Originally one room, additional chambers would be added in the MB IIC (Stratum II), and the cultic center would remain in use well into the LB IA period (Stratum I) (M. Dothan 1981: 76; D. Cole 1984: 89).

A foundation deposit of silver and bronze figurines was found under the Stratum IV stone altar (M. Dothan 1981: 76), while many other cultic objects were discovered embedded in the stone platform. They resemble those from its first phase and include offering stands and hundreds of votive vessels such as seven-cupped offering bowls and seven-spouted lamps. Figurines of doves, monkeys and cattle were common. Semi-precious stone beads, bronze, silver and gold jewelry and zoomorphic amulets were also found. The courtyard contained numerous cooking pots and animal (predominantly goat) bones (M. Dothan 1957: 122; 1977b: 909–11). Stone molds and metal residues were remnants of an on-site workshop for the manufacture of figurines and weapons (M. Dothan 1957: 123; 1981: 77).

The typical Middle Bronze Age goddess figurine was popular at Nahariya and was closely related to those from Byblos, Ugarit and Megiddo (Negbi 1976: 106; M. Dothan 1977b: 912). Architectural similarities among the sanctuaries at these sites have also been noted (Dothan 1957: 123–24; 1981: 77–78; A. Mazar 1992b: 161–62).

Gezer and Dan

A foundation deposit was found near the MB IIC High Place at Gezer. The silver female figurines in it resemble silver and gold statuettes found elsewhere on the site, and at MB IIA Megiddo and Nahariya (Negbi 1976: 81–82).[14] Similarly, a cultic offering deposit was found at Tel Dan (Ilan 1992a: 263). The figurines at both these sites may have once been part of sacred installations destroyed in antiquity, or still undiscovered.

Bat Yam

The excavation of Bat Yam, a small site 2 km inland from the Mediterranean coast north of Jaffa, revealed a poorly preserved building of more than 4.30 × 3.30 m. Its identification as sacred rests upon its cultic paraphernalia, which include a hollow stand, a seven-cupped offering bowl and the dove-shaped head of a zoomorphic vessel. Animal bones and pottery were also found (Gophna and Beck 1981: 53–54, fig. 1 [site #7]).

Kfar Shemaryahu

Kfar Shemaryahu is located several kilometers inland from the Mediterranean coast, within the territory of Aphek on the Sharon Plain (Gophna and Beck 1981: fig. 1 [site #18]). A *tabun* or jarstand was set into the floor near the southwestern corner of a three-roomed rectangular building (Kaplan 1971: 305). This MB IIA site was identified as cultic because of an offering deposit, and because of similarities between its building and the MB IIC–LB I residential structure at Nahariya.

Tell el-Hayyat

Tell el-Hayyat, a half-hectare site in the eastern Jordan Valley, was occupied from the EB IV (Phase 6) through the late MB IIC period (Phase 1). Hayyat contained a sequence of fortress sanctuaries that dated from the MB IIA (Phase 5) into the MB IIC (Phase 2). Houses were located outside the walled sacred precinct in its final three phases, transforming the isolated rural sanctuary into a small village (Falconer and Magness-Gardiner 1989: 341–42).

The original sanctuary, a small square building with an entryway created by projecting piers, was expanded and developed over the years as it attained the plan of a typical *migdal* or fortress temple. Inside the building were a low bench, a mudbrick altar, and, eventually, a stone pedestal. One or more undecorated *maṣṣebôt* surrounded by flat-lying stones stood in the courtyard throughout much of the life of the building (Falconer and Magness-Gardiner 1989: 342–43).

The Tell el-Hayyat temple was enlarged in the MB IIC period and a large niche was set into its rear wall. Some part of the plastered façade was painted red. A deposit of votive bowls and oil lamps was placed just outside the entryway and the stone column base was moved into the courtyard (Falconer and Magness-Gardiner 1989: 342–43).

The animals most commonly sacrificed were sheep and goat, their bones found in significantly higher concentrations in sacred than in domestic contexts. Crucibles and molds, metal by-products and finished products including an anthropomorphic figurine and miniature "oxhide" ingots were found in and around the sanctuaries and provide evidence for a metallurgic workshop. A pottery kiln and ceramic manufacturing debris were also discovered (Falconer and Magness-Gardiner 1989: 343–44, figs. 8, 13, 14).

Summary: Middle Bronze IIA

Although the full story of Egyptian involvement in MB IIA Canaan is not yet known, it is clear that there was a unique relationship between Egypt and the coastal sites of Nahariya, Ugarit and Byblos, as well as with Megiddo farther inland. It may be no coincidence that these four sites were virtually the only MB IIA sites in Canaan with firm architectural evidence for religious observance.[15]

Very early in the Middle Bronze Age, probably in response to the economic stimulus provided by Middle Kingdom Egypt, rather unique sanctuaries were constructed at Megiddo, Byblos, Nahariya, and possibly at Ugarit. Similarities in architecture and in sacred assemblages demonstrate the close relationship between these religious sites. Egyptian influence, apparent in the obelisk clusters in the various courtyards, merged with an indigenous Canaanite worship characterized by the erecting of *maṣṣebôt*. A successful religious forum dominated by an emerging priesthood and supported by the wealth of offerings was thereby created. This, in turn, stimulated the growth of the ruling classes that would emerge in the MB IIB–MB IIC.

Tell el-Hayyat in the remote Jordan Valley is the single exception to the testimony of Egypt's importance in stimulating the MB IIA religious revival. The temple at Hayyat, lacking evidence of Egyptian involvement, is best understood as a regional cult center administered by local tribal groups. The influence there was from Syria, the fortress temple being an inland type known from contemporary Ebla.

Evidence for temple industry was uncovered at Nahariya and Tell el-Hayyat although presumably temple workshops existed at other sites as well. The important link between commerce and religion is also apparent from the votive offering deposits uncovered at Byblos, Ugarit, Nahariya, Gezer, Megiddo and Dan. These deposits, offerings for the deities, contained valuable objects including sheet metal figurines, weapons, stickpins and jewelry, stone blades, ceramic and stone beads, and miniature votive vessels. Control over metal supply, production and trade was critical for sustaining the social and religious elites of the MB IIA period (Ilan 1992a; 1992b; and references therein). From a religious perspective, those with metal resources were able to offer the very best to their gods and to receive the best in return (see Levy 1995 for a discussion of similar mechanisms in the Chalcolithic period). The imposing image of the fortress temple, with its high elevation and defense-style architecture, likewise suggests priestly access to wealth and the need to protect it.

CANAAN IN THE MIDDLE BRONZE IIB PERIOD

The MB IIB (1800/1750–1650 B.C.E.) has been described as a era of continuing and impressive reurbanization. It is a period characterized in particular by "the expansion and fortification of sites already settled in the MB I [= MB IIA]; the development of a more distinctly local 'Canaanite' culture … with somewhat fewer foreign contacts; and the standardization of such industries as the manufacture of pottery and bronzes" (Dever 1992a: 10).

In terms of religion, the MB IIB witnessed the continuation of traditional religious structures at the Syrian sites. The best known is Ebla, at which all earlier temples remained in use. In Canaan, the regional cult centers at Nahariya and Tell el-Hayyat were enlarged in the MB IIB, as was the Megiddo sacred area. New temples or religious installations were also built at Hazor, Givat Sharett, Tell Kittan and Kfar Rupin(?).

Hazor

The Galilean site of Hazor was founded in the MB IIB (Stratum 4), but no temples can be dated to that period. However, rock-cut tombs and tunnels similar to those from Ebla Area B were found in Area F in the Lower City (Yadin et al. 1960: 127–28). Later, in the MB IIC (Stratum 3), they may have been used to bury royalty residing in the palace constructed over them (A. Mazar 1990a: 214).[16]

In addition, some religious statuary and furnishings known from their association with later temples were produced in the MB IIB and illustrate Hazor's connections with Syria. These include a basalt seated male figure,[17] stone offering and libation tables[18] and a carinated basalt krater.[19]

Givat Sharett

The hilltop village of Givat Sharett, 1 km southeast of the fortified city of Beth Shemesh, was occupied for several decades in the MB IIB and then abandoned. This well-planned village was protected by a row of houses aligned so that their common rear wall formed a defensive barrier, while a second row of houses flanked a lane leading to the top of the hill. Artifacts from both large and small houses indicate Givat Sharett's agrarian economy, while grave goods found in three nearby burial caves were of as high a quality as those from Beth Shemesh (Bahat 1978).

A sacred building with two rooms was located at the top of the hill. In the larger of the two rooms, stone benches lined the walls. Cult objects including incense burners, fragments of *kernoi*, miniature votive vessels and a seven-branched vessel were scattered on the floor. An altar area was situated along the back wall of the stone-paved smaller room. A stone pillar stood in its center and miniature votive vessels and a seven-spouted lamp lay around it (Bahat 1978).

Tell Kittan

The eight-dunam site of Tell Kittan, located on a strategic hilltop overlooking the Jordan River some 12 km north of Beth Shean, was a regional cultic center. The first sanctuary was constructed in the MB IIB period (Stratum V). It was a small room, measuring 4.3 × 4.6 m. Piers extended from two walls to form a shallow entryway and two pillars flanked the entrance. Parallel to the sanctuary façade and 5 m in front of it stood a row of stone *stelae* separated by three small square pits, perhaps socles for additional *stelae*. Two larger *stelae* stood elevated behind the first row. The central *stele* was carved to represent a nude goddess cupping her breasts, and with her facial features distinct (Eisenberg 1977: 77–78).

Later in the MB IIB (Stratum IV), a new sanctuary, enlarged to 11.5 × 14.3 m, was built over the original one. Piles of ash containing animal bones were heaped around a semi-circular bench in the courtyard. Four crudely carved stone figurines lay near a basalt slab and two basalt bases. A *temenos* wall surrounded the complex, which now included several houses. Information about the MB IIC occupation at Tell Kittan is ambiguous, but later, in the LB I, a new sacred complex was constructed over that of the MB IIB period (Eisenberg 1977: 79–80).

Kfar Rupin

The farming village of Kfar Rupin was 17 km south of Tell Kittan, on the west bank of the Jordan River. The settlement, several courtyard houses grouped along narrow alleys and sharing common walls, is tentatively dated to the MB IIB (Gophna 1979: 28).

Building C, at the village center, was unique. It was a 6 × 5 m room whose walls were twice the width of those of other buildings. The entrance opened into an enclosed courtyard that measured 12 × 6 m. The building's orientation, central position within the village, thick walls and rectangular plan facilitated its identification as a sanctuary. In its floor plan and pottery, it resembled the fortress temple at Tell Kittan (Gophna 1979: 29–32).

Tell el-Dabʿa

Tell el-Dabʿa in the eastern Nile Delta is identified with Avaris, the Hyksos capital of Egypt. Beginning early in the MB IIA (12th Dynasty), the material culture of this fortified city was primarily Canaanite (Dever 1985a: 74, fig. 1). Its importance in international trade, initially with the Syrian coast and later, in the MB IIB, with Canaan, has been documented (Ilan 1995: 308).

Not much is known of the MB IIA (Stratum G) sanctuary. Two Canaanite-style temples were constructed in the MB IIB (Stratum E/3).

Temple III was a tripartite building with a recessed niche in its rear wall, and double walls 4–5 m thick. Communication between Temple III and the adjacent Temple V, which was narrower and possibly bipartite, was facilitated by side doors (Bietak 1979: 247–53, figs. 8–9).

A rectangular mudbrick altar covered with ashes and bones stood in the large (21.5 × 33.8 m) courtyard in front of the two temples. *Favissae* were filled with bones and pottery. The sacred area also included a small sanctuary, a narrow mortuary temple flanked by two cemeteries (among the burials were teams of donkeys) and some small residences (Bietak 1979: 250–52).

Later in the MB IIB (Stratum E/2), a new mortuary temple displaying Egyptian and Canaanite features was constructed in the sacred area, and new cemeteries were dug nearby. The three partitions within this new Mortuary Temple I may have been related to the three major family tombs to its south, tombs that also included donkey burials (Bietak 1979: 256–58; fig. 8, 10).

Summary: Middle Bronze IIB

Religion in the MB IIB period reflects several critical elements within society and culture. A synthetic Egypto-Canaanite cult continued to be celebrated at Nahariya and at Megiddo, while at Egyptian Tell el-Dabʿa the same situation is apparent in reverse. The fortress temple at Tell el-Hayyat was enlarged and similar structures were constructed at Tell Kittan and Kfar Rupin, also in the Jordan Valley. Like Nahariya on the coast, these Jordan Valley sanctuaries were regional cult centers staffed by religious professionals and used by kin groups residing in the area or traveling through it. The small sanctuary at Givat Sharett illuminates religious life in a village setting. Finally the tombs and tunnels at Hazor reflect a cult of ancestor worship that had its origins in the Syrian north.

The MB IIA–B changes in funerary customs also indicate the changes in social structure that typified this period. The single burials of the EB IV were now replaced, as family groups claimed control over individual burial spots and used them for multiple interments. A study of Tomb 1181, a burial cave at Hazor, highlights social and economic changes. Grave goods indicate interregional trade, an economic surplus, status items, technological developments and the accumulation of wealth. All this demonstrates a "multi-level, hierarchical societal structure" (Maeir 1997: 323), very much at one with other documented developments in the MB IIB.

CANAAN IN THE MIDDLE BRONZE IIC PERIOD

The MB IIC (1650–1500 B.C.E.) was an era of internal development in Canaan typified by the proliferation of large walled cities. At the same time, international relations were complex, not in the least because of the dominant role played by Canaanite "Hyksos" in Second Intermediate Period Egypt.

Changes in religious practice reflected these changes in politics and social structure. Large fortress temples were constructed in the walled cities of Hazor, Megiddo, Shechem, Tel Haror and Pella while smaller shrines were built at Tel Mor and in the gateway areas at Ashkelon and Tell el-Farʿah (N). The regional sanctuaries at Nahariya, Tell el-Hayyat and Tell Kittan remained in use. Others were built at Gezer, at Shiloh, and perhaps at Jebel el-Rubka as well. At Tell el-Dabʿa, sacred structures of the MB IIB period were used until the destruction of the city at the end of the MB IIC period.

Hazor

The MB IIB funerary complex at Hazor suggests the presence of a clan group whose mortuary practices indicated social organization and control. The scale of occupation grew in the MB IIC and, with the larger population, there is evidence for increased social complexity, seen, for example, in Hazor's many sanctuaries.

Recent excavations at Hazor have uncovered part of an MB IIC temple under the Late Bronze Age palace in Area A in the Upper City. A niche was set into the back wall of its single large room; its elegant stonework emphasizes its importance. A large *favissa* containing votive vessels, incense burners and chalices, ash and bone, was cut into the floor. The *favissa* and niche together indicate that this building was a temple and it has been dated to the transition between the MB IIC and the LB I (Ben-Tor 1999c: 272–73).

The Bipartite Temple in Area H in the Lower City was nestled inside the MB IIC (Stratum 3) rampart (Yadin 1975: 118). It was large (19.75 × 18 m), with walls over 2 m thick. The back room had a cult niche set into one wall and the front room was subdivided into a central entryway flanked by two small, tower-like chambers. Outside the building, an elevated mudbrick platform was reached by several basalt steps. To its south lay a large open court, finely paved with small pebbles. It is likely that the orthostats found in the later LB IIA Orthostat Temple originated in this MB IIC structure (Yadin 1975: 118; Yadin et al. 1989: 213–19, pl. 37).

A badly preserved building constructed over the Area F tombs and tunnels in the Lower City has been called the "Double Temple" Yadin 1975: 70). However, neither architectural remains nor finds confirm the identification of this building as a temple (Yadin et al. 1989: 138, pl. 28). Originally Yadin, its excavator, suggested that the Area F building was a palace (1976b: 476). This interpretation seems to be correct, particularly in light of the associated subterranean tombs used to bury Hazor's royalty (A. Mazar 1990a: 210).

In summary, in MB IIC Hazor the clan group involved with the MB IIB "ancestor cult" in Area F constructed a large residence over the tunnels and burial tombs. Elsewhere in the Lower City, people with links to Syria built a sanctuary of their own. They brought sacred objects and cultic paraphernalia from inland and coastal sites and set them up in their new Area H Bipartite Temple. They would remain prominent in Hazor until the end of the Bronze Age. Finally, the clan that had controlled Hazor's Upper City since the MB IIB built themselves a new royal sanctuary in Area A.

Megiddo

The excavators of Temple 2048 dated this building to the LB II (Stratum VIII–VII) (Loud 1948: 102–5, fig. 247), but subsequent research demonstrated that Megiddo's fortress temple was constructed in the MB IIC (Stratum X).[20] Other buildings constructed at the same time as Temple 2048 include Building 2005, a service building for cultic personnel, and Palace 5019.[21] Houses were constructed in the vicinity as well.

Temple 2048 was built on a platform that covered the earlier sacred structures of Megiddo Area BB and elevated the sanctuary to a height of 1 m above its surroundings. Its exterior measured 21.5×16.5 m and its walls were 4 m thick. Initially, Temple 2048 was fronted by two small chambers that were eventually modified into towers flanking the entrance. In this way, a classic fortress temple was created (Kempinski 1989a: 182).

Religious practice in Temple 2048 is attested by decorated cultic vessels and a small bronze snake found east of the sacred area, as well as by pottery and animal bones (Davies 1986: 49). Temple 2048 remained in use throughout the Late Bronze Age and even into the Iron I (Stratum VIIA).

Shechem

The MB IIC (Stratum XVI/Temenos 6) was a period of vigorous building activity at Shechem. The massive city wall with its monumental gateway was constructed at that time, as was the royal palace (Seger 1975: 38*; Toombs 1976: 57–59). Several sanctuaries including the Fortress Temple, a small royal chapel within the palace complex and the extramural Mt. Gerizim Square Temple coexisted in MB IIC Shechem.[22]

The Fortress Temple was located just inside the north city gate (Bull 1960: 116; G. E. Wright 1978: 1085 top). Built on a large stone base, its outside dimensions were 26.3 × 21.2 m and its walls were over 5 m thick. Two large towers containing staircases flanked the entrance to the temple. Two *favissae* or cisterns, one lined with plaster to hold liquids, were set into the floor of the inner chamber (G. E. Wright 1965: 87–91). Over time, the plan of the building was altered, as access to the *cella* became indirect and *maṣṣebôt* flanked the entrance to the temple (G. E. Wright 1978: 1085 bottom).[23] The base of a large altar was found in the courtyard east of the temple (G. E. Wright 1965: 93).

Late in the MB IIC, the Square Temple was constructed on the lower slope of Mt. Gerizim, some 300 m from the city of Shechem. This 18 m^2 building consisted of rooms arranged around a central chamber or courtyard, within which were a stone pillar and the foundation for an altar. Objects found within the building suggest its cultic function (Boling 1969).[24]

Shechem was a city of growing social complexity in the MB IIC, as reflected by its vigorous building campaign. Religious diversity is evident in its three places of worship, the royal chapel, the Fortress Temple and the extramural sanctuary on Mt. Gerizim. It is curious that within the walled city the major sanctuary was fortified, but outside the extramural sanctuary on Mt. Gerizim stood in a vulnerable location. The lack of political integration within the Central Highlands (Bunimovitz 1993b: 7) and the struggle among competing social groups may be reflected in the somewhat unusual distribution of sanctuaries at Shechem.

Jebel el-Rubka

An open-air sanctuary dating to the Middle Bronze Age was located on a high mountain peak south of Shechem. The Jebel el-Rubka sanctuary consisted of an isolated oval platform measuring 16 × 19 m, created by constructing a meter-high wall and filling it with small stones (Finkelstein 1998: 359). More information is necessary to fully assess this possible pilgrimage sanctuary.

Pella

The city of Pella was walled in the Middle Bronze Age, and occupation continued there throughout the Late Bronze Age and into the Iron I (Hennessy and Smith 1997: 257). A fortress temple was constructed early in the MB IIC, a period during which Egypt displayed a marked interest in the site (Knapp 1989: 64). This temple was in use until the ninth century B.C.E. Recent excavations have revealed four architectural phases. Those of the Late Bronze Age are the best known. The temple measured 32 × 24 m, larger than that at Shechem but similar in plan. It included a towered façade, a central pillared hall and a holy-of-holies (Bourke, et al. 1998: 196–97; Bourke 1999).

Beth Shean

Beth Shean was a small, unfortified settlement in the MB IIC period. Recent excavations have revealed a courtyard that may have been associated with a so far undiscovered cult place or shrine (A. Mazar 1992a: 6; 1997a: 66).

Shiloh

Shiloh, in the Central Highlands, was first occupied in the MB IIB period. In the MB IIC period, massive defense works guarded the site. No sanctuary has been found, but in Area F a group of storage rooms, the only structures that can be dated to the MB IIC period, contained materials that suggest one stood nearby. The pottery assemblage includes numerous storejars, as well as votive bowls, cultic stands and a zoomorphic vessel in the form of a bull. There were, however, almost no domestic vessels. Bronze axes and silver jewelry, including several North Syrian or Anatolian pieces, were also found. One silver pendant was decorated with the symbol of a Hittite deity. The storerooms were destroyed at the end of the MB IIC period (Finkelstein 1988: 212–16).

Gezer

The High Place at Gezer was constructed in the MB IIC period (Stratum XIX), at the same time as the city's massive "Inner Wall" system; it was reused in the Late Bronze Age (Stratum XVIII) (Dever 1976a: 426). This unique and highly visible High Place was accessible only from within the city walls (Dever 1976a: 426, plan on 429).

The Gezer High Place consists of ten large stone *maṣṣebôt* and a partially hollowed stone block, erected in a north–south line. The surface in front of the *stelae* was plastered and the complex was surrounded by a low wall. The many burned animal bones associated with the pavement led the excavator to suggest that the High Place had been the site of outdoor covenant renewal ceremonies, perhaps for a ten city-state league (Dever 1973: 69–70; 1997c: 397; for city-state leagues, see Campbell and Wright 1969 and references therein). In the absence of supra-city-state organization in the MB IIC, however, it might be better to relate the ten *stelae* to clan groups resident in and around Gezer than to a League of Ten as suggested by Dever.

Tel Mor

Tel Mor, a port associated with the nearby city of Ashdod, contained a sanctuary used from the MB IIC (Stratum XII) into the LB I period (Stratum X). All that remains of the building is a courtyard floor cut by a *favissa* filled with broken pottery of "cultic character." At one point late in the MB IIC period, animal horns surrounded by votive vessels, chalices and a seven-spouted lamp lay on its floor. The ceramic and artifactual assemblage contained typically Canaanite elements, but also suggests close relations between Tel Mor, Egypt, and Cyprus (M. Dothan 1959: 271; 1960: 124; 1977a: 889–90).

Ashkelon

A small sanctuary dated to the MB IIC was found near the base of the massive rampart surrounding the port of Ashkelon. This sanctuary was located outside the city wall, on a path leading from the

Mediterranean Sea to the much elevated northern gate. Little is known about the sanctuary itself. Its prize find is a small silver-plated bronze calf, found in one of its storerooms. The calf stood inside a cylinder-shaped ceramic model shrine, its opening fitted with a clay door large enough for the calf to fit through. When in use, the model shrine would have been placed on a small platform within the sanctuary (Stager 1991: 25-29).

Tel Haror

Tel Haror, a large MB IIC walled city on the north bank of Wadi Gerar in the Negev Desert, contains a well-preserved fortress temple and cultic complex. A mudbrick wall enclosed buildings, a courtyard and various installations. One room, 10 × 10 m contains niches and low offering benches. The benches and the floor were covered with ash, animal bones and cultic vessels. Analysis of the bones revealed that 62% were sheep and goat and, unusually, as many as 5% were dog bones (as is also the case at Mari). Cylindrical stands with red and blue paint on a white background, topped by large bowls, were found with other vessels at the entrance to the room (Oren 1993; 1997).

Elsewhere in the courtyard were various installations including niches, an offering table, hearths and cultic vessels. *Favissae* filled with ash, bone, offering tables and the red-painted arm of a large statuette were uncovered. In the second phase of use, *favissae* contained complete bird and puppy skeletons, hundreds of votive vessels, clay objects with seal impressions, seven-spouted lamps, vessels with snakes and bulls in relief, and imported Cypriote wares. Hundreds of votive vessels were also found in many nearby chambers. An elite residence, perhaps a palace like those at contemporary Tel Seraʿ and Tel el-ʿAjjul, was also found (Oren 1993; 1997).

Tell el-Farʿah (N)

In the MB IIC, Tell el-Farʿah (N) was a large walled city (Level B5). Its Field II Gateway Shrine, situated just within the western gate, consisted of a small, partially encircled, slab-lined installation, understood as a cultic basin or hearth. A fragment of a ceramic mask once used in religious ceremonies was found 10 m away (Mallet 1988: 81).[25]

Tell el-Dabʿa

The sacred area at Tell el-Dabʿa remained in use throughout the MB IIC (Late Stratum E/2–Stratum D/3), although the material culture at the site was now less typically Canaanite. During this period, the population of the city encroached upon the sacred area and in particular upon the cemeteries. Mortuary Temple I went out of use and warriors' tombs were constructed near the main temple. Late in the MB IIC (Stratum D/2), during the final years of Hyksos occupation, the sacred area was maintained but worship took place elsewhere (Bietak 1979: 260-68).

Summary: Middle Bronze IIC

Religion in the MB IIC was typified by a trend toward the construction of sacred structures in large fortified cities. Worship at Shechem and Hazor took place in multiple sanctuaries, indicating complex socio-political relationships, while Megiddo, Pella, Tel Mor, Tel Haror, Gezer and Beth Shean(?) seem to have contained only one sacred place. Gateway shrines were used at Ashkelon and Tell el-Farʿah (N). Finally, regional sanctuaries at Nahariya, Shiloh, Jebel el-Rubka(?), Tell Kittan and Tell el-Hayyat provided continuing religious services to rural residents.

SUMMARY: SANCTUARIES OF THE MIDDLE BRONZE AGE

As we have seen, many of the Middle Bronze Age sanctuaries (at sites including Byblos, Ebla, Alalakh, Ugarit[?], Megiddo, Shechem, Tel Haror, Tell el-Dabʿa and Hazor[?]) were situated near palaces but often these cities had other temples as well. Ashkelon and Tell el-Farʿah (N), both large cities, had shrines in their gateway areas. The Gezer High Place, an open-air cultic installation inside an MB IIC city, remains an anomaly.

Rural sanctuaries were also popular in the Middle Bronze Age. They were found within villages or towns (Givat Sharett, Tel Mor, Kfar Rupin, Beth Shean[?]) and in isolated cultic centers such as Tell el-Hayyat, Tel Kittan, Nahariya, Jebel el-Rubka and Shiloh. It is difficult to clarify the plan and function of some rural sacred sites, Kfar Shemaryahu and Bat Yam, for example.

It is not possible to classify the architectural forms of Middle Bronze Age sanctuaries by reference to their location. Fortress temples, for example, were found in urban sites ranging from Ebla in Syria to Tel Haror in southern Canaan and Tell ed-Dab'a in Egypt. They were also located in a cluster of urban sites—Shechem, Hazor, Megiddo and Pella—and rural sites—Tell el-Hayyat, Kfar Rupin, and Tel Kittan—in and near the Jordan Valley. Elements of the monumental symmetrical temple architecture as known from northern sites such as Ebla, Mari, Byblos and Alalakh, were employed at the southern sites of Hazor, Megiddo and Shechem as well, often as part of the architecture of the fortress temple. Inasmuch as styles were not regionally determined and since multiple building types coexisted at a number of sites, other explanations for this surprising diversity must be sought.

RELIGION AND SOCIETY IN THE MIDDLE BRONZE AGE

Increasingly, scholars have looked to archaeological data to learn about socio-cultural institutions and processes of change. In regions other than the Levant, social archaeology has concentrated on the study of complex societies whereas in the Levant its focus until recently was on prehistoric periods and unstratified societies.

Studies of Middle Bronze Age and Late Bronze Age Canaan commonly explain patterns of material remains through recourse to historical events, "ignoring the fact that these patterns were created by a social system—the Canaanite society—whose behaviour and adaptation to a changing environment is by no means *sui generis*" (Bunimovitz 1993a: 1–2). Bunimovitz used settlement pattern studies to explore the process of socio-cultural change in Middle Bronze Age and Late Bronze Age Canaan. Relationships between and among cities and their hinterlands, urban and rural populations, sedentary and settled populations, Egypt and the city-states of Canaan, together formed the basis for discussion. Bunimovitz's highlighting issues of socio-political organization suggests ways to clarify the diversity—and shared features—found among the Canaanite sanctuaries.

Despite the tendency of urban elites to control various socio-economic and political functions, the importance of rural populations in the continuing regeneration of Canaanite society should not be minimized. "Social reproduction was not simply a prerogative of the 'rural countryside' ..., but rather of those structures which underlay both urban and rural forms, and which perpetuated settlement and society at both ends of the settlement continuum, the kin-based group" (Joffe 1993: 85). Insofar as the cultural institutions of Bronze Age Canaan depended upon Canaan's many kin groups, who resided both in cities and in the countryside, it is to these groups that shared belief systems (represented by their sacred structures, iconography and cultic paraphernalia) must be attributed.

An urban religious center may have been a place of worship uniting clan groups within and outside of the city. So too may city-dwellers have traveled to countryside shrines to fulfill religious obligations. The concept of the city as a "central place" and the countryside as "periphery" may, therefore, not be applicable to the study of religion and the social group. As Marfoe noted in his study of the complexity of the social landscape of the Lebanese Biqaʿ:

> local groups are characterized by both a social cohesiveness and a flexibility that transcends fixed socioeconomic roles or identification by residential permanence .... Once we are freed from the notion of residential definition of social groups, the history of settlement and land use in the Biqaʿ can be seen to be no more than a record of this fluidity, i.e., of periodic shifts along a spectrum of available economic strategies and sociocultural roles (1979: 8).

These ideas underscore our inability to understand society and social process in Canaan without reference to its tribal components. It can be expected that relationships among clan groups were reflected in the structure of their religion.[26] Inasmuch as centralized control over tribal elements was limited, some sort of religious coexistence was necessary in order to maintain the delicate balance upon which the emergent city-states of the Middle Bronze Age were dependent.[27]

Insofar as Syro-Canaanite religious architecture exhibited a degree of uniformity, this was typified by two sacral traditions. The first was a coastal/near-coastal tradition that reached its peak early in the Middle Bronze Age and retained adherents throughout the first half of the second millennium. The second was a tradition with deep roots in Syria and in the Jordan Valley. Throughout the Middle Bronze Age, its followers grew in power and influence and it came to typify religious practice in the cities of the MB IIC period.

The coastal/near-coastal Obelisk/*Maṣṣebôt* tradition, seen at sites such as Nahariya, Byblos, Ugarit, Megiddo, Gezer and perhaps Dan, originated in the MB IIA period. It was typified by worship in open courtyard places, by obelisks or *maṣṣebôt* and by special assemblages of figures, predominantly female, cast and hammered in precious metals. Worship practices at these sites were influenced by Egyptian traditions, particularly that of erecting obelisks. Religion also resonated with Canaanite ritual practices that had been observed by the indigenous population for many centuries.

The second religious tradition was typified by worship at the fortress or *migdal* temple, known from such sites as Ebla, Alalakh, Megiddo, Hazor, Shechem, Pella, Tel Haror, Tell el-Hayyat, Tell Kittan and Kfar Rupin.[28] In Canaan, this temple type first appeared at Tell el-Hayyat in the MB IIA. In the MB IIB, its use in the Jordan Valley expanded to include the small sites of Tell Kittan and Kfar Rupin(?).

The Tell el-Hayyat fortress temple reached its peak in the MB IIC period. At that time, the fortress temple came to be used in important Canaanite cities, highlighting the complicated urban phenomenon at Shechem, Megiddo, Hazor, Tel Haror and Pella. This may be attributed to the increasing importance of adherents to its cult, the long-time residents of the Jordan Valley. Metalworking at the Hayyat temple might explain the prominence and success of that site as control over metallurgy was an important mechanism in the creation of Middle Bronze Age elites.

The fortress temple was so named on account of the unusual thickness of its walls, important for defending each sacred building and its precious contents. This is curious when considered in relation to contemporary sacred places in undefended rural locations such as Nahariya that endured for centuries protected it would seem by nothing more than communal respect for their sanctity.

What accounts for the unusual configuration of the fortress temple, and for its popularity? Despite the thickness of the temple walls, these buildings were not impregnable. Whether or not the walls could be breached easily is a moot point, since people defending a fortress temple could not have endured a lengthy siege and the buildings therefore remained vulnerable. On the other hand, their bastion-like plan expressed symbolic power, representing a major deployment of resources and personnel and, more importantly, the invincible home of an invincible god.

In Canaan, the fortress temple was a regional phenomenon, almost exclusively restricted to rural and urban settings in the Jordan Valley and environs.[29] Its proliferation can be related to the interrelationships among the tribal groups that populated the cities and countryside of Middle Bronze Age Canaan. The clan groups that worshipped in the various fortress temples may have had varying subsistence strategies, but each one had successfully adapted to life in and around the Jordan Valley.

Several important conclusions can be drawn from this discussion of the two main religious traditions of Middle Bronze Age Canaan. The first relates to their regional quality. In general, cultural influences and traditions were localized (Dornemann 1981: 67–68), and the same can be said of religious influences and traditions. Next, the relationship between the tribal group and religious organization is underscored. From this perspective, the interplay between urban centers and rural hinterlands becomes apparent, as the study of Middle Bronze Age religion highlights social and economic dynamics.

The Role of the Emerging Urban Elite

The large-scale state bureaucracy and sharply-defined socio-political functions typical of the urban centers of Syria and Mesopotamia had no place in the relatively small cities of Middle Bronze Age Canaan.[30] There, the emerging urban elite exercised both sacral and secular leadership roles though for all practical purposes these two roles were not differentiated (see Marfoe 1979: 15–16; see too Ilan 1995: 306).

In Canaan, traditional groups came into conflict with new urban elites who tried to channel kin-based socio-cultural patterns into religion-based ideologically bonded units. Insofar as the elite maintained the perceived social order through the central symbolic role of the palace-temple organization, it had an important means of mobilizing diverse human resources and of securing their loyalty (Marfoe 1979: 35).

By restructuring the symbolic order, the new urban elite deployed local resources for its own ends and to secure the loyalty of traditionally organized groups. This restructuring was made possible because residents of cities, villages and remote hamlets, along with their seminomadic brethren were, presumably, all members of the same social or ethnic groups.

Demographic fluidity and flexibility in sociocultural identification were and are found throughout the Levant, as cities moderate between village farming and pastoralism. Rather than being at an extreme, cities function within a societal continuum (Marfoe 1979: 9). In other words, urban elite (whether king, priest, trader, administrator or military leader), agriculturalist and pastoralist may all have shared kin affiliation and thus religious beliefs, despite their different places of residence, subsistence strategies and degrees of wealth and status.

As we have seen, social structure was reflected in the planning of Middle Bronze Age cities. The many neighborhoods in large cities like Ebla and Hazor, each with its own special sanctuary, reflected the residences of kin groups with semi-autonomous infrastructures designed to serve their own needs and beliefs. Urban superstructures, signaled by royal complexes (including temple, palace and perhaps burial chambers), also served the needs of the dominant group within each city, as well as the needs of society at large. Inasmuch as clans were interrelated not only within cities but also between cities and rural areas, city planning, and in particular the position and style of sacred structures, reflected those complex relationships.

CONCLUSIONS

Small sanctuaries or sacred installations were found at MB IIA Nahariya, Kfar Shemaryahu, Bat Yam, Megiddo, Dan(?), Gezer(?) and Tell el-Hayyat. In the MB IIB period, sanctuaries were built at Tell Kittan, Tel Haror, Kfar Rupin(?) and Givat Sharett, while at Hazor Area F, burial tombs and tunnels were used. The fact that most of these places of worship were in unfortified countryside locations, accessible to the population at-large, underscores the non-urban orientation of the first two phases of the Middle Bronze Age.

In the large city-states of Syria, Ebla, Alalakh, Ugarit, Byblos and Mari), the construction of multiple temples occurred as early as the MB IIA period. In Canaan, on the other hand, it was not until the MB IIC that sanctuaries, let alone multiple sanctuaries, were erected in major cities. This is when the urban temples and sacred installations of Hazor, Shechem, Pella, Ashkelon, Tel Mor, Gezer and Tell el-Far'ah (N) were constructed. There are a few exceptions, including Megiddo, where there was some degree of cultic continuity from the Early Bronze Age through the Middle Bronze Age, and Tel Haror, where urban temple construction may have been related to the social complexity demonstrated by the Hyksos experience at Tell el-Dabʿa.

That these building activities took place together with intensive urbanization and fortification suggests that one result of the crystallization of an urban elite was an increasing exclusivity of worship. Since sacred construction in the MB IIC period took place within and not outside urban areas, the manipulation of religion for the purpose of social control by the expanding power elite can be assumed.[31]

It has long been recognized that the cultural institutions of Bronze Age Canaan were based upon its indigenous tribal components. Reaching back, at a minimum, to the Chalcolithic era, the kin-based structure of Canaanite society has been documented. The complex urban world of the Early Bronze Age was made possible by certain of these kin-groups' attaining elite status through political, religious and economic domination. The attendant social stratification empowered the urban centers and assured their survival for hundreds of years.

In the small cities of Early Bronze Age Canaan, control over religion and politics had often coincided, for centralizing elites maintained their vested interest in the social order by emphasizing the quintessential symbolic role of the combined palace-temple organization. Religion, inasmuch as it presented the urban elite with an important means for mobilizing diverse human resources and for securing their loyalty, would continue to provide a relatively enduring forum for social unification.

Following the collapse of this urban world late in the third millennium, it was the agriculturalists and pastoralists of the Canaanite countryside who provided resiliency and the substance for social regeneration. This rural component of society, retaining elements of its own religious practice and belief, continued to serve as a counterbalance to the cyclical failures of the urban elites.

Consequently, the non-urban orientation of religion early in the second millennium should come as no surprise. Despite the incipient regeneration of Canaanite cities in the MB IIA period, places of worship were built in unfortified countryside locations in this period. Sacred installations of various sorts were found at rural Nahariya, Kfar Shemaryahu, Bat Yam and Tell el-Hayyat. That at Megiddo (Cult Room 4040/High Place) was part of a village settlement.[32]

It can be no coincidence that (with the exception of Tell el-Hayyat in the Jordan Valley) early second millennium Canaanite religious installations displayed evidence for Egyptian involvement. The Obelisk

Temple at Byblos contained dedications to Egyptian rulers and gods. Material remains from Nahariya on the coast and from Megiddo on the Via Maris demonstrate the important relationship between Egypt and Canaan in the MB IIA period, while similarities in form and content link these sacred places to the smaller shrines at Kfar Shemaryahu and Bat Yam. As Egyptian traders, envoys and administrators became increasingly involved in Canaan, they stimulated the reformulation of a Canaanite elite, which in turn moved to control forms of religious expression by establishing centrally located places of worship.

In the Jordan Valley, the interior passageway between Syria and Canaan, the situation was similar.Tell el-Hayyat's sanctuary, geographically vulnerable to inland influences, more closely resembled contemporary Temples D and N at Ebla and for nearly a millennium the fortress temple would typify architecture in and around the Jordan Valley. The rather isolated Hayyat sanctuary was, like its Canaanite contemporaries in the MB IIA period, a center for regional worship.

Thus religion, presumably organized at the local level during the rural EB IV, came with the budding urbanism of the MB IIA to be organized around pilgrimage to sacred installations. The reformulation of the social order, indicated by this increasing religious centralization and by its concomitant burgeoning hierocracy, would eventually evolve into the urban-based religion of the MB IIC period.

Most of the MB IIA regional temples were used throughout the MB IIB period, while new places of worship were also built. The material culture of the Givat Sharett sanctuary resembled its coastal contemporaries while inland, the fortress temple predominated and was now also found at Tell Kittan and Kfar Rupin. The sacred necropolis in Hazor Area F is attributed to this period as well.

For the most part, it was not until the MB IIC period that temples were constructed in the major urban centers of Canaan.[33] As in the Syrian cities of Ebla (Temple D), Alalakh and Mari, temples at Shechem (the Fortress Temple and the Royal Chapel), Hazor (Area A), Megiddo (Temple 2048), Tel Haror and Tell el-Dab'a (Temple III and Temple V) were associated with palaces. The siting of the fortress temple in Pella is not yet clear. Smaller sacred structures were built in the gateway areas of Ashkelon and Tell el-Far'ah (N). It is unlikely that the anomalous High Place was Gezer's only sacred site, but too little is known of its MB IIC period to be certain. Gezer notwithstanding, in every large MB IIC city for which we have knowledge of sacred architecture, at least one temple can be associated with the ruling clan. At the same time Shechem (Mt. Gerizim) and Hazor (Area H) contained alternative places for worship.

While the rural sanctuaries of MB IIB Nahariya, Tell Kittan, Tell el-Hayyat and perhaps Shiloh were reused in the MB IIC, in general the MB IIC was an era of religious reorientation.[34] Religious practice came to be centered almost exclusively within municipal areas, increasingly dominated by powerful aristocracies. That this important shift took place together with intensive urbanization and fortification suggests that one result of the crystallization of an urban elite was its increasing control over access to worship. Ultimately, the Middle Bronze Age trend of placing forms of religious expression in the hands of an expanding elite demonstrates the manipulation of religion for the purpose of social control.

At the end of the Middle Bronze Age, Canaan underwent a century or more of warfare and destruction, resulting in the disruption of the "Canaanite" way of life that had predominated for the past half-millennium. It would be incorrect to suggest that the resumption of order in the Late Bronze Age would bring with it entirely new social structures. Certain traditional elements of Canaanite life would survive the catastrophic decades of the mid-second millennium as evinced materially in the continuity of ceramic forms from the Middle Bronze Age into the Late Bronze Age. However, the destruction and/or abandonment of many large cites, major population shifts, the ascendance of new empires at Canaan's borders, the economic and social traumas brought about by the collapse of Middle Bronze Age urban centers and the disruption of the rural way of life all would contribute to the formation of a society different in many ways from its predecessor.

NOTES

[1] In a study of *maṣṣebôt*, Graesser described them as "markers, reminders, jogs for the memory." He noted that the *maṣṣebâ* could perform any of four functions, memorial, legal, commemorative and cultic (marking places where the deity could be found). Finally, "a single stone was not limited to a single function but often carried out several at one and the same time" (1972: 36–37).
[2] See Ilan 1995: 313–14 for a discussion of religious continuity from the Neolithic to the Middle Bronze Age.
[3] During the Middle Bronze Age, the seven major political-territorial units in Israel's northern coastal plain included both fortified urban centers and rural

sites (Gophna and Beck 1981: 76–77). For example, the coastal plain south of the Yarkon was a "large, comparatively integrated urban system" while the socio-political organization of the Central Highlands consisted of localized city-states (Bunimovitz 1993b: 7).

[4] According to Dever, the first phase of the Middle Bronze Age (Dever's MB I = Albright's MB IIA) encompassed the first quarter of the second millennium (*contra* Weinstein 1992, where an early nineteenth century date for the beginning of this period was suggested) (1992a: 2–10).

The second phase of the Middle Bronze Age (Dever's MB II = Albright's MB IIB) includes the century from 1750–1650. Finally, the third phase (Dever's MB III = Albright's MB IIC) refers to the years from 1650–1500, with a brief transitional period into the LB IA (until the mid-15th century) (Dever 1992a: 10–14).

[5] For typological studies of temples, see G. R. H. Wright 1971; Dever 1992c; A. Mazar 1992b; Bonfil 1997; Nakhai 1997; and references therein.

[6] The monumental symmetrical temple was a large freestanding building situated within a sacred precinct. Its symmetrical plan was arranged along a long central axis. A cult statue could have been placed within its well-defined holy-of-holies (A. Mazar 1992b: 166–67).

[7] Similar tunnels were found in MB IIB Hazor.

[8] McClellan (1989 and references there) has summarized the problems of the Alalakh chronology. The slight shift in the location of the Level VII temple and the change in its architectural layout (Woolley 1955: 59) corresponded with the break between Period 1 (Level 10/XI–X, IX and VIII) and Period 2 (Levels VII, VI and V), as demonstrated through ceramic analysis.

[9] The main temples of the Early Bronze Age were located at the heart of the city, around the Sacred Lake. They included the Baalat-Gebal Temple to the northwest, the *Enceinte Sacrée* to the west and the Obelisk Complex to the southeast. Later in the Early Bronze Age, the Sacred Lake was filled in and the temples reoriented. New sacred structures, including the *Champs des Offrandes*, the Megaron XVII in the extreme south of the city, the tower temple(?) on the west and an unpublished temple in the southeast facing the palace, were constructed (Saghieh 1983: 1–2).

[10] According to Albright, the main function of the Obelisk Temple was as a mortuary shrine (1966: 26).

[11] The great majority of these were male figurines, found in seven separate deposits (Negbi 1976: 122–23).

[12] The reign of 12th Dynasty Pharaoh Sesostris I was one of large-scale construction. From now on, Egyptian temples would be built of stone, to create eternal monuments to the gods and to commemorate the kings who built them (Franke 1995: 738–39). Sesostris I constructed a solar temple near Hieropolis

and erected several pairs of obelisks there to commemorate his jubilee (Aldred 1987: 54, 130–31, fig. 28).

[13] The tel of Nahariya, as yet unexcavated, lies 800 m south of the sacred site, while Acco and Achziv, fortified towns of the MB IIA, are both located within 10 km of it.

[14] Unlike at Megiddo and Nahariya, no Egyptian material was uncovered at Gezer (Weinstein 1975: 4).

[15] Although some details remain obscure, architectural and artifactual parallels from the sites of Kfar Shemaryahu, Nahariya and Bat Yam relate them to each other and to other MB IIA coastal sites.

[16] Similar royal tombs were uncovered under Palace Q in Ebla, at Late Bronze Age Ugarit and at Megiddo, suggesting the celebration of an ancestor cult at these sites (A. Mazar 1990a: 214, 230 n. 44).

[17] This figure was found in a pit near the LB II Orthostat Temple in Area H. Its provenance was probably a workshop in the Aleppo-Alalakh region; its style and iconography in keeping with the Old Syrian tradition found at such sites as Ebla (Beck 1989c: 322–24).

[18] Stone altars and libation tables found in and around the LB II Orthostat Temples of Area H are similar to those from inland Syria, in particular from MB IIB Ebla (Temple D and Sanctuary B2), Alalakh and Carchemish (Beck 1989c: 330–34).

[19] This krater, although found in an LB IIB context, originated in the MB IIB period. It resembles metal and ceramic vessels from coastal Syria (Beck 1989c: 329–30).

[20] See Davies 1986: 49 and references there. Alternately, a large sanctuary constructed along the lines of the later Temple 2048 may have stood in the sacred area at Megiddo throughout the MB IIB and MB IIC periods (Epstein 1965: 220–21).

[21] Later, in the LB I period (Stratum IX), Temple 2048 was associated with Palace 2134.

[22] The so-called Courtyard Temples (G. E. Wright 1965: 103–22) have more recently been understood as an MB IIA–MB IIC palace (A. Mazar 1992b: 164) or other non-sacred public structure (Dever: personal communication).

[23] It is unclear whether these *maṣṣebôt* originated in the first phase of Temple 2048.

[24] G. R. H. Wright suggests that a prototype for the Mt. Gerizim Square Temple stood in the northern part of Shechem's "Sacred Area" prior to its MB IIC relocation outside the city walls (1975: 57–61). However, his reconstructed building does not have the box-like shape that typifies the Mt. Gerizim building and the small finds do not suggest sacred activities. Alternatively, Oren suggests that the Mt. Gerizim and Amman Airport buildings resembled Egyptian-style "governors' residencies" of the Canaanite Late Bronze Age

(1984: fig. 2), although the Amman Airport building is now understood as a mortuary shrine (see chapter 5).

[25] Locus 559, de Vaux's Temple 1–3 (1976: 400) is now understood to have been a partially subterranean granary, like that at MB IIA Gezer (Dever 1989: 156).

[26] Those explaining the "gods of the fathers" in the biblical patriarchal narratives have postulated different gods for the different Israelite patriarchs, each of whom was understood as the leader of a different patriarchal clan. In these reconstructions, as Israelites, members of the original clan groups, moved to unite, their new god Yahweh inherited the qualities of the old clan gods. Many of these studies are outdated but their linking of religion to inter-clan relationships is correct. For a study of this patriarchal material, see Dever 1977 and references therein.

[27] In the Iron II, as the prevalent political structure shifted to that of the nation-state, attempts were made to enforce centralized religious uniformity (see chapter 6). The results were often disastrous.

[28] A. Mazar classifies the temples somewhat differently, looking in particular at longroom temples with symmetrical plans, typified by Megiddo 2048, Hazor A Long Temple, Hazor H Bipartite Temple, Tell Kittan IV and the Shechem Fortress Temple. He attributes their proliferation to cultural and ethnic ties among the West Semitic states of the Levant and North Mesopotamia (1992b: 167–69).

[29] Hazor's setting in the Galilee makes the city easily accessible to the Jordan Valley, as does Megiddo's Jezreel Valley location.

[30] Hazor may provide the single exception to this statement.

[31] The social implications of religious organization must be distinguished from its theological implications. In terms of belief, significant issues are expressed physically by the relationship among enclosed and open spaces, by exterior form and interior organization of space (Herzog 1980), by decoration, iconography, access to the holy-of-holies and by sacred objects.

[32] While there may have been MB IIA sanctuaries at Dan and Gezer, in the absence of firm evidence they cannot be included in this discussion.

[33] Tell el-Dabʿa was the only large city of the MB IIB known to have contained temples. Given its location in the eastern Delta, it cannot be considered a typical site.

[34] Not enough is known of the Jebel el-Rubka open-air shrine to include it in this discussion.

CHAPTER FIVE
THE LATE BRONZE AGE

The discontinuity between the Middle Bronze Age and the Late Bronze Age can be seen in the disruption of religious services to the Canaanite populace, but interestingly, this did not take place on a large scale until well into the LB I. Eventually, however, a newly oriented religious order became apparent. Canaan was increasingly the subject of external imperial strategies, divided between Hittites to the north and Egyptians to the south. Northern sites such as Hazor continued to reflect Syrian influences. Domination by Egypt was reflected in the construction of Egypto-Canaanite temples at sites ranging from Beth Shean in the Jordan Valley to Lachish in the Shephelah.[1] Whereas religion in Middle Bronze Age Canaan reflected issues of social structure, in the Late Bronze Age it became increasingly dominated by international politics (fig. 3).

A number of schemata for establishing the chronology of the Late Bronze Age have been proposed (Weinstein 1981; Ussishkin 1985: 217–20; see also Leonard 1989: 6–7). I will continue to follow that of Dever (1992a: 14–18, fig. 1) whose framework presupposes a "post-destruction" phase early in the Late Bronze Age (his MB III/LB IA). During this period (1500–1450 B.C.E.), some sites experienced the ongoing ramifications of warfare with Egypt while at others an occupational gap resulted from its previous military expeditions against Canaan. The LB IB period (1450–1400 B.C.E.) has often been considered a period of post-destruction recovery yet, as Dever (1992a: 16) and Gonen (1984) have noted, "recovery" took a century and more.

The LB IIA period (1400–1300 B.C.E.), Egypt's Amarna Age, was "the zenith of cultural development in Palestine in the Late Bronze Age" (Dever 1992a: 17). During the LB IIB period (1300–1200/1150 B.C.E.), Egyptian control over Canaan was at its peak and this included the exploitation of local religion in the service of imperial needs. The end of the Late Bronze Age is linked to partial destructions and occupational gaps commonly blamed on incursions by "Sea Peoples," '*apiru*, *shasu*, disenfranchised Canaanites and others, but they must

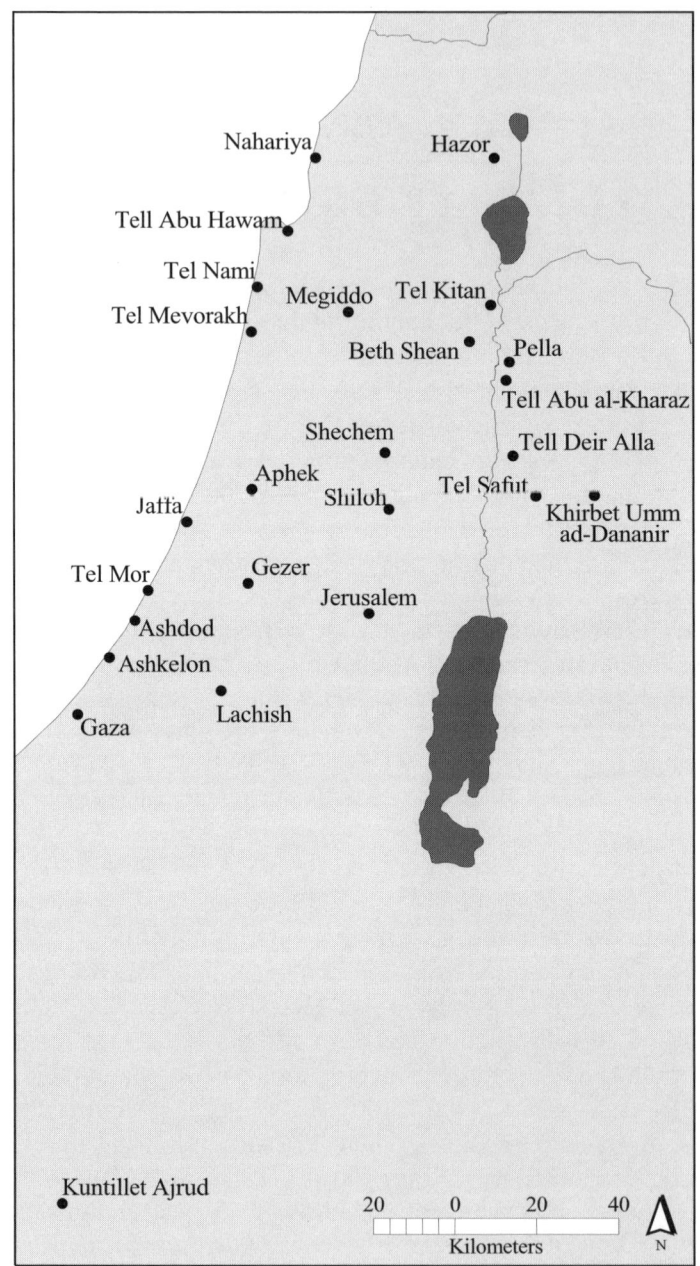

Fig. 3 Map showing the location of Late Bronze Age sites. Map by Marcy H. Rockman.

also be related to chronic Egyptian interference in Canaan throughout the Late Bronze Age.

Egyptian control of strategically located Canaanite city-states in the 18th, 19th and early 20th Dynasties has long been acknowledged, although the degree to which Canaan was materially exploited by Egypt has been the subject of some debate. Most scholars now agree with N. Na'aman, who suggests that during the Late Bronze Age, Egypt deliberately exploited Canaanite wealth, importing both tribute and "gifts" from its subjugated territories (1981; see also Knapp 1989 and Bunimovitz 1995). This process began when, following his victory at Megiddo (ca. 1457 B.C.E.), Thutmosis III established a highly structured means of collecting tribute from western Asia and in particular from Canaan. "He appointed new princes for each town—but not before each took a loyalty oath—and Palestine soon became a giant storehouse for Egypt." Over time, Egypt "came to appreciate the potential economic benefits of annual Canaanite contributions to the coffers of the god Amon" (Leonard 1989: 12–13).[2]

The Egyptian administration became increasingly entrenched and a growing body of archaeological evidence documents Egyptian control under the later pharaohs of the 19th Dynasty. Increasingly, Canaan was administered by Egypt from its district capital at Gaza and even exploited by Egypt for its agricultural and human resources. According to Singer's reconstruction of this colonial process (1988), sites such as Ashdod and Aphek, strategically located along the Via Maris, were turned into Egyptian bases during the long thirteenth century reign of Rameses II.[3] Subsequently, under Merneptah's rule, Ashkelon and Gezer, the remaining major Canaanite city-states in the south, were conquered.

Finally, early in the twelfth century, Rameses III turned his attention to the Central Highlands, annexing Lachish, Tell esh-Shariyah and possibly Tell es-Safi. Egyptian domination, characterized by exploitative economic institutions, did not survive the subsequent and dramatic decline in Egyptian power (Singer 1988).

Severe food shortages began during the reign of Rameses II and continued during that of Merneptah. Information about the exploitation of Canaanite agricultural resources to alleviate these shortages comes from a letter found at Aphek. It documents a transaction that took place in Jaffa, an Egyptian administrative center that maintained royal granaries. A shipment of fifteen metric tons of wheat was one of several such consignments sent from Jaffa to Ugarit. This shipment highlights the problem of food shortages in Hatti, shortages that resulted in serious famine late in the Bronze Age.

To mitigate its effects, New Kingdom Hittite rulers attempted to procure large quantities of grain from Egypt, either directly or involving Ugarit, whose merchant fleet was essential for its transportation (Singer 1983: 3–5). The Jaffa–Ugarit shipment noted above is but one example of the agricultural resources of Canaan being used to support not only Canaan's native population and its Egyptian overlords but also people residing in foreign lands. It will be seen below that Egypto-Canaanite temples at a number of Canaanite sites were used specifically to support these colonial needs.

The effect of Egyptian domination—and exploitation—of Canaan is critical for understanding culture and religion during the Late Bronze Age. Large cities in the north, cities able to maintain relative autonomy in the face of imperial demands, displayed a cultural and religious heterodoxy that placed them at variance with smaller sites in the south. In the north, Syro-Mesopotamian traditions prevailed.[4] In the south, on the other hand, one observes an incremental growth in the use made by Egypt of Canaan's religious institutions, as they became increasingly important for the fulfillment of Egyptian imperial designs.

KINGDOM OF UGARIT

The port city of Ugarit was one of the most important sites of the Late Bronze Age due to its remarkable collection of tablets and to the vast amount of architectural and artifactual information revealed by decades of excavation and publication. Our ability to study the structure of this Late Bronze Age city-state is much enhanced by its many mythological, ritual, economic and administrative texts. These combine with archaeological data to expand our understanding of Ugarit's socio-political, economic and religious world. They also suggest the workings of other smaller city-states to its south, especially the Canaanite stronghold of Hazor.

The kingdom of Ugarit extended over approximately 360 km^2. Within it, social, political, religious and economic ties linked some two hundred towns and villages to the capital city (Heltzer 1976: 7; Dornemann 1981: 67). Despite its dependence upon, and subordination to, the Hittite Empire, Ugarit's pivotal location among the city-states of the Levant,

Anatolia, the Mediterranean and Egypt ensured its unique role (Heltzer 1978: 99).

Ugarit was one of only two Hittite vassal states that remained under the rule of a native dynasty. The other was Amurru, further south in Lebanon (Astour 1981: 24). While from a political perspective Ugarit looked north, its ceramic assemblage resembled that of Canaan (Dornemann 1981: 68). Ugarit's political ties with the Hittites, its wide-ranging trade relations, its connections with southern contemporaries, and the broad extent of its territory combined to create a cosmopolitan capital characterized by social, ethnic and religious diversity.[5]

In the city of Ugarit, neither cultic organization nor religious economy functioned independently. Instead, cultic personnel, together with certain other professionals, were royal dependants. As in Late Bronze Age Alalakh, the Hittite Empire, Kassite Babylonia, Middle Assyria and Egypt, the needs of the state temple were for the most part supplied by the royal treasury. In these regions, "the temple and its personnel were in the hands of the royal power and possibly Ugarit was one of the most distinguished examples" (Heltzer 1982: 138–39).

There were two venues for religious observance for the residents of the kingdom of Ugarit. Villages were required to contribute to, and to participate in, national cults but according to the texts, worshippers in at least some villages also participated in local cults. Village sanctuaries at which local priests officiated were dedicated to local gods. These in turn were subordinated to El, head of the Ugaritic pantheon (Heltzer 1982: 71–73). This is reflected in administrative texts that discussed personnel and the disbursement of provisions. They indicate that priests were supported by their local sanctuaries, but that they also were connected to the royal palace (Rainey 1965: 123).

All this accords well with what we might expect in this period of transition. Throughout the Late Bronze Age, clan affiliation became a decreasingly important criterion for status and authority, as Ugarit's well-entrenched royalty gradually undermined the economic, social and religious self-sufficiency of the city-state's many clan groups. The power of tradition and the desire for autonomy may also explain some of the many sacred structures found in the city of Ugarit and in the rural countryside, structures that ranged from royal sanctuaries to neighborhood and rural chapels.

Of Ugarit's many temples, the Temples of Baal and Dagan are the best known, but mythological texts and archaeological excavations have revealed others too (Schaeffer 1939; Yon 1984: 41, 47). The "Hurrian Sanctuary" or "Sanctuary of the Mitanni Axe" was part of a well-protected royal complex that included the huge royal palace, an arsenal and other buildings. The plan of this two-roomed sanctuary resembled those of the two acropolis temples and its furnishings were evocative of a sacred place. However, the poor state of preservation precludes a more detailed description (Yon 1984: 47; 1992: 26; 1997: 260, fig. 2).

The Temples of Baal and Dagan were located at the highest point on the acropolis, at some distance from the royal palace and administrative headquarters. First constructed early in the Middle Bronze Age, they remained in use until the extensive destruction of the city at the beginning of the twelfth century (Yon 1984: 45, figs. 1, 2).

The two-roomed Temple of Baal measured 22 × 16 m and was enclosed by a *temenos* wall. The remains of an altar were found in its courtyard (Schaeffer 1931: fig. 2; 1933: fig. 14). The sanctuary's height, accentuated by a tower, and its position at the apex of the site, ensured that it was visible from the sea. Its importance for the religion of maritime Ugarit, a city dependent upon trade and vital international connections, was underscored by its visibility from the nearby sea and by the many stone anchors found within it.[6] Stelae discovered in the sacred precinct attest to the sanctuary's dedication to the god Ba'al (Yon 1984: 43–45; 1997: 260).

To its east stood the Temple of Dagan, similar in scale and form to that of Ba'al, but more massively constructed (Schaeffer 1935: pl. 36). Its almost completely ruined condition precludes other than the most general description, but like the Temple of Baal it had two main chambers and a tower. The objects found in both these sanctuaries hint at their original richness (Yon 1984: 45–46; 1997: 260).

The House of the High Priest (or, perhaps, the Library) stood between the Temples of Baal and Dagan, indicating that the area around the temples was not conventionally residential. Finds from this building included bronze weapons and utensils with dedications to the "chief of the priests," and important mythological texts (Yon 1997: 260).

Elsewhere on the tel, residential neighborhoods were "interspersed with shops, workshops, and religious structures" (Yon 1992: 27). For example, the Rhyton Sanctuary was located in a residential district in the center of the city. This small, bench-lined sanctuary had a three-tiered altar on its rear wall. Among its significant artifacts were a *stele* and a cult stand with elements similar to the "Baal of Lightning" *stele* found in the Baal Temple. Also important were its numerous Syrian, Cypriote, Mycenaean and Minoan *rhyta*. The Rhyton Sanctuary was used throughout most of the Late Bronze Age (Yon 1984: 48–50; figs. 1, 3).

Other sanctuaries were excavated within Ugarit's various residential neighborhoods. Some were identified by their architectural configurations, but in others it was the constellation of cultic objects that indicated that the structures were sacred. Religious artifacts, including *stelae*, figurines, liver and lung models used for divination, inscribed tablets, cult stands and *rhyta* were found in the "House of the Magician Priest" on the south acropolis and at numerous other places throughout the neighborhoods of Ugarit. Other interesting assemblages, which were found in the nearby port city of Minet el-Beida, commonly included small altars. Domestic cults were indicated by the presence of small ceramic figurines or pendants bearing religious iconography discovered within residential structures (Yon 1997: 260). Taken together, these data point the way toward the many additional sanctuaries that were part of the complex social and religious fabric of Late Bronze Age Ugarit (Yon 1984: 47, fig. 1).

The multiple sanctuaries at Ugarit underscore the complexity of religion in this Late Bronze Age capital city. The central and dominating position of the Temples of Baal and Dagan, their long centuries of use, their massive size, rich artifactual assemblages and their link to the maritime community all suggest that these sacred buildings provided the central focal point of worship for local residents, for travelers and traders, and even for foreign dignitaries.

The various clan groups and residents from afar who lived at Ugarit worshipped in sanctuaries within their own neighborhoods. The Hurrian Sanctuary, part of the palace complex, was used by Ugarit's ruling clan. The Rhyton Sanctuary, the "House of the Magician Priest" and the numerous constellations of sacred objects found around the city and in neighboring Minet el-Beida all demonstrate the richness of Late Bronze Age religion.

CANAAN IN THE LATE BRONZE AGE

Nahariya, Gezer and Tel Mor

Farther south, in Canaan, the transition from the Middle Bronze Age to the Late Bronze Age displayed some elements of continuity, as demonstrated by religious institutions that endured into the fifteenth and even the fourteenth centuries B.C.E. Several MB IIC period open-air sacred sites including the Gezer High Place (Dever 1973: 244) and that at Nahariya (M. Dothan 1977b: 910) remained in use during the LB IA period. The new sanctuary built at Tel Mor late in the Middle Bronze Age remained in use until the fourteenth century B.C.E. (Level IX) (M. Dothan 1959: 271).

Hazor

At 840 dunams, Hazor was more than four times larger than Lachish, the next largest Late Bronze Age settlement and over sixteen times larger than the average Canaanite town of fifty dunams. In the LB II period, Hazor incorporated some forty percent of the settled area of Canaan (Gonen 1984: 68) and was one of only a few cities that were fortified (Bienkowski 1987: 52). Despite intense destruction in some areas of MB IIC Hazor, in other areas the first Late Bronze Age stratum (Stratum XVI=3) reflected continuity with its predecessor (Ben-Tor 1997b: 4). Greater change marked the transition from the end of this LB IB stratum (Stratum XV=2) and its LB IIA successor (Stratum XIV =1B). Stratum XIV was then destroyed, perhaps by Seti I at the end of the 14th century B.C.E. The LB IIB occupation (Stratum XIII=1A) showed a marked decline in the standard of living for the residents of the city (Ben-Tor 1997a: 3).

Late Bronze Age Hazor was anomalous on account of its size and also its rather autonomous position in the face of imperial Egypt.[7] Like Ugarit in the north, Hazor contained multiple places of worship throughout the Late Bronze Age including the well-known sanctuaries in Areas C, H and A and the cultic installations in Areas A, K, F and P. The religious complexity at Hazor during these centuries may be attributed to the relative security of its diverse communities, as they managed to remain independent of Egyptian overlords.

With the onset of the LB I period, significant changes were made to the MB IIC Bipartite Temple in Area H in the Lower City. Its courtyard was enlarged, surrounded by a *temenos* wall and enhanced by the addition of special cultic installations (Yadin et al. 1989: fig. 4, pl. 38). A ceremonial gate divided the now-enclosed area into two courtyards, the inner of which contained two stone altars surrounded by animal bones and ashes. Numerous cultic vessels and fragments of clay liver models, one with an Akkadian omen inscription, were found nearby. A slanted, paved surface and a drainage channel (partially made up of discarded incense stands) helped maintain cleanliness in this sacrificial courtyard (Yadin 1975: 113–14). A pottery workshop produced votive vessels for use in religious ceremonies.

The MB IIC temple in Area H had been bipartite, with a *cella* at its rear. In the LB I, the exterior of this 13.5 × 20 m building remained unchanged but its interior was modified significantly. Benches were added to the main hall, the *cella* was closed from public view and a stand for a cult statue was placed at one side (Yadin 1972: 79). The growing complexity of the courtyards, including their many installations and the pottery workshop, and the increased seclusion of the sanctuary, together point to the growth of a specialized clergy that officiated over worship in the LB I temple while limiting public participation in its sacred cult.

Following its destruction, the Area H temple was reconstructed. The LB IIA building was now tripartite, as a front room was added to the old bipartite plan (Yadin et al. 1989: fig. 5, pl. 39). Lion orthostats, one found buried in the courtyard, flanked the entryway to the new front hall and basalt orthostats lined the interior walls.[8] The courtyard was reduced in size and many of the LB I cultic installations were eliminated.

In the innermost room, a seated basalt figure was found in a *favissa* located between two pillar bases. This statue, manufactured in a workshop in the Aleppo-Alalakh region, dates to the seventeenth century B.C.E. and displays "the traditional Syrian iconography of a seated figure holding a cup in its right hand." It may represent a king or dignitary rather than a god (Beck 1989b: 323). There were also two basalt libation tables.

In the LB IIB period, the walls of the front room and of the innermost chamber were lined with basalt orthostats originally created for use in earlier sanctuaries (Yadin 1972: 89). A tall basalt incense altar was decorated with a four-rayed disk, a motif typical of religion in the north. An offering table and four libation tables, also of basalt, were found too. Some have parallels in Syrian offering tables, in particular those from Alalakh and Carchemish, while the large altar in Area F may have served as the prototype for the rectangular offering table. Other basalt objects included a basin and a krater.

A headless sculpture was found in a layer of ash just inside the innermost chamber with its head lying nearby. The ash and the nearby bowls indicate that this statue received offerings made by temple worshippers. The figure's intentional decapitation was offered as evidence of its special status.[9] "As there is no indication of the figure's divinity, it may be considered as representing a revered ancestor (perhaps a deceased king), as was suggested by Yadin and others" (Beck 1989b: 326–27). Unlike the LB IIA sculpture, that from the LB IIB was produced locally in a style that drew on both Egyptian and Syrian prototypes. As at Ebla, the offering tables in the Orthostat Temple were placed in front of *stelae* and statues to receive the offerings (Beck 1989b: 326–34).

Vessels stacked on benches and a partition wall set up in front of the *cella* also attest to religious activities within the innermost chamber (Yadin et al. 1989: fig. 6, pl. 40). Figurative pieces included bronze representations of a female figure, a snake and a bull. Votive offerings included beads, shells, a faience scarab and a collection of Syrian and Mittanian-style heirloom cylinder seals, several centuries old (Yadin 1972: 92–94; Beck 1989a: 319–21).

A second sculpture, also headless, was found in pieces in front of the LB IIA Orthostat Temple. The male figure, wearing a four-rayed disk emblem similar to that on the incense altar, stood on a bull. As with much of the material from the temple, this statue may have been made in Syria and first used in an earlier sanctuary at Hazor (Beck 1989b: 337).

Almost the only metal figurines found at Hazor are those that came from the Orthostat Temples. They include four solid bronze male figures, four sheet-metal female figures, a sheet-metal snake and a solid bronze bull (Negbi 1989: 348–50).[10] According to Negbi, the sheet metal and peg figurines were prophylactic or apotropaic in function while the solid bronze "smiting" males and the bull were "effigies of the 'smiting god' and his animal attribute" (1989: 354). These small figures may have been copies of the cult statue, whose image was also found in the stone and cylinder seal assemblages. Parallels between the Hazor assemblage and its larger counterparts in the Kamid el-Loz Temples 3-1 and in coastal Syria, especially Ugarit and Byblos, have been noted (Negbi 1989: 351–57; Beck 1989b: 329).

The statue of the male on a bull, the emblem on his chest and the one on the incense altar, the bronze "smiting god" figures and the bronze bull have together led to speculation about the deity to whom the Orthostat Temple was dedicated. Yadin suggests "the storm-god, whatever his actual name was in Hazor" (1972: 95). Recently, Bonfil supported this suggestion, identifying the Orthostat Temple with the worship of the storm god Hadad (1997: 101).[11]

The LB I Orthostat Temple was the largest in the five hundred-year sequence of temples in Area H. Many rituals were enacted in the large outdoor courtyards while inside the cult was increasingly removed from public view. The combination of expanded cultic acts attested by the courtyard installations and the workshop for the manufacture of votives suggests an enlarged staff of cultic personnel. The increased secrecy of indoor worship also documents an increasing stratification among this staff, with only certain clergy entitled to officiate indoors. That many cultic objects including orthostats, statues, altars and offering tables found in the subsequent LB IIA Orthostat Temple had been produced in inland Syria a century or more earlier indicates a fraternity between the priesthood of the Orthostat Temple and brethren in the north.

The strong ties between the Orthostat Temple priesthood and its inland Syrian counterpart may have been perceived as a threat to Egyptian interests in Canaan, placing those officiating in the Area H sacred structure under some pressure to restrict their public observances. As a result, many open-air ritual activities were eliminated in the LB II Orthostat Temple, as was the votive workshop. The building itself was reconfigured. Three rooms replaced two, thereby moving the central cultic focus farther from public view. The enduring attraction of Canaanite worship was reflected in the statues imported from Syria and in their local replication.

In Area F in the Lower City the situation was different. In the LB II, the wealthy residence[12] went out of use and the area was transformed into an open-air cult place (Yadin 1972: fig. 25). A five-ton altar was placed at the eastern end of a large open square. A narrow channel linked two depressions in the altar's upper surface. Cattle bones lay nearby. Cooking pots, a baking tray and a cow's skull rested on a platform at one end of the square and an alabaster goblet was found in a nearby niche.

The ceramic assemblage included nested bowls, incense stands, "cup-and-saucers," *kernoi* and rattles. A drainage channel at the southern end of the square was used to help maintain the cleanliness of this sacrificial area. A basalt table, *pithoi*, large kraters, cooking pots and Mycenaean pottery were found in nearby buildings (Yadin 1972: 101).

In Area C in the Lower City, a small shrine known as the Stelae

Temple (Locus 6136) was found nestled in the Middle Bronze Age rampart close to a densely settled residential neighborhood (Yadin et al. 1958: pl. 181; 1960: pls. 207, 219).[13] Little is known of the shrine's first phase (LB IIA) since much of the building and its paraphernalia were later reused. The doorway was lined with at least one basalt lion orthostat, and a semicircular cult niche containing a ceramic jug was set into the rear wall of this small (6.0 × 4.5 m) building. Unhewn stone benches lined its walls and two well-dressed stones may have been offering tables. Together with pottery, small finds included a pair of bronze cymbals found resting in a bronze bowl (Yadin 1972: 67–69; 1975: 47–48).

In its second phase (LB IIB), the cult niche was altered to form a raised platform. Ten basalt *stelae* now lined the back of the niche. The relief on the only decorated *stele* shows two upraised hands under an upturned crescent cupping a disk. Below the crescent are two small tassel-like circles. Yadin's suggestion that this was the symbol of the shrine's deity, the moon god Sin, (1972: 69–72) has been challenged (Ahlström 1975: 72), but recently received support from Bonfil in her analysis of the Hazor temples (1997: 101). According to Yadin and Albright, the *stelae* were representations of the dead, commemorated in the Area C Temple (Yadin 1972: 74).

A decapitated basalt statue of a seated man, his head lying nearby, was also found in the niche. This statue resembled the decapitated statue from the Orthostat Temple and again the intentional beheading is considered indicative of the individual's special status (Beck 1989b: 323–27). A roughly finished basalt offering table was also found.

Scattered nearby were three roughly formed basalt figures (Yadin et al. 1958: pl. 162: 5–7). According to Beck, "their interpretation as 'ancestor idols' ... means that their function is equal to that of *stelae* as a means of commemorating the dead, thus strengthening the arguments in favour of the interpretation of the Stelae Temple at Hazor as related to the cult of the dead" (1990: 94).

The ceramic assemblage found in and around the Stelae Temple included small bowls, miniature votives, decorated chalices and jugs, stands, trays and imported Cypriote and Mycenaean pottery (Yadin et al. 1958: pls. 90–92; 1960: pls. 117–24). Seventeen additional *stelae*, some only partially worked, were found on the slope outside the small sanctuary. A pottery workshop supplied the sanctuary with cultic objects, including an unusual clay mask similar to one found in an Area D cistern.

Large quantities of pottery, much of it identical to the pottery from the Stelae Temple, were found in several of these buildings.

A unique silver-plated bronze standard was discovered in nearby Building 6211. It had been placed in a special jar, which lay beneath three ceramic bowls. The standard, once thought to depict a woman ornamented with snakes and holding a snake in either hand (Yadin 1975: 49–55), has since been subjected to X-ray radiography. Its decoration is now described as "a geometric design of a rectangle with a double base and with two bent lines projecting from each of the lower corners. Two dots are seen between the double lines of the base" (Tadmor 1989: 197*).

The jar in which the cult standard was found resembles one from Ugarit. That one is decorated with a snake motif (Yadin et al. 1960: 109). Tadmor describes the jar as a pottery snake house and suggests that the image on the standard depicts a snake house as well. In her opinion, the building in which the standard was found might have been a shrine (1989: 197*). Daviau on the other hand considereds it to be a storeroom or shop (1993: 227–28).

Some two-thirds of the artifacts uncovered in the Stelae Temple could have been used in domestic settings, while some nearby homes contained cult objects (Daviau 1993: 220–24). The layout of this Area C neighborhood, its proximity to the Stelae Temple and the evidence from Building 6211 highlight the importance of the small sanctuary for the worship practices of its community. Attention to domestic cult seems to have been important too.

A temple was located in Area A in Hazor's fortified Upper City. According to its excavator, the Long Temple, a 16.2 × 11.6 m building (Yadin 1975: 260; 1976b: 482), had been constructed in the MB IIC period (Stratum XVI) and then rebuilt in the LB I period (Yadin 1969: 52). However, recent excavations suggest that the temple's founding should be placed in the LB I period (Ben-Tor 1997b: 4; Bonfil 1997: 89).[14]

The entrance to the Stratum XV sanctuary was lined with orthostats including one that depicts a lioness. The many additional orthostats found nearby suggest that its interior walls may also have been covered with orthostats (Yadin et al. 1989: 18; Beck 1989b: 328–29). With its rectangular plan and thick walls, the sanctuary resembled contemporary sacred structures at Megiddo and Shechem, which were also located near palaces. A statue of a deity with a cult symbol carved on its chest was found near the entrance to the Area A palace. This stone statue measuring more than 1.2 m high is the largest such statue found in Canaan (Ben-Tor 1997a: 9). The god worshipped in the Area A temple has been identified with El, the head of the Canaanite pantheon (Bonfil 1997: 101).

The Area A temple was destroyed in the LB IB period and although it was never reconstructed, the sanctity of the area was preserved. In the LB IIA and LB IIB periods, open-air cultic installations were set up around the perimeter of the destroyed building (Yadin 1975: 259–61; 1989: pls. 4, 7; Ben-Tor 1997a: 3). One of these comprised a tall basalt *stele*, several small *stelae* (like those in Area C) and an offering bowl. Votive bowls and the remains of sacrificial animals lay in pits and piles around the ruins of the Area A temple (Yadin 1975: 261–62). A solid bronze statue of an enthroned male worshipper, like the one in the Area H Orthostat Temple, was found nearby (Negbi 1989: 359).

Cultic Installation 5006 adjoined the LB IIA city gate in Area K in the Lower City (Yadin et al. 1961: pl. 142). This installation consisted of a somewhat circular stone pavement, near which lay small bowls, a lamp, a storejar, a *bilbil*, basalt pestles and *stelae*. The *stelae* resembled those from the Stelae Temple and from the Area A cultic installation (Yadin et al. 1989: 292).

An LB II sacred installation was excavated in Area P in the Lower City, at Hazor's easternmost gateway. There, a number of orthostats and libation tables were found near a ruined building (Yadin 1969: 61).

Religion in Late Bronze Age Hazor can be summarized as follows. In the MB IIB–MB IIC periods, several large clan groups had dominated politics—and religion—at Hazor. Their presence was evident in the observance of an ancestor cult in Area F, in the royal Long Temple in Area A and in the Area H Bipartite Temple with its close ties to inland Syria.

The abandonment of the Long Temple in Hazor's Upper City at the end of the LB I period suggests that Hazor's traditional ruling family lost some of its control over the city, perhaps as a consequence of Egypt's destabilizing incursions into Canaan. In Area H, on the other hand, religious continuity is demonstrated as the worship of the Canaanite god *par excellence* continued without interruption throughout the Late Bronze Age. This fact attests to the strength and adaptability of those residents of Hazor who had long looked to Syria for support and inspiration.

Religious practice in Late Bronze Age Hazor also highlighted the individuation of minority groups. These included the indigenous clans that were increasingly alienated from the weakening royal authorities. They worshipped at some of the cultic sites found throughout the city, including the Area C Stelae Temple and the sacred installations in Areas C, K, P, F and A. People coming to Hazor from elsewhere in Canaan to find refuge from Egyptian domination may also have worshipped in them. The vast scale of Hazor throughout the Late Bronze Age both ensured, and reflects, its relative autonomy in the face of increasing Egyptian domination.

Megiddo

The Late Bronze Age at Megiddo was an era of religious continuity and socio-political change. Enduring sacred traditions were demonstrated by the Late Bronze Age use of Temple 2048, originally constructed in the MB IIC. Shifts in Megiddo's socio-political structure are also shown through the dislocation of the earlier palace.

Scholars have long assumed that after his well-documented victory over a coalition of Canaanite kings, Thutmosis III established his authority over the city of Megiddo. His takeover, however, was not attested by an increase in Egyptian objects at the site, suggesting that the imposition of Egyptian authority did not require a large occupation force. It may rather have been reflected in the change in funerary practices. Burials, once intramural, were now extramural, perhaps a consequence of Egyptian beliefs and aesthetics (Gonen 1987: 97). The fact that the Middle Bronze Age palace was not occupied in the LB I period and that no other palace has been discovered on the site may also reflect this shifting geopolitical reality.

Despite its restricted size and lack of defensive wall, LB I Megiddo represented a pinnacle of affluence and stability that was shared by many residents of the city (Gonen 1987: 89, 94).[15] Wealth, once centered in the palace complex, was now dispersed throughout Megiddo's residential neighborhoods. However, while the traditional monarchy and its elite brethren were no longer politically dominant, the religious hierarchy retained its authority and became the bearer of continuity within this Late Bronze Age city.

The rebuilding of the originally MB IIC Temple 2048 at various points throughout the Late Bronze Age demonstrates this continuing religious authority. Some of Canaan's earliest header-stretcher masonry typified the renovations done to Temple 2048 early in the fifteenth century B.C.E. (Level IX).[16] Two large stone towers separated by a columned portico now stood at the front of the building, (A. Mazar 1992b: 170–71; Loud 1948: fig. 247).[17] New residential neighborhoods were constructed nearby.

Few changes were made to Temple 2048 in the LB IIA (Level VIII). Perhaps in response to the pressures brought about by continuing Egyptian control, a new palace was built. Despite a century of abandonment, this new palace followed the lines of its Middle Bronze Age predecessor. Now, however, the city gateway became part of the palace compound (Gonen 1987: 89–91), perhaps in an effort to control access to the city.

In the mid-thirteenth century B.C.E. (Level VIIB), Temple 2048 underwent important alterations.[18] Inside, the niche in the back wall was covered and replaced by an offering bench in which three Middle Kingdom Egyptian statues were buried (Loud 1948: pls. 265–66; Singer 1988/89: n. 12). Basalt slabs, one with rounded depressions in its top, were set into the newly plastered floor (Gonen 1987: 94). A *temenos* wall now surrounded the entire sacred compound (Loud 1948: fig. 247; A. Mazar 1992b: 171).[19]

The palace underwent alterations as well. Most intriguing was the construction of Room 3013, a small room in its western wing. This room contained a raised platform reached by a small flight of stairs. Although no objects were found in it or in the surrounding rooms, analogy with architectural elements in Temple 2048 led to the suggestion that Room 3013 was a "household shrine" (Loud 1948: 30, fig. 383; Gonen 1987: 94). If so, the construction of this small royal chapel may have been necessitated by the alienation of Megiddo's rulers from the new religious practices now enacted in Temple 2048.

The Level VIIB occupation of Megiddo ended in a massive destruction. The new twelfth century B.C.E. (Level VIIA) settlement followed the general lines of the previous stratum (Gonen 1987: 94). The painted floor in the new palace, almost 2 m above its predecessor, may have resembled that of the contemporary Stratum VI Summit Temple at Lachish (Singer 1988/89: 101, n. 1). The cache of more than 300 ivories and other precious objects found in Treasury 3073 (Loud 1939) demonstrates Megiddo's continuing importance as a strategic Egyptian stronghold on the route to Hatti (Singer 1988/89).

Major changes took place in the Stratum VIIA Temple 2048. Reconstructed a meter and a half over its predecessor, its walls were narrower and its towers built along a different plan. The offering bench along the rear wall, now reached by six steps, was covered with a layer of rough stones and plaster, and a projection came out from its center. A niche was recessed into the rear wall (Loud 1948: fig. 247; Kempinski 1989a: 183; A. Mazar 1992b: 172).

Once again, a statue of an Egyptian monarch (in this case, the mid-twelfth century king Rameses VI) stood in the Megiddo sanctuary (Singer 1988/89: 106–8, n. 12; Ussishkin 1997b: 464). This suggests that the suborning of Canaanite religious leaders was a problem that intermittently challenged the rulers and inhabitants of Megiddo throughout the Late Bronze Age and after. When Megiddo's traditional configuration of royal, sacred and secular architecture was destroyed ca. 1130 B.C.E., ending centuries of Egyptian domination at Megiddo and in Canaan (Ussishkin 1997b: 464), it was soon replaced by the poorly constructed houses of the Israelite Iron Age.

Like Beth Shean (see below), Megiddo was continuously occupied by Egypt throughout the Late Bronze Age and into the Iron Age. Even though those clan groups that had ruled the city in the Middle Bronze Age were controlled or replaced by Egyptian authorities early in the Late Bronze Age, worship had continued in Megiddo's traditional sacred structure, Temple 2048. However, the introduction of Egyptian statuary into this fortress temple, the construction of a small chapel in the Megiddo palace, and the changes in burial practices all suggest the impact of Egypt on traditional Canaanite religion.

Tel Kittan

At Tel Kittan, new construction took place on the site of the Middle Bronze Age sanctuary. The new LB I (Level III) building, now oriented toward the north, retained elements of its fortress-style predecessor (Eisenberg 1977: 80). It included a hall and two small service rooms, each of which contained many ritual vessels and precious objects, including jewelry displaying religious emblems. A circular heap of stones and broken pottery lay in the courtyard nearby. Several small buildings, presumably the residence of the temple clergy, were situated south and east of the temple (Eisenberg 1981: 159; 1993: 881). The abandonment and destruction of the village and its sanctuary has been attributed to Thutmosis III as he campaigned to establish supremacy over the Beth Shean Valley (Eisenberg 1977: 80).

The exertion of Egyptian military power over this small village should not be considered arbitrary, but rather an extension of Egyptian imperial interests. As we have seen, the Middle Bronze Age fortress temple was a locus of authority for those clans that controlled territory in and around the Jordan Valley. The subjugation of potential dissidents in this cosmopolitan and strategically critical region was a critical factor in New Kingdom Egypt's imperial design.

Beth Shean

In antiquity, Beth Shean was a city of imposing size that was occupied almost continuously from the Chalcolithic period. The appeal that it held for its frequent foreign occupiers can be attributed to its strategic location between the Jezreel and Jordan Valleys. Excavations to date have revealed little of the Middle Bronze Age city (James and Kempinski 1975: 207–12) and so a discussion of religion at Beth Shean must begin with the Late Bronze Age.

Early in the Late Bronze Age, a new sanctuary was constructed on the acropolis (Area R) near the city gate. It was the first of five sacred structures to be built on that location over the next 500 years. The bench-lined sanctuary of Stratum R3 measured 11.7 × 14.6 m and had an unusual asymmetrical plan, one that resembled those at the roughly contemporary Tel Mevorakh sanctuary and the Lachish Fosse Temple. It comprised three chambers, an anteroom, a shrine and a trapezoidal holy-of-holies. Small finds include several scarabs and the broken leg of a striding god statue. Animal sacrifices were offered in the nearby courtyard. The LB IA sanctuary was badly damaged and underwent several stages of repair before it was abandoned, leveled and covered by an artificial fill (A. Mazar 1990b: 108*, fig. 4–8; 1992a: 6–8, fig. 4; 1993a: 215–16; 1997a: 67).

Following Thutmosis III's move to control the Jordan Valley, Beth Shean became a key Egyptian stronghold in Canaan (Leonard 1989: 11). The construction of a new sanctuary in the LB IB (Stratum R2/ Stratum IXB) reflected this shift from Canaanite to Egyptian authority. The new sanctuary, Rowe's Building 10, was part of an extensive complex that included rooms, courtyards and a number of altars.

Building 10 measured 7.5 × 5.5 m. At its rear was a small niched room. Among the small finds were many Egyptian objects including a *stele* dedicated to Mekal, the Canaanite god of Beth Shean, erected by the Egyptian Pa-Ra-em-Heb in memory of his father Amen-ep. Other finds include more than one hundred pottery vessels, mostly offering bowls and kraters, decorated in Canaanite and Egyptian motifs, and two Canaanite bronze daggers. No parallels to this sacred precinct have been found (Rowe 1940: fig. 1/Room 10; McGovern 1985: Map 4/ Locus 1230; James and Kempinski 1975: 209–13; A. Mazar 1992a: 8).[20]

Evidence indicates that an LB IIB (Stratum VIII) temple at Beth Shean was founded during the reign of Seti I, under whose authority 19th Dynasty Egypt renewed its hold on Canaan. The layout of the LB IIB site served as the basis for subsequent LB IIB (Stratum VII) and Iron I (Stratum VI) construction, and so the Stratum VIII temple was used in Stratum VII as well (A. Mazar 1992b: 173–76; 1993a: 217).[21]

During much of the thirteenth century, Beth Shean was home to an Egyptian garrison that used the site as a collection depot for the taxes that the indigenous Canaanite population was required to pay to its Egyptian overlords. Evidence for this comes from the Stratum VII public granary and from the Egyptian governor's fortified residence (James and Kempinski 1975: 214; F. James 1966: 4; Ottosson 1980: 43). In addition, LB IIB Beth Shean had the highest concentration of Egyptian-style architecture of any site in Canaan. Together with Deir el-Balah, it also had the most Egyptian-style pottery, and with Timna the greatest quantity of Egyptian-style objects (Higginbotham 1996: 162).

With these Egyptian influences, it is no coincidence that the Stratum VII sanctuary (Rowe 1940: fig. 3; James and Kempinski 1975: 212 top) at Beth Shean was similar in plan to the Egypto-Canaanite Summit Temple at Lachish (see below). The roofed building was accessed through several entrance rooms. Its bench-lined main hall was approximately 14 m^2 and contained two columns and a brick altar (A. Mazar 1992b: 173). Plastered pits that may have been used for grain storage were located in two corners and a *stele* depicting a horned goddess was found near one of them (Rowe 1940: 8). The holy-of-holies at the back of the main hall was reached by ascending seven steps. Under them, a foundation deposit contained numerous finds, including cylinder seals and pendants. Many of the small finds from the Stratum VII sanctuary indicate the strength of Beth Shean's ties with Egypt (A. Mazar 1993a: 217). At the same time, northern influences are demonstrated by Syro-Hittite seals and by a Syro-Hittite axehead (Rowe 1940: 8–9, pls. 41–43).[22]

A single chamber at the rear of the Stratum VII sanctuary was probably a treasury, while a second small room containing a *tanour* and a baking mold(?) may have been used to prepare sacred bread. Little is known of the courtyard area except that it contained an altar surrounded by a large quantity of ash and animal bones (A. Mazar 1992b: 173–75). Finds on the sanctuary floor suggest its destruction late in the thirteenth century B.C.E.

Throughout the Late Bronze Age, Egyptian forces occupied Beth Shean but the cult celebrated there combined both Canaanite and Egyptian elements.[23] With the increasing exploitation of Canaan in the LB IIB, the sanctuary at Beth Shean (like some others in Canaan) became a locus for Egyptian imperial designs. In this way, religion and the politics of imperialism were inextricably combined.

Pella

The excavation of the fortress temple at Pella is not yet complete, but preliminary evidence indicates that the Late Bronze Age was best-preserved phase of this MB IIC–Iron II structure. Artifactual remains include fenestrated stands, jewelry, weapons, furniture inlay, a votive snake, and glyptic pieces. The ceramic assemblage includes bowls, jugs and jars bearing the sacred tree motif, cultic vessels and imported ceramic wares. Cultic figures include a representation of Reshef and a life-sized basalt head. The range of international contacts documented by these finds shows contact with Egypt, Syria, Mitanni and Babylon, as well as with Canaanite sites (Bourke et al. 1998: 194–201; Bourke 1999).

Tell Abū al-Kharaz

An extramural temple dating to the LB IIA period (Stratum 3) has been excavated at Tell Abū al-Kharaz, south of Pella in the Jordan Valley. The sacred chamber (Room 5) contains installations, artifacts and pottery that suggest its possible cultic function. It was part of a larger building that may have included a potters' workshop. Much of the pottery, some of which was found around an altar or offering bench, was of high quality and Cypriote imports were found together with decorated Canaanite wares. Cultic objects include ceramic stands, one of which was fenestrated. While the full extent of the building is not yet known, preliminary evidence suggests a structural resemblance to the first two Lachish Fosse Temples (Fischer 1991a: 44–45; 1991b: 79–81, figs. 4b, 10–12; 1999: 13).

A metal figure of a warrior god, which displays an interesting combination of feline and human features, was found in an Iron Age pit but may have originated in the Late Bronze Age sanctuary (Fischer 1996: 103–4). Other cultic objects dating to the Iron Age (Fischer 1996: 103; 1997: 132; 1998: 221) suggest continuity of worship at the site.

Tell Deir 'Alla

A sanctuary stood at Tell Deir 'Alla throughout the Late Bronze Age. Its fourth and final phase, destroyed in an earthquake, is the best known. The plan included an elevated *cella* with particularly thick walls, a raised podium and two stone pillar bases. A storeroom was located on one side of the sanctuary. A "treasury" across a small courtyard contained twelve clay tablets, nine marked with small holes or dots and three inscribed in a still undeciphered script. They pertain to matters of temple administration. Many interesting finds came from the last phase of the sanctuary. They include ritual vessels, fenestrated pottery shrines, cylinder seals, beads, a gold ring, fragments of bronze armor plating and an imported Egyptian faience vase with the cartouche of the late thirteenth/early twelfth century Queen Taousert (Franken 1975: 322; 1997: 137; van der Kooij 1993: 339).

Similar objects were uncovered in a nearby residential complex. The proximity of the houses to the sanctuary and the specialized objects found in them indicate that the complex housed cultic personnel. Its isolated but strategic location suggests that the Tell Deir 'Alla sanctuary was a regional sanctuary, used by tribes living in and around the Jordan Valley (Franken 1969: 19–20; 1975: 322).[24] However, its many foreign imports, ceramic and other, suggest a broader use. Twenty percent of the local pottery was produced offsite, in the mountains of Gilead and the nearby plateau. This might suggest that the site was pivotal in trade between Gilead and Egypt, a place to which Gileadites could bring their flocks, produce and other goods, perhaps for export to Egypt. The sanctuary was central to this international trade effort (van der Kooij 1993: 339–40; Franken 1997: 137–38).

Although little is known of the earlier phases of the Deir 'Alla sanctuary, it may have functioned as a regional cultic center throughout much of the Late Bronze Age. As Egypt moved to consolidate its control over the strategic Jordan Valley, it used the Deir ʿAlla sanctuary as a place where it could make contact with and exert control over the Jordan Valley tribes that worshipped there.[25] The profitable trade that ensued as a result of this contact must have been an added benefit.

Tell Ṣafuṭ and Khirbet Umm ad-Danānīr

Two Baqʿah Valley sites contain evidence for Late Bronze Age sanctuaries. At the walled site of Tell Ṣafuṭ, a red-plastered room contained several cultic objects including a footed ceramic vessel and a bronze figurine of a seated deity. The god depicted was unique. He wears a flat crown and his extended arms are wrapped in gold. The heads of female clay figurines were found elsewhere on the site (Wimmer 1997).

At Khirbet Umm ad-Danānīr, a building destroyed in the LB II resembled the mortuary structure at the Amman Airport (see below). A "dedicatory fill" under the plastered floor contained miniature pottery vessels, jewelry, burned and unburned animal bones, and whole parts of animal bodies. It also contained an altar 60 cm × 60 cm. A fireplace lay between it and a "massive centrally located column" (McGovern 1993: 146).

Shechem

Shechem was the major fortified city of the Central Highlands in the Middle Bronze Age. Despite its destruction and subsequent abandonment at the end of the MB IIC period, the site remained attractive and it was reoccupied early in the LB IB period.

As part of this reoccupation, a new fortress temple was built over Fortress Temple 1. Fortress Temple 2a (Temenos 8/Stratum XIV–XII/ 1450–1200 B.C.E.) (Toombs 1976: 58) measured 16.0 × 12.5 m. Inside the main hall, two sets of steps led to a podium set against the rear wall. *Masseboth* 2 and 3, originally used in Fortress Temple 1, stood in the Fortress Temple 2a courtyard, which may have also held a mudbrick altar (Wright 1965: 95–100).

Later, in the Iron I period (Temenos 9/Stratum XI/1200–1150/1125 B.C.E.), Shechem underwent many repairs (Toombs 1976: 58). Those at Fortress Temple 2a included the reconstruction of the podium its the main hall. A new floor was laid in the Temple 2b courtyard and an altar of hewn stone was added. The city of Shechem, including its ancient sanctuary, was destroyed in the second half of the 12th century B.C.E. (Toombs 1976: 98–102). The site of the Fortress Temple would remain abandoned until the Iron II, when a granary was built over it (Bull 1960: 115).

Building 5988, a second Late Bronze Age sanctuary, was located in Field IX, a residential neighborhood at the center of the city. This small sanctuary stood near a multi-roomed house with a courtyard, separated from it by an alley. Inasmuch as that alley provided access to the sanctuary (Bull et al. 1965: 11), it may be that the house was used by temple personnel. Originally dated to the Iron I (Bull et al. 1965: 11–15), Building 5988 was recently redated to the LB IB–LB II (Campbell, personal communication, 1991; 1993: 1352).[26]

In its first phase, Building 5988 was a stone structure with a crude brick platform along its northern wall. A stone jar containing thirteen beads, a lamp and four astragali was found under the altar and adjacent to it stood the base of a ceramic stand. In its second phase, the floor and altar were plastered and a partially worked stone *maṣṣebâ* weighing 250 kilograms lay on the floor. Building 5988 was reused in the Iron I, but its altar and *maṣṣebâ* were covered over by a plastered floor, indicating that it no longer served as a sanctuary (Bull et al. 1965: 11; Campbell, personal communication, 1991; 1993: 1352).

In summary, the reoccupation of Shechem in the LB IB included the reconstruction of its old Fortress Temple, which remained in use throughout the Late Bronze Age and into the Iron I. Even as the Fortress Temple with its commanding location served as the municipal center for worship, at least one neighborhood sanctuary was used by some Shechemites in the LB IIB. The destruction of Shechem, including its Fortress Temple, marked the end of Canaanite control in the Central Highlands.

Shiloh

Evidence for a Late Bronze Age renovation of Shiloh's Middle Bronze Age sanctuary is tenuous and it seems unlikely that there was an actual settlement or sanctuary there in the Late Bronze Age. Instead, the site seems to have functioned as an open-air shrine. A 1.5 m thick accumulation of earth, stones, broken pottery, ashes and animal bones represents the remains of offerings made in the Late Bronze Age and dumped in their present location in the Iron I. The discovery of hundreds of shallow bowls dating primarily to the LB I and broken into unusually large pieces suggests that the breaking and burying of these sanctified vessels was deliberate. Several intact or nearly intact vessels were filled with bones and ashes. A cylinder seal impression on a jar handle, a female figurine and a piece of gold jewelry in the shape of a fly were also found (Finkelstein 1988: 218–19; 1993: 1367).

More than 92 percent of the animal bones at Shiloh belonged to sheep or goats, indicating that this cultic center served the needs of pastoralists in the surrounding countryside. Ceramic evidence suggests that worshippers were particularly active at Shiloh in the LB I, and this may be because the memory of the Middle Bronze Age sanctuary was freshest at that time. Judging by the decrease in pottery throughout the Late Bronze Age, it seems that ritual activity steadily diminished until the site was abandoned prior to the end of the period (Finkelstein 1988: 218–20).

Tell Abu Hawam

Tell Abu Hawam,[27] a Late Bronze Age port, was a conduit for Mediterranean goods intended for redistribution throughout Canaan and into Transjordan (Leonard 1987: 261, 264, fig. 3).[28] Two sacred structures, Building 50 and Building 30, were identified by its excavator (Hamilton 1935: 10–13). Building 50 dated to the LB IB–IIBperiod; Building 30 was its Iron I successor (Hamilton 1935: 10; Balensi 1985: 68, n. 20; A. Mazar 1992b: 180).[29]

Building 50 was a small rectangular building with unusual exterior buttressing and a small entrance room on its eastern end. Four columns supported the roof and a shallow depression lined with flat stones was set into the floor at the center of the building (Hamilton 1935: 12; Gershuny 1981: 38–39; A. Mazar 1992b: 180).

Two residential complexes stood between Building 50, on the eastern side of the tel, and a second public building on the western end (Hamilton 1935: 12; Gershuny 1981: 38–40, fig. 1). The sanctuary was sited so that it pointed toward the sunrise in early summer.

> Such a cosmic orientation, with access from a waterway, matched Egyptian religious symbolism

and illustrates the ideal prescriptions for the establishment of a sanctuary. It was proposed that temple 50 be interpreted as the solar shrine of Rabant. The original site thus combined maritime architecture with the image of a primeval mound emerging from the holy lake of Horus: the Shihor of the Hebrew Bible (Balensi et al. 1993: 114).

Architectural parallels between Egyptian chapels (such as that at El Kab) and Building 50 have been noted (Balensi 1985: n. 15).

Among the ceramic finds were Mycenaean, Cypriote, Late Helladic and Minoan wares (including *kernoi* and bull *rhyta*) and local pottery. Artifacts such as mace heads, flint and metal knives, cylinder seals, gold jewelry, gaming pieces, and faience cups and *rhyta* were found. The figurines include a horse, a lioness and a gilded bronze statuette of a seated male in a cone-shaped helmet. Parts of several other statuettes were found, as well. The wide assortment of small finds from Building 50 highlights Tell Abu Hawam's importance as a central redistribution point for Aegean materials, and especially for Cypriote copper, being traded with inland sites (Leonard 1987: 264; Balensi et al. 1993: 14).

Tel Nami

The port of Tel Nami lay farther south along the Mediterranean coast. There, an LB IIB cultic precinct was located on the summit of the mound, connected with the Late Bronze Age rampart. A courtyard, 10 × 6 m and partly covered, was paved with broken pieces of ceramic incense burners. In it, four flat stones were configured to form a square and a large basalt basin stood on a basalt pedestal. Pottery associated with this cultic area included a seven-spouted lamp, a *kernos*, kraters, lamps and votive bowls. The many pieces of bronze, silver and gold were seen as evidence of Tel Nami's important role in the maritime-based business of metal recycling. The site was destroyed early in the twelfth century (Artzy 1993a: 635–37; 1993b; 1997).

Tel Mevorakh

Tel Mevorakh is located farther to the south, 2 km east of the Mediterranean coast. In antiquity, the site was accessible from the coastal branch of the Via Maris and from a route connecting this coastal road with the main branch of the Via Maris, farther inland. While Tel Mevorakh was an important regional sanctuary, the coastal city of Dor, 10–12 km to the north, was the area's economic and administrative center (Stern 1984: 1, 44).

Tel Mevorakh was home to a sequence of three sanctuaries dated to the LB IB (Stratum XI), LB IIA (Stratum X) and LB IIB (Stratum IX). The sacred precinct was protected by a Middle Bronze Age rampart and by a newly constructed stone wall (Stern 1984: 31), but its accessibility was highlighted by the location of its entrance on a spot where the incline up the mound was the most moderate.

In addition to the sanctuary, there were several other buildings within the area bounded by the *temenos* wall. They may have been used for storage, or as residences for cultic personnel and as lodging for worshippers. Cobbled courtyards surrounding three sides of the sanctuary may have provided a setting for ritual acts and for the exchange of goods among travelers and with the local population.

The three sanctuaries were similar, although with each rebuilding the structure was somewhat enlarged. The Stratum XI sanctuary was the best preserved of the three (Stern 1984: figs. 2, 24). The walls and floor of its main hall, which measured 5×10 m, were thickly plastered. At least one column supported the roof. The slanted floor and the drain in one wall (Stern 1984: 4–6) suggest indoor sacrifices that required later cleanup. Some sacrifices were undoubtedly made on the stone libation table with two depressions on its upper surface that came from a secondary context at Tel Mevorakh (Stern 1984: 27) and was similar to those from the Hazor Orthostat Temples.

The Stratum XI sanctuary was lined with offering benches. A stepped altar, partially covered, was constructed along its rear wall and the bottom half of a storejar was embedded in one of its lower surfaces. A *favissa* was found at the center of the room (Stern 1984: 4–5, 15). Alterations made to the Stratum X (Stern 1984: fig. 23) and Stratum IX (Stern 1984: fig. 25) sanctuaries related primarily to the process of its enlargement.

The most common vessel in the Tel Mevorakh sanctuary was the bowl, often found *in situ* on the altar, on offering benches and on the floor. Cypriote and Mycenaean pottery was found in each stratum and "Ionian" bowls were found in Stratum XI as well (Stern 1984: 16, 20). Other Stratum XI vessels included chalices, goblets, jugs, juglets, cooking pots, lids, a tankard, a lamp and a store jar handle with a potter's mark. In Stratum X the tankard and lids disappear and dipper juglets, Canaanite storejars, kraters, *pithoi* and votives appear.

The many jugs and juglets must have been used for the transportation of honey, oils and perfumes to the sanctuary and for the presentation of liquid offerings. However, the majority of vessels were open in form, appropriate for food presentation and consumption but not useful for transportation and storage.

Most Stratum XI bowls were plain, carelessly shaped and undecorated. A review of the Stratum XI pottery plates suggests that the Tel Mevorakh bowls fell into uniformly sized groups. In Stratum X, seventy percent of the bowls were crudely manufactured and had string-cut bases (Stern 1984: 10, 13). Now, standardization was facilitated by the "throwing-off-the-hump" method of production. The ceramic evidence suggests that offerings were presented in predetermined quantities, presumably controlled by the Mevorakh cultic officials. As we will see, a similar mechanism was employed at the contemporary Lachish Fosse Temples.

Many precious offerings were found in the Tel Mevorakh sanctuaries, on the altars, offering benches and elsewhere. They include bronze arrowheads, cymbals, a knife, a dagger, a snake, jewelry, cylinder seals and a calcite votive bowl. The absence of cult statues or figurines should be attributed to their deliberate removal as the sanctuaries went out of use rather than to their original absence.

Two crucibles, one containing copper slag, were found in a temple courtyard. They were used to produce the many bronze pieces, including the snake figurine, that were used in cultic celebrations. A bronze pendant embossed with an eight-point star was found nearby. Seashells from the courtyard area were used for dying fabric (Stern 1984: 12, 23–24, 106).

The artifactual evidence from the Tel Mevorakh temples attests to the importance of on-site industries at this regional sanctuary. The lithic assemblage with its high proportion of sickle blades, the *pithoi* and Canaanite storejars, cooking pots, a mortar and a silo indicate that agricultural products were raised in the vicinity of the sanctuary and processed on-site. A number of other objects, including ceramic vessels, dyed fabrics and bronze cult pieces were manufactured in small sanctuary workshops.

Who was worshipped in the Tel Mevorakh sanctuary? According to its excavator,

> the one and only possible hint is the discovery of the bronze snake figurine which is often considered one of the attributes of the goddess 'Ashtoret .... We shall perhaps not be far from the truth in our proposal that this typical Canaanite temple was the house of the most popular pair of Canaanite deities of the age: Ba'al and 'Ashtoret (Stern 1984: 35).[30]

The triad of major Canaanite goddesses, Asherah, Astarte and Anat, their Egyptian hypostatization Qudshu and the Egyptian goddess Hathor shared many characteristics. Among them was an association with snakes and with lions. The bronze snake found in the Mevorakh sanctuary suggests this association, as do the bronze arrowheads which may symbolize leonine qualities.[31] Tel Mevorakh's function as a regional place of worship serving a mixed community may indicate that the sanctuaries were dedicated to a hypostasized goddess, celebrated in the manifestation desired by the individual worshipper. Whether a male deity was also worshipped cannot be determined from the excavated evidence.

Lachish

Lachish is located on the south side of the Wadi Lachish, on the border between Israel's Shephelah and the southern Highlands. During the Late Bronze Age, it was home to a sequence of typically Canaanite sanctuaries. Eventually, when Lachish fell under Egyptian imperial control, an Egypto-Canaanite temple was built at the center of the city.

In the mid-fifteenth century B.C.E., the first in the sequence of three Fosse Temples was constructed on an otherwise abandoned site (Tufnell et al. 1940: 14). Strategically located near the road, Fosse Temple I (LB I) was a roadside sanctuary at which travelers and traders stopped and made offerings, hoping to secure the success of their ventures. As the sanctuary became popular, drawing an increasing number of staff and devotees from the surrounding countryside, interest in settling on the mound grew.

The growing importance of the site in the fourteenth century is attested not only by the increased size of Fosse Temple II (LB IIA), but also by letters from Lachish found in the Amarna archives in Egypt (Singer 1988: 5; Ussishkin 1978a: 18). The LB IIB (Fosse Temple III) development of the site was precipitated by increased Egyptian interest in the region and may have resulted in the construction of a second temple on the tel (Level P-1/Level VII). However, a major conflagration dated to the end of the thirteenth century placed the entire mound in ruins (Tufnell et al. 1940: 45; Ussishkin 1985: 216).

Over the centuries the form and content of the Fosse Temples remained essentially the same although the structure grew to 10×10.4 m from an initial 10×5 m (Tufnell et al. 1940: pls. 66–68). The floor plan consisted of a main hall and two or more auxiliary rooms that were used as entry rooms and storage areas. Furnishings included an increasing number of offering benches, storage niches and altars (Tufnell et al. 1940: 36–43).

Spacious courtyards cut by an increasing number of *favissae* and refuse pits surrounded the temple. These courtyards provided the setting for the exchange of goods that took place at this sanctuary, a place in which traders, travelers and area residents all congregated. Auxiliary structures for storage, production and domestic purposes were constructed nearby. Metal objects and pottery were produced within the temple precinct (Tufnell et al. 1940: 43–44, 81).

The pottery of the Fosse Temples is characterized by the large number of bowls found in the sanctuary and in the surrounding *favissae* and pits (Tufnell et al. 1940: 77–79), many of which had been deliberately broken in order to prevent their reuse. The finely crafted bowls of the early Fosse Temple were soon replaced by mass-produced vessels (Tufnell et al. 1940: 28). Together with bowls, the ceramic assemblage consisted of other containers used for food and drink, including pilgrim flasks, chalices, kraters, goblets and cooking pots.

Artifactual remains from the Fosse Temple consisted primarily of jewelry, together with a few seals and scarabs (Tufnell et al. 1940: 65–75). A bronze food whisk suggests the cultic preparation of food. Animal bones, primarily those of sheep and goats, were found in the temples and in the pits outside. All came from young animals and most identified were the metacarpals of right forelegs (Tufnell et al. 1940: 93–94).

While few figurines are associated with the Fosse Temple, those found indicate a cult based on the worship of traditional Canaanite deities. The inscription on the late thirteenth century Lachish Ewer, a jug decorated in the palm tree and ibex motif, declared this vessel to have been an offering to the goddess Elat, probably to be identified with the biblical goddess Asherah (Tufnell et al. 1940: 47–54; Cross

1984: 75; Hestrin 1987b). Bronze and ceramic figurines depicted Reshef (Tufnell et al. 1940: 67), and a recent reading of the inscription on the ewer found Reshef's name as well (Puech 1986: 22–24).

In summary, the Lachish Fosse Temple experienced steady growth throughout the Late Bronze Age. Enactment of the cult consisted primarily of the offering agricultural products and animal sacrifices that were presented in bowls, poured from juglets and burned in hearths. Analysis of vessel types suggests that sacral meals were also consumed in the temple. The gods worshipped there included Elat and Reshef, both known from the Ugaritic pantheon.[32]

Following the thirteenth century destruction of the tel, Lachish fell under the jurisdiction of 19th Dynasty Egyptian kings, then in the process of expanding their control over strategically located Canaanite city-states (Singer 1988: 5). A great deal of construction took place on the western side of the city, where the Summit Temple and other public structures were built. The new temple there may have been part of the palace (Ussishkin 1978b: 10–12, fig. 3; 1997a: 318). In contrast to the isolation of the Fosse Temple, the Summit Temple with its cunning blend of Canaanite and Egyptian architectural forms was well integrated into the political core of the city.

The Summit Temple consisted of a large main hall measuring 16.5 × 13.2 m. At its rear, a monumental stone staircase led to the *cella*. To the left of the staircase were three small stone column bases[33] and to the right, a large stone tub. Six pottery stands stood along the back wall of a storeroom that contained most of the known temple equipment. A wide doorway provided access to additional storage and other rooms, and to several courtyards (Ussishkin 1978b: 12–18). The plan of the temple resembles that of the Level VII–Lower VI temples at Beth Shean, a major Egyptian administrative center throughout the Late Bronze Age (Ussishkin 1978b: 24–25).

A number of *favissae* or pits contained large quantities of sherds. Most vessels were small badly shattered bowls, although cooking pots, cup-and-saucer lamps and storejars were also found (Ussishkin 1978b: 19). Jars, juglets, goblets, chalices, flasks, single-spouted lamps and miniature votives typically found at Canaanite temples were missing from the Summit Temple ceramic assemblage. Faunal remains, including pigeon, duck, dog and large sea fish (Ussishkin 1978b: 21), likewise differed from the faunal assemblage typical to the traditional

Canaanite temple, which would have contained a preponderance of sheep, goat and even cattle bones.

Small finds were few and fragmentary and included Egyptian furniture, textiles, stone vessels and jewelry (Ussishkin 1978b: 20). A crumpled gold plaque depicts Astarte, identified in Egypt with the goddess Qudshu. There in 19th Dynasty representations, she commonly stood between the Canaanite god Reshef and the Egyptian god Min (Clamer 1980). Graffiti figures of Reshef similar to those found in Egypt and at Beth Shean were found scratched into several stone slabs from the doorway (Clamer 1980: 161; Ussishkin 1978b: 18).[34]

Documentation for a *šmr* or harvest tax, paid in the form of grain offered at the Summit Temple, comes from hieratic inscriptions on fragments of bowls. Similarly inscribed bowls were found at Tel Seraʿ, Tell el-Farʿah (S), Tel Haror and Deir el-Balah (Gilula 1976; 1982; 1984; 1991; Goldwasser and Wimmer 1999: 41). In some instances, payment may have been made at local Egypto-Canaanite temples; elsewhere, goods might have been shipped to the Egyptian temple in Gaza or even to the Temple of Amun at Karnak. The inscribed bowls may have served as "vouchers" or receipts for these payments (Wimmer 1990: 1090).

In this context, the barley, grapes, vetch and olive pits, and the large concentration of wheat found on the floor of the Summit Temple (Ussishkin 1978b: 21) are significant. They indicate the range of agricultural products brought into the temple, symbolizing the quantities of produce collected by Egypt from Canaanites in the territory of Lachish.

The high proportion of bowls in the ceramic assemblage, the scarcity of other vessel types, and the absence of cattle, sheep and goat bones all indicate that ritual in the Summit Temple emphasized the presentation of agricultural products. In fact, it was precisely *for* the collection of such products that Lachish, in an easily accessible and extremely productive agricultural region, was elevated to the status of an administrative center for the Egyptian empire in Canaan.

Traditionally, the support of the priestly class had been one of the consequences, if not the motivating intentions, of the Canaanite rites of offering and sacrifice, rites well documented in the Fosse Temples. The goal of the Egyptian harvest tax was the agricultural exploitation of Canaan. Toward this goal, Egyptian officials altered traditional worship practices to suit their own needs. They exploited Canaanite rituals, ensuring that Egyptian grain requirements were met by co-opting the indigenous Canaanite religious establishment and by manipulating the pre-existing system of food offerings.

Here, when contrasted with the worship of Elat at the Fosse Temple, the choice of Astarte, so popular in Egypt, as the goddess to whom the Summit Temple was dedicated, is instructive. The decision to worship Canaanite deities well-known in the Egyptian pantheon facilitated the cooperation of the local population. As a result of its payment of the grain tax and the loss of its religious autonomy, the native population here, as elsewhere, must have become impoverished and alienated.

Egypto-Canaanite temples existed at a number of other sites, including Gaza, Ashkelon, Ashdod, Aphek and Jerusalem. Their presence demonstrates the extent of Egyptian domination and the efficacy of its efforts to manipulate religion in order to actualize imperial goals.[35]

Gaza

The Great Papyrus Harris I mentions a temple in Gaza, the major Egyptian administrative center on the Canaanite coast. The text can be dated to the reign of Rameses III, the last time that Gaza appeared in the official records of New Kingdom Egypt (Katzenstein 1982: 113). It emphasized the critical role of Gaza for New Kingdom pharaohs, stating that Canaanites brought tribute to their Egyptian overlords at the temple "Amun of Ramesses" in Gaza (Pritchard, ed. 1969: 260–61; Giveon 1978: 22; Singer 1988: 3; Wimmer 1990: 1086–88, 1097; Keel and Uehlinger 1998: 110–14).

Ashkelon

An ivory plaque from the Megiddo Treasury (mid-thirteenth to mid-twelfth century B.C.E.) mentions an Egyptian temple in Ashkelon (Giveon 1978: 23), probably built after Merneptah's conquest of the city (Singer 1988: 3; 1988/89: 105).[36] The inscription on this plaque suggests that this temple was dedicated to the Egyptian god Ptah (Pritchard, ed. 1969: 263; Katzenstein 1982: 113; *contra*, see Wimmer 1990: 1093–95).

Ashdod

A small LB IIB (Stratum XIII) cult area was discovered at the northern edge (Area G) of the Canaanite port of Ashdod. Sherds and bones lay on a plastered brick altar. Nearby, the stone base for a round pillar may originally have supported a cult image (M. Dothan 1979: 127–28). Egypt dominated LB II Ashdod and Ashdod's sacred site should be understood as Egypto-Canaanite.

Jaffa

A small sanctuary measuring 4.4 × 5.8 m stood near the late-thirteenth/early-twelfth century citadel in Area A. The Stratum III building contained the embalmed skull of a lion once adorned with amulets and jewels, found lying on the plastered sanctuary floor. A broken scarab with the name of Queen Tiy, wife of Amenophis III, and two small bowls lay nearby. The sanctuary may have been destroyed by Merneptah and later rebuilt by Jaffa's new residents, the Sea Peoples (Kaplan 1972; Kaplan and Kaplan 1976; Kaplan and Ritter-Kaplan 1993).[37]

Aphek

Aphek, strategically located on the Via Maris, was subjugated by Thutmosis III and by Amenophis II. Archaeological evidence indicates that the city was still under Egyptian control in the first half of the thirteenth century, after which it was destroyed (Owen 1981: 50–51). Despite the lack of architectural evidence for a Late Bronze Age temple, a faience foundation tablet found in a secondary context alluded to a Temple of Isis (Kochavi 1978: 50–51). Its hieroglyphic inscriptions included the prenomen of Rameses II(?) together with several epithets of the goddess Isis. In Egypt, foundation tablets of this type were always found in the temple of the god to whom the tablets were dedicated. For example, the Papyrus Wilbour mentions a temple of Isis founded by Rameses II, probably located in Memphis (Giveon 1978: 26–27; Owen 1981: 51).

Jerusalem

A number of objects, many found over a century ago north of Damascus Gate, are remnants of a 19th Dynasty Egypto-Canaanite temple. They include a fragment of an Egyptian *stele* that mentioned Osiris and depicted an offering scene, an Egyptian style offering table, two Egyptian alabaster vessels, a small stone statuette of a seated figure and a number of architectural fragments including Egyptian lotus capitals. The temple probably stood on the main road leading from Jerusalem to the Central Highlands, a region known to have had contacts with Egypt in the LB IIB (Barkay 1990; 1996; 2000).

SUMMARY: LATE BRONZE AGE[38]

Nearly all the sanctuaries of the LB IA period continued in use from the MB IIC. This may be attributed to the general turmoil of the era, when the struggle to survive Egyptian invasions and inter-urban warfare was the chief cultural priority. Hazor withstood the Egyptians, possibly with the support of Hurrian and Mittanian groups from the north. At Hazor, the Area H temple of the MB IIC survived throughout the Late Bronze Age while a new temple was built in Area A. At Megiddo, Temple 2048 remained important, but the palace that had long stood near it was now moved to the gateway area.

A new urban sanctuary was built at Beth Shean, a city that was becoming increasingly important to Egypt. Worship at the Pella fortress temple continued uninterrupted during this transitional period, but the sanctuaries or sacred installations at Tel Mor, Gezer, Nahariya and Tel Kittan went out of use by the end of the LB IA. New regional centers for worship were established during the LB IA at Shiloh and Tell Deir ʿAlla.

In contrast to the warfare of the LB IA, the LB IB and the LB IIA period were spent in consolidation and renewal. Egyptian control of Canaan was primarily economic and political. Military power was not often used. Worship during the LB IB period reflected these new socio-political realities. At Megiddo, Shechem and Hazor, extant temples were modified and reused. Nearby, Shiloh remained a pilgrimage center. Building 10, the new sanctuary at Beth Shean, reflected the now permanent Egyptian presence in that city. The new sanctuaries at Lachish and Tel Mevorakh, both located along trade routes, show the important role of trade in reviving local elites.

At the start of the Middle Bronze Age, the growth of countryside sanctuaries was one of the first signs of the recovery from urban desolation. In the LB IB period, similarly a period of recovery and regeneration, most sacred sites were urban. This demonstrates the increased solidity of the indigenous urban tradition, due in part to the long-term entrenchment of clan leadership.

The enlarging of sacred installations at some LB IIA sites and the construction of others can be attributed to the relative peace and prosperity that resulted from less oppressive Egyptian policies. Renovations took place at the temples in Megiddo, Beth Shean, Tel Mevorakh, Lachish and Shechem.

Hazor remained an enclave of Canaanite culture throughout the Late Bronze Age. Egyptian control was indirect at best, counterbalanced by local authority and perhaps by continuing Hittite interests, as well. This is particularly evident in Area A, which had contained royal sanctuaries since the MB IIC period, but held only an open-air installation in the LB II period. The Area A Long Temple was replaced as Hazor's main sanctuary by the Area H Orthostat Temple with its many Hittite elements. New sacred buildings and installations including the Stelae Temple and Shrine 6211 in Area C, the outdoor altar in Area F and open-air installations near the gateways of Area P and Area K, were constructed. The complexity of religion in Late Bronze Age Hazor reflects the scale of this major Canaanite stronghold, the social and ethnic diversity of its population and the need for accommodation that affected the lives of all those living in the city and its environs.

One characteristic of religion in the LB IIB period was the doubling of the number of sacred sites over that of the previous periods. During the LB IIB period, increasing Egyptian demands forced many cities in Canaan not only to acquiesce to Egyptian overlords but also to sustain Egyptian garrisons and even to export food to Egypt or its allies. Certain Canaanite religious institutions were exploited to further these goals. New Egypto-Canaanite temples, at least some of which were used to facilitate grain collection, were constructed at Lachish, Beth Shean, Jerusalem, Tell Abu Hawam, Aphek, Ashdod, Jaffa, Ashkelon and Gaza. Temple 2048 at Megiddo fell under the authority of Egyptian administrators, and this may be why a private chapel was now constructed in Megiddo's royal palace.

At Lachish, the new Egypto-Canaanite Summit Temple served as a collection center for the grain tax and the traditional Canaanite Fosse Temple went out of use. As local leaders were replaced by Egyptian officials, the intimate connection between politics and religion was highlighted once again.

Beth Shean is the parade example of an Egypto-Canaanite city of the LB II period but the constellation of sacred and secular architecture and small finds from that city underscores the complexity of life in thirteenth century Canaan. The city was controlled by an Egyptian governor and supported an Egyptian garrison. It contained a temple with many Egyptian elements. Other materials, though, demonstrated on-going Canaanite influences. In addition, the influence of Hittites, evident at sites from Hazor in the north through the Jordan Valley as far south as Amman, can be seen in the materials from the LB IIB sanctuary at Beth Shean.

The Fortress Temple at Shechem remained in use in the LB IIB period, but now a neighborhood sanctuary was also used. The Deir ʽAlla sanctuary contained texts in an Aegean script. Excavations in the Baqʽah Valley, at Tell Ṣafuṭ and Khirbet Umm ad-Danānīr, are beginning to reveal information about Late Bronze Age temples farther east in Jordan. At the port of Tell Abu Hawam, the sanctuary resembled an Egyptian chapel, and another coastal sanctuary was excavated at Tel Nami.

In the Late Bronze Age, Canaanite culture, under pressure from international powers, was forced from the cyclical patterns and tensions inherent in the indigenous urban-rural dichotomy of the Early Bronze and Middle Bronze Ages. The changes required by external leaders necessitated changes in socio-political structure that would eventually culminate in the new state system of the Iron II period. Kin-based affiliations became less significant in determining social organization and so kin-groups were increasingly unable to control society's religious dimensions.

The royalty and its followers, often controlled or backed by foreign rulers, were at times complicit in the expropriation of organized religious practice for secular purposes. Acrimony between royal and clan-based religion is apparent throughout the Hebrew Bible. Inasmuch as it described the first millennium conflict between the royal cults of the Israelite and Judaean monarchies and the local clan and community-based cults, the Bible may be the last document to record vestiges of the tumultuous changes of the Canaanite Late Bronze Age.

NOTES

[1] These temples blended Egyptian structural or decorative elements with Canaanite architectural forms. Egyptian ritual and other objects were found alongside Canaanite cultic paraphernalia. Iconography often exhibited

qualities of synthesis rather than exclusivity, but in general the gods and goddesses of Canaan prevailed. Quantitative and qualitative comparisons of Egyptian and Canaanite elements suggest the complexity of worship at each individual temple. For a discussion of Egyptian temples in Canaan and the Sinai, see Wimmer 1990.

[2] According to Ahituv (1978), on the other hand, Egypt was not interested in systematically exploiting Canaan's many resources. Instead, the eventual demise of Canaanite culture should be attributed to constant warfare and to the small-scale burden of supporting the local Egyptian colonial administration.

[3] For an alternative view that postulates limited Egyptian military and administrative authority see Higginbotham 1996. Her interpretation allows for Egyptian oversight and suggests that the Canaanite elite provided a great deal of willing support for Egypt.

[4] According to Na'aman,

> the Phoenician coast and Palestine (apart from its northern parts) were one administrative unit while southern Syria (including Bashan and the kingdom of Hazor) were treated separately. This structure was apparently the outcome of the events of the Middle Bronze Age, when southern Palestine and the Phoenician coast were under Egyptian influence (though not necessarily direct rule), while southern Syria and northern Palestine were grouped with the Syro-Mesopotamian West Semitic kingdoms. The latter thus acquired an altogether different administrative and cultural tradition from the other territories of Canaan, and was organized within a separate framework (1981: 183).

[5] The Mediterranean style of housing in the *Ville Sud* neighborhood south of the acropolis is but one example of Ugarit's cosmopolitan fabric (Callot 1983: 76–77, fig. 1).

[6] "As the most effective tool capable of saving life and cargo if a vessel was caught in one of the Mediterranean's sudden storms, the anchor was valued by ancient mariners not only for its functional ability but also as a piece of psychological, reassuring equipment" (Raveh and Kingsley 1991: 200; see too Wachsmann 1996).

[7] "The paucity of Egyptian material should lead us to consider whether Hazor may have been outside the arc of effective Egyptian control by the Amarna period. There is no doubt that it was nominally part of the Egyptian empire"

(Bienkowski 1987: 58). See also Na'aman 1981: 183; Daviau 1993: 255. Recently, however, fragments of five Late Bronze Age royal Egyptian statues were uncovered at the site (Ben-Tor 1999b: 5*).

[8] The orthostats were found *in situ* in the Stratum 1b Orthostat Temple. At the time the original field report was written, the excavators thought that this was the construction phase for which they were created (Yadin et al. 1989: 241). However, continued excavation and analysis, the discovery of similar but stratigraphically earlier orthostats in Area A, and the close similarity between the Stratum 3 and Stratum 2 Orthostat Temples indicates that these stone wall facings were first used in the MB II (Yadin et al. 1989: 212–13).

[9] The statue may have represented an individual of such power that he had to be ritually "killed" to neutralize him, just as sacred vessels were often ritually broken prior to being discarded. Alternatively, these basalt statues may have been decapitated or otherwise disfigured by the conquerers of Canaanite Hazor at the end of the Late Bronze Age (Ben-Tor 1997c: 123–24).

[10] Recently, four bronze bulls were found in a Late Bronze Age palace (Ben-Tor 1999a: 2*).

[11] Others have mentioned "the Canaanite storm god Baal" (Mazar 1990a: 248) and the god El (Beck 1989b: 337). Another view is that his identity may never be ascertained (Negbi 1989: 357–58).

[12] In Yadin's opinion, the MB IIC building in the Lower City Area F was a "Twin Temple." It was therefore natural for him to define the LB I (Stratum 2) building on the same spot as also sacred (1972: 98–100). Similarly square, the Amman Airport "temple" provided the basis for Yadin's reconstruction of the poorly preserved Stratum 2 building in Area F (Yadin et al. 1989: 153). More recent studies have shown that the MB IIC "Twin Temple" was in fact a palace and its LB I successor was patrician housing (A. Mazar 1990a: 257).

[13] The size of the houses in Areas C and F and their many rooms point to a comparison with Ugarit in the north rather than to smaller Canaanite sites. Neighborhood layout and house plans indicate "a complex social organization of extended families" (Daviau 1993: 255).

[14] The Middle Bronze/Late Bronze Age palace was located in Area A (Ben-Tor 1997a: 3; 1997c: 122).

[15] A comparable situation existed in Late Bronze Age Hazor (Yadin 1972: 125).

[16] The original excavators of Temple 2048 discerned only one floor, and pottery of the Iron I lay on it. In consequence, it has been difficult to assess the absolute dates of the major changes in this building (A. Mazar 1992b: 170–71).

[17] *Contra*, see Davies 1986: 60–62, fig. 14. In his opinion, Level VIII construction in Megiddo Area BB represented the foundations of the Level VIIB sanctuary, constructed when Megiddo fell under the control of Amarna Age Shechem. The result was the replication on a smaller scale of the Shechem Fortress Temple.

[18] See Kempinski 1989b for a reconstruction of the temple façade based upon contemporary ceramic house models.

[19] The cultic objects found in Late Bronze Age Temple 2048 include a bronze figurine of a seated deity wearing a crown and holding a standard embossed with a four-pointed star, and two ceramic liver models (Loud 1948: pls. 238.30, 255.1). A clay female figurine, gold and bronze crescent-shaped pendants, four small bronze cymbals and a typical array of pottery were also found. A collection of bronze objects buried beneath the floor may have been a foundation offering (G. Davies 1986: 63).

[20] A second sanctuary thought to have stood north of Building 10 (Rowe 1940: 10–11) was more likely a royal palace (Ottosson 1980: 65–66).

[21] An older chronology had dated the foundation of the Stratum VII sanctuary to the reigns of Amenophis III and Amenophis IV, somewhat earlier in the fourteenth century (James and Kempinski 1975: 213–14).

[22] Hittite influence can also be seen in a contemporary Hittite-style mortuary installation, the so-called Amman Airport Temple (see n. 37 below).

[23] Wimmer suggests the Egyptian worship of Canaanite deities at Beth Shean, as indicated by the religious imagery on the Mekal Stele and on an Egyptian cylinder seal depicting Rameses II. Both show that worship, even by Egyptians, was dedicated to the Canaanite gods Mekal/Reshef and Astarte (1990: 1079–80).

[24] Franken, excavator of the site, suggests that each fenestrated pottery shrine from the sanctuary once "contained a 'document' that testified to special bonds between the sanctuary and certain groups, such as families or tribes. Each pot may have represented a priestly family whose duty it was to serve during a certain period in the temple" (1997: 137).

[25] The growing body of information about Egypto-Canaanite temples led Negbi to document the similarities among the Tell Deir 'Alla sanctuary, the Lachish Summit Temple and the Beth Shean temples in Levels VII–VI (1991: 213, 227). Egyptian control over the latter two sites is well-documented, and the comparison suggests its control over the Jordan Valley regional sanctuary, as well.

[26] My thanks to Prof. Campbell for sharing his unpublished manuscript with me.

[27] Tell Abu Hawam has been identified with Canaanite Rabant/Rabana and with biblical Shihor libnah (Balensi et al. 1993: 8) or Achshaph (Dever 1997a: 9).

[28] Despite the importance of Egypt at Tell Abu Hawam (Balensi 1985: 68, n. 15), the site was not an Egyptian naval base. That role was filled by nearby Acco, which fell into Egyptian hands during the reign of Rameses II (Weinstein 1980: 45).

[29] Local and imported wares found in a *favissa* outside the western wall suggest the foundation of Building 50 just after 1450 B.C.E. LB IIB pottery ascribed by

Hamilton to Building 30 (Hamilton 1934: 76–77) actually represented the final occupation of Building 50 (Balensi 1985: n. 20). *Contra*, see Gershuny 1981, who dated both buildings to the Late Bronze Age.

[30] There was in fact no Canaanite goddess named 'Ashtoret. This name was derived from the consonants in the name of the Canaanite goddess 'Ashtarte, to which biblical writers added the vowels from the word בֹּשֶׁת (*bošet*), meaning shame, thereby creating the false and condemnatory 'Ashtoret (McCarter 1980: 143).

[31] On Asherah, see Reed 1949; Patai 1967: 29–100; Cross 1973; Dever 1984; Olyan 1988; Smith 1990: 80–114; Keel and Uehlinger 1998: 177–281 and references therein. On inscribed arrowheads, see Cross and Milik 1954; Dever 1990: 135–36; Keel and Uehlinger 1998: 126–28; and references therein.

[32] It is possible that the worship of El was implied by the worship of Elat, whose name was the feminine form of that of the male deity (Cross 1984; see also Puech 1986: 24).

[33] These bases may have been pedestals for statues of the Summit Temple gods (Gittlen 1982: 68*–69*).

[34] A proto-Canaanite inscription was found on a sherd from a Level VI pit in the city center, not far from the Summit Temple (Ussishkin 1983: 155–57). According to Cross, "the inscribed bowl bore the record of a gift—perhaps even a *stele*—presented to a temple, or placed on display in a sacred precinct, honouring *'il 'ib*, the divine ancestor" (1984: 75). This suggests that the Canaanite ritual of erecting *stelae* in honor of sacred ancestors continued despite Egyptian involvement in local religious practices.

[35] The relationship of sites with hieratic inscriptions documenting taxation through grain payments to the temples that received those payments is unclear. For a discussion of whether these temples were located in those cities in which hieratic inscriptions were found, or whether payments from those cities were made to the temple in Gaza, or even shipped directly to Egypt, see Goldwasser and Wimmer 1999 and references therein.

[36] *Contra*, see Weinstein 1981: 19–20.

[37] Not everyone agrees with the identification of this building as a temple (A. Mazar 1992b: 180).

[38] The discovery of an unusual building filled with luxurious imported items in Markeh near the Amman Civil Airport sparked a great deal interest, in no small part because Transjordan was thought to have been uninhabited for much of the second millennium. Initially, the late thirteenth century B.C.E. building was considered a temple (Hennessy 1966; G. R. H. Wright 1966) and, more specifically, a tribal sanctuary. It was compared to the MB IIC Tananir/Mt. Gerizim building (Boling 1969); both were interpreted as shrines for tribal

league ceremonies (Campbell and Wright 1969). Alternatively, it was compared to the Shechem Field VI *temenos* area, which was thought to provide it with an architectural prototype (G. R. H Wright 1975: 60–61), and to the LB I Area F "temple" at Hazor (Yadin 1972: 98–100). It has also been described as domestic rather than sacred (see A. Mazar 1990a: 209–10, 257). A building with some architectural similarities was discovered at nearby El Mabrak, but this building likely served a domestic, not a religious function (Yassine 1988a). The eastern building at nearby Rujm al-Henu was nearly square and again parallels with the Amman Airport Building were noted. However, it has been difficult to assess the Rujm al-Henu building's function and date of occupation (McGovern 1983).

More recent excavations of the Amman Airport Structure have increased our knowledge of the site, and have led to a shift in interpretation. The well preserved square stone building measured 15 × 15 m, with exterior walls approaching 2 m in width. It was composed of an outer square that boxed in an inner square chamber. Several partition walls turned the corridor between the two "boxes" into a casemate-like series of chambers (Hennessy 1966: fig. 2). Its excavators have determined that the Amman Airport "temple" served as a mortuary. The building was a fortified repository for luxury burial goods and the nearby "Structured Rock Pile" a funeral pyre.

This interpretation is supported by the specialized and rich assemblage of stone and ceramic vessels, as well as the weapons and jewelry, objects typical of funerary contexts. The large number of imported goods is surprising, and so is the fact that they ranged from the MB II through the Late Bronze Age, even though the local pottery was exclusively thirteenth century.

Analysis of the many human skeletal remains indicates the cremation of more than 1127 adults. Their partial articulation suggests that at least some of the cremations were primary burials (Herr, ed. 1983; Herr 1997a). Significantly, several Late Bronze Age burial caves have also been discovered in the area. The anomalous configuration of architectural, artifactual and human remains in the Amman Airport Mortuary Site has tentatively been attributed to the presence of Hittites in LB IIB Transjordan (Herr, ed. 1983: 29–30). Excavations suggest a contemporary Hittite presence at Tell es-Sa'idiyeh as well (Negbi 1991: 211–12).

Building 490 at Tell el-Far'ah (N), once thought to have been an Late Bronze Age (Level VIIa) temple (de Vaux 1957: 574–77), is now understood to have been an Iron I house (Chambon 1984: 20).

Sanctuaries, cultic installations and religious texts dating to the Late Bronze Age were found at Timna and Serabit el-Khadim (Beit-Arieh 1987; Rothenberg 1988). These sacred places dedicated to Hathor (Giveon 1978;

Wimmer 1990: 1066–70) were constructed for Egyptians working at the Aravah and Sinai mines, as well as for those Canaanites who also worked there (Beit-Arieh 1987; Puech 1984: 22). They were removed from the cultural sphere of Canaan, having been "erected for the religious needs of Egyptian mining expedition personnel" (Weinstein 1981: 19).

CHAPTER SIX
ISRAELITE SACRED PLACES OF THE IRON AGE

In modern times as in antiquity, the *bāmâ* (במה) has had a special ability to evince controversy, for archaeologists and biblical scholars have been unable to arrive at a uniform description. Perhaps in consequence, assumptions about the *bāmâ* have been more common than have investigations into its form and function. Recently, however, interest in the role of the *bāmâ* in Israelite religion has increased (Barrick 1975; 1980; 1992; 1996; Vaughan 1974; Emerton 1997; Nakhai 1994; Catron 1995; Gleis [in Barrick 1999]).

Chapter Three discussed the Bible's treatment of the *bāmâ* and suggested that its role in Israelite and Judaean society was different than the Deuteronomistic editors would have had their readers think. Contrary to biblical descriptions, it was an institution of the monarchy and not a populist manifestation of vestigial Canaanite cult practices. In this chapter I will demonstrate that by using a social science-based approach to archaeological and textual data, we arrive at an understanding of the *bāmâ* as a legitimate element in Israelite worship. We also expand our knowledge of the socio-political world within which the *bāmâ* was embedded.[1]

THE BIBLICAL *BĀMÂ*

The *bāmâ* (plural במות; *bāmôt*) is generally considered to have originated in the world of Canaanite worship, despite the fact that the term had no sacred association in Canaanite dialects (Barrick 1975: 36). G. E. Wright describes *bāmôt* as country sanctuaries for "common" Canaanite worship which in his opinion emphasized base sexual desires (1960: 13–15). Dever describes the *bāmâ* as "a platform or Canaanite-style high place of the sort mentioned in several biblical passages" (1990: 133). De Vaux likewise assumes a Canaanite origin for the *bāmâ*, while his rather broad treatment of the "high place" encompasses many of its scholarly definitions (1961: 284–88). Still the idea that the biblical *bāmâ* was Canaanite in origin has not gone unchallenged. In his study of the sacred complex at Tel Dan, Biran suggests that the *bāmâ* may have been an Israelite concept (1981: 142).[2]

Although the word *bāmâ* (or its plural, *bāmôt*) appears approximately one hundred times in the Hebrew Bible, primarily in reference to cultic sites, its meaning remains unclear. The Hebrew root ב.מ.ה. (*b.m.h.*) had cognates in several Semitic languages. In Ugaritic it meant the back of a body. In Akkadian, the singular meant back but the plural referred to terrain, possibly hilly (Barrick 1980: 51; 1992: 196–97). The Vulgate rendered *bāmâ* as *excelsus*, leading to the popular English translation "high place" which, although inaccurate, has colored our understanding.[3]

Until recently, four interpretations of the *bāmâ* have prevailed: (1) a primitive open-air installation on a natural hilltop equipped with some combination of *ʾašērâ* (sacred pole), *maṣṣebôt* (standing stones) and possibly altar(s),[4] (2) an artificially raised platform upon which religious rites took place,[5] (3) a sacrificial altar[6] and (4) a mortuary installation.[7] It is the first interpretation, that of the elevated open-air cultic site, which has been most widely accepted.[8]

Unfortunately, none of these interpretations fully corresponds with the rather scant biblical evidence concerning the *bāmâ* and the religious activities that took place there. The sources of this problem are twofold. In part, confusion stems from some scholars' perception of the *bāmâ* as the site of rather bawdy Canaanite rituals, rituals that the chronically unfaithful Israelites allegedly revived, as they were unable to adhere to "normative" Jerusalem-centered Yahwism.[9] Also, scholars have linked various combinations of architectural or artifactual cultic materials with the ill-defined *bāmâ*. Almost any unroofed space used for religious activities could be described as a *bāmâ*, since "open-air" and "elevated" were considered its only requisites.[10]

Emerton calls for caution in the face of conflicting textual evidence. Discussing the uncertainty over its form (open-air or building), he concludes that "perhaps the wisest policy is simply to regard any local sanctuary as possibly a *bāmâ* but recognize that we cannot be certain …. We do not know whether the word could be used of any sanctuary, or whether there was something that differentiated *bāmôt* from other sanctuaries" (1997: 130).[11]

Seeking to overcome these ambiguities by developing a systematized approach, Barrick details the essential features of the *bāmâ* as known from the HB. He concludes that the textual evidence remains "slender at best" and that reliance upon it can yield only partial understanding of the biblical *bāmâ* (1980: 57; 1996: 641–42). Even so, he determines that the *bāmâ* was a multi-roomed structure in an urban environment, one in which worshippers sacrificed and burned incense (1980; 1992: 198–99). He also defined a distinction between the phrases *bêt bāmôt* (בית־במות) or *bêt bāmôt* (בתי־במות), and *bāmâ* or *bāmôt*. He suggests that biblical authors used the former to describe non-Judahite installations and that it was part of the vocabulary of the northern nation of Israel, while the latter expression was part of the language of Judah (Barrick 1996: 642).[12]

For the most part, previous studies of the *bāmâ* have been textually based, relying upon the HB as their primary reference. Important archaeological data and methodological advances have been ignored. However, a more comprehensive approach, one that utilizes archaeology and texts together with social science studies (Bunimovitz 1993a; Meyers 1983: 414–15; 1987: 357–58) can further elucidate the biblical *bāmâ*.[13] To this end, the *bāmâ* is examined in the context of those social structures within which it was embedded.[14] This provides a model for the *bāmâ* against which archaeological data can be tested. Inasmuch as the material evidence mirrors that model, then we can conclude that we have not only correctly assessed the function of the *bāmâ* but have accurately identified a number of actual Israelite *bāmôt*.[15]

A Social History of the Bāmâ

For the most part, the HB condemned worship at *bāmôt* and lauded their destruction. Its Deuteronomistic editors advocated the exclusive legitimacy of a Jerusalem-centered religion by vilifying the alternatives. However, the HB also contains a different perspective, one made evident through an examination of the *bāmâ's* setting in Israel and Judah.

As one might expect in a clan-based society and even in a nascent nation-state, Israel's first places of worship were essentially local phenomena. The HB describes Israelite worship at numerous open-air sites, at various places where the Ark was situated, at a domestic sanctuary (Judg 17:4–5), at a cultic center (Judg 18:30–31) and at the sanctuary in Shiloh. The earliest, and fullest, written references to the *bāmâ* come from the tribal period, the era of the Judges.[16] 1 Sam 9:11–25 describes religious rites at a *bāmâ* in an unnamed city within the district of Zuph, and 1 Sam 10:5 describes a processional of prophets leaving a *bāmâ* in Bethel.

The HB attests to the *bāmâ* in the period of the Judges and then skips to the reign of Solomon. The silence about *bāmôt* in the Davidic era is curious, since the nation of Israel underwent enormous changes in political and social structure during David's reign in the early tenth century. These changes surely had important implications for religion in Israel. What can we theorize concerning David's institutionalization of Israelite religion?

Under David's rule, the United Monarchy expanded from a small nation-state into an empire as he consolidated his forces within Israel and then subjugated kingdoms to the north, west and east. His empire building was greatly facilitated by his deliberative efforts toward the centralization of his kingdom. These included:

1) State building: Malamat describes David's imperial strategy as five-fold. A tribal kingdom, then a national kingdom, a consolidated territorial state, a multinational state and finally an empire were created as a result of David's well-defined administrative, military, political and diplomatic objectives (1984: 164–68).

2) Military conquests: David's military conquests close to home and at Israel's borders are well documented. Of particular interest is the conquest of Moab (2 Sam 8:2) and Ammon (2 Sam 10:1–11:2; 12:26–31), those nations closest to Israel's eastern border, nations to whose gods Solomon is said to have later constructed *bāmôt* in Jerusalem.

3) Economic organization: The economic centralization of David's empire has recently been documented. Heltzer suggests that 1 Chr 27:25–31 is an excerpt from an archaic documentary chronicle. It describes how agricultural produce and the breeding of livestock were managed according to specialized programs, subsequent to which goods were distributed in accordance with state policy (1989: 200*).

4) Temple building: David's role as the creative energy behind the Jerusalem Temple has been demonstrated (C. L. Meyers 1987). Documentation for this is found in 1 Chr 22, which describes his organization of materials and a work force to be used by Solomon when building the Jerusalem Temple. That David would have initiated construction of a centralized place of worship accords with what is known about his other efforts at national consolidation.[17] Furthermore,

David's attempt to increase his control over worship outside of the capital city should be expected.

To be sure, textual evidence for David's involvement in the organization of religious practice outside of Jerusalem is elusive, just as his role in preparations for the construction of the Jerusalem Temple was downplayed. However, as it becomes increasingly apparent that 1 Chronicles contains texts relevant to the study of early monarchical Israel (Halpern 1981), the description in 1 Chronicles 15 of David's organization of a large body of priests and Levites becomes significant. If, as has been suggested, the list of Levitical cities in Joshua 21 originated during David's reign (Aharoni 1967: 269–73; 1969: 117), then 1 Chr 15 and Joshua 21 together may be understood as a plan for the resettlement of Levites throughout the realm. The aim of this clerical reorganization was the strengthening of national solidarity and the promotion of loyalty to the crown through the promulgation of the official cultus in outlying areas.[18]

According to the Deuteronomistic Historians (DH), use of the *bāmâ* continued until the construction of the Jerusalem Temple, as Solomon and the Israelites worshipped at the great *bāmâ* in Gibeon (where Yahweh appeared to Solomon) and at others (1 Kgs 3:2–5). DH's great complaint about Solomon was that once the Temple (in their opinion, the only appropriate place for Yahwistic worship) was complete, Solomon nonetheless built *bāmôt* for his non-Israelite wives and for the gods of Sidon, Ammon and Moab (1 Kgs 11:4–8), the latter two Davidic conquests. Sanctuaries dedicated to their gods Milchom and Chemosh were constructed in the heart of the Israelite capital as a means of obtaining Ammonite and Moabite cooperation.[19] The construction of *bāmôt* for Solomon's foreign wives, acquired as spoils of war or through treaty making, would have served the same purpose.

These references make it clear that worship at *bāmôt* was an Israelite custom, one that prevailed during the Settlement and early monarchical periods. Also significant is the fact that kings could initiate *bāmâ* construction. These points will be developed, but first the social history of the *bāmâ* during the Divided Monarchy must be considered.

Jeroboam I, first king of the northern kingdom of Israel, constructed royal sanctuaries at Bethel and Dan in order to break the ties between his Israelite subjects and the crown in Judaean Jerusalem, and in order to organize the rural population in Israel (1 Kgs 12:25–33).[20] In addition, control of Dan and Bethel, strategically located at Israel's northern and southern borders, was crucial for Jeroboam as he struggled to establish his authority and to strengthen his nation's borders. To obtain undisputed control, he had no choice but to enfranchise the Levitical priesthood that had dominated religious practice at Dan since the Settlement period.[21] He had to involve the priests, and by extension the residents of Dan and its environs, in the national cult, in order to link them to the Israelite monarchy.

The establishment of this urban royal cult did not, however, sufficiently guarantee the people's loyalty and so Jeroboam also constructed *bāmôt* throughout his kingdom. These *bāmôt* were serviced by priests from all population groups except, deliberately, the Levites (1 Kgs 12:31). The obedience of the new *bāmôt* priests was reinforced by the fact that they also had to serve at the royal sanctuary in Bethel (1 Kgs 12:32). That this new priestly group was non-Levitical suggests that Jeroboam's religious revolution was not the construction of the *bāmôt* sanctuaries (so, for example, Cross 1973: 75), for *bāmôt* had long been legitimate places of Israelite worship. Instead it was the disenfranchisement of the Levitical priests who in the days of the United Monarchy had been dispatched to the *bāmôt* sanctuaries.[22] As a result, the biblical condemnation of Jeroboam may speak as much to the pro-Levitical stance of the much later Deuteronomistic authors of Kings as to their hatred of the institution of the *bāmâ*.

In the southern kingdom of Judah as well, the royal cult alone had not adequately met the socio-political goals of the rulers. Judah's monarchs therefore established a *bāmôt* system similar to that in Israel. The *bāmôt* system of the Divided Monarchy is described in 2 Kings 23, a passage that chronicles Josiah's cultic reforms.[23] Verse 5 mentions the *bāmôt* priests whom the kings of Judah had appointed. Verse 9 notes that following Josiah's destruction of the *bāmôt*, the *bāmôt* priests did not worship in the Jerusalem Temple but rather joined with others of their own clans, underscoring the position of the *bāmôt* priesthood within the residual clan elements of the Judaean population.

Additional evidence for the long-lived legitimacy of the *bāmôt* system comes from the late eighth century. During his campaign against Judah, the Assyrian king Sennacherib sent several of his chief officers to Jerusalem to negotiate a peaceful resolution to his imperial designs (2 Kgs 18:17–37; 2 Chr 32:9–19). Addressing both administrators and residents of the capital city, the Assyrian officers argued for Judaean support of Assyria because, in the face of Hezekiah's apostasy, Sennacherib had been chosen by Yahweh to redeem Israel.

Among the charges leveled at the Judaean monarch was that, through his destruction of Yahweh's *bāmôt* and his insistence upon worship exclusively in Jerusalem, Hezekiah had undermined devotion to the very god from whom he was now claiming support. The accuracy of these charges and their destructive potential was underscored by the Judaean ministers' request that the Assyrian officers speak in Aramaic rather than Hebrew to prevent nearby Judaeans from understanding their conversation.

In summary, two-tiered religious hierarchies were set up in Israel and in Judah. First, royal cults, celebrated in Jerusalem in the south and in Bethel and Dan in the north, were established.[24] They served the dual purpose of permitting the monarchy a sense of Canaanite-style grandeur and permanence and of forcing centralization upon Israelite and Judaean worship. The royal cults were complemented by the traditional *bāmôt* system of regional worship. The *bāmôt* provided the people of Judah and Israel with access to local religious centers. In the beginning, they also served to neutralize otherwise disenfranchised and potentially fractious priestly groups by presenting them with alternate status positions. That they ultimately bore some responsibility for the creation of a priestly underclass, one removed from the vortex of royal power, is also significant. The Levitical priests, prevented from serving at northern royal sanctuaries and *bāmôt*, may eventually have become the core of the Deuteronomistic group (Boling 1992a: 1013). In their writings, they espoused an unequivocal condemnation of the *bāmâ*, the very institution from which they had earlier been excluded by royal decree.

It is apparent that the *bāmâ* was for the most part an accepted place for Israelite worship, one that met the needs of the northern and southern monarchs and of the Israelite and Judaean citizenry. However over time the *bāmôt* priesthood grew increasingly independent of the monarchy and of the royal clergy. At least in part to eliminate the threat that they posed to royal authority, Hezekiah and Josiah waged campaigns against the rural *bāmôt*, hoping to eradicate the *bāmôt* priesthood's power base.

In doing this, they received support and even religious legitimization[25] from those elements within the population who opposed the *bāmôt* sanctuaries because of the way in which they had contributed to their exclusion from the matrix of Israelite and Judaean religion. As they influenced those kings whose political aims included exerting tight centralized control, they advocated the primacy of the Jerusalem Temple and the destruction of the *bāmôt* sanctuaries. From their anti-*bāmôt* stance one can see the tensions inherent in the traditional dual-access approach to Yahwism.

THE CHALLENGE TO ARCHAEOLOGY

The Bible's complex, obscure and fascinating description of the *bāmôt* system challenges archaeologists to search widely for relevant material remains and highlights the difficulty of that task. Now that our analysis of biblical texts has shown the fundamental position of the *bāmâ* in the political and religious world of ancient Israel, it is possible to investigate the physical evidence in light of this new understanding.

So far discussion has centered on textual evidence. Now it can focus on archaeological evidence. A number of sacred structures and installations from the Iron I (Settlement Period) and from the Iron II (United and Divided Monarchies) have been discovered (fig. 4). They present us with material evidence for the organization and practice of religion in first millennium Israel and Judah.[26]

The Iron Age (1200–587 B.C.E.) in Israel and surrounding lands was a period of change in the social and political landscape of western Asia and the eastern Mediterranean. Following the significant disruptions to urban life and the demise of Egypt's New Kingdom empire in Canaan that marked the mid-thirteenth to mid-twelfth centuries B.C.E., new political, economic and in some cases religious organizations came to prevail.[27]

The Iron I (1200–1000 B.C.E.) was an era of important transitions. Residents of coastal Lebanon and northern Israel retained their traditional way of life, providing the core of the great seafaring Phoenician city-states. Farther south, coastal settlements by the "Sea Peoples" resulted, *inter alia*, in the formation of the Philistine Pentapolis. Elsewhere, the situation was different. In Israel and Jordan, numerous towns and villages appeared in previously little settled territory. In Israel, these new settlements clustered in the Central Highlands, the area that would later provide the core for the tenth century nation of Israel.

Eventually, the rural settlements of the earlier era became integrated into the nation-states that were typical of the Iron II period (1000–587 B.C.E.). Israel and Judah, Ammon, Moab and Edom, all rose to importance in the south while farther north in Syria, the development of the Aramaean states followed a similar pattern.

ISRAELITE SACRED PLACES OF THE IRON AGE

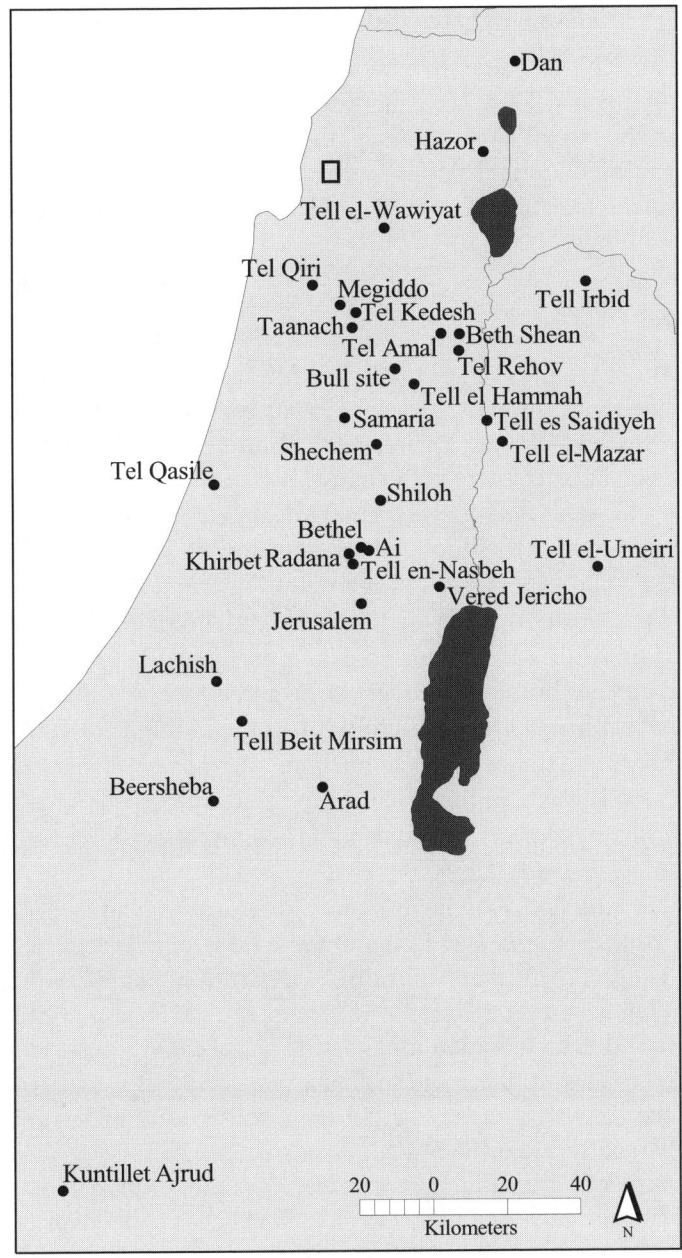

Fig. 4 Map showing the location of Iron Age sites.
Map by Marcy H. Rockman.

IRON I: THE SETTLEMENT PERIOD

It is difficult to generalize about the architecture of worship sites during the Iron I. They are found in a wide range of locations, from mountaintops to villages, and even those found in villages share little by way of architectural features. Often what identifies these sites as sacred is their assemblage of cultic objects, which might include ceramic stands with relief decoration, chalices and other specialized vessels.

Bull Site

The Bull Site, the earliest of the Israelite sacred places, can be dated to the twelfth century (A. Mazar 1999a; see Finkelstein 1998 for a Middle Bronze Age date for this site). Built on a hilltop in Manasseh near the road that connected Dothan and Tirzah, it was situated within a cluster of small villages and commanded a view of some of the most important mountain ridges in northern Israel. Among the poorly preserved stone installations found within the sacred enclosure was a *maṣṣebâ* or altar, in front of which were several offerings. Cultic artifacts found at the Bull Site included a small bronze bull, a fragment of a ceramic incense burner or model shrine and a bronze object that may have been a mirror. Other small finds included cooking pots and bowls, animal bones and flints. The location of the site and its cultic installations suggest that it was a regional sanctuary used by Israelite clan groups residing in neighboring villages and throughout the district (A. Mazar 1982: 26–37; 1993b).[28]

Similar bull figurines have been found at Canaanite sites of the Middle Bronze Age (Ashkelon) and the Late Bronze Age (Ugarit and Hazor, which has five bull figurines), at twelfth century Beth Shean and at tenth century Tel Reḥov. According to A. Mazar, the excavator of the Bull Site, its mountaintop location and the bull figurine together suggest the worship there of the Canaanite god Baal Hadad, of "Bull El," of the Israelite Yahweh, or, perhaps, of "the Bull of Jacob" of the patriarchal narratives (1982: 40).

The story of Gideon in Judges 6 describes the worship of Baal by a group of Israelites living in the district of Manasseh, the district of the Bull Site. It is not possible to connect this story directly with this site. However, the evidence of the bulls from Canaanite and Israelite sites, the biblical narrative and the Bull Site itself together underscore the significance of this archaeological site for understanding the Canaanite background of early Israelite religion.[29]

Shiloh

According to the biblical tradition (Josh 18:1–10; 21:1–3; Judg 21:19–21 and 1 Sam 1–3), Shiloh was the main cult center for Israelites in the premonarchical era, particularly important as the home of the Ark, Israel's central cult symbol (Halpern 1992: 1214). The recounting of events at Shiloh in 1 Sam 9:1–10:16 provides us with our most detailed description of the *bāmâ* (Barrick 1992: 199). The many settlements around Shiloh in the Iron I help explain its preeminence as a regional sanctuary in the pre-Temple era (Milgrom 1992: 460).

Although no architectural evidence for an Israelite sanctuary has been found, artifactual remains suggest that it was located on the summit of the mound (Finkelstein 1988: 228).[30] The pillared buildings of Area C were part of the sanctuary complex. Their scale, complex architecture and contents (a rich ceramic assemblage with numerous large *pithoi*) suggest public rather than domestic use. Cultic materials included vessels with animal reliefs. Altogether, the sanctuary and associated buildings would have occupied a large portion of the tel, indicating that, as in the second millennium, religion was the principle business at Iron I Shiloh (Finkelstein 1988: 220–34, 291).

Hazor

At Hazor, mid-eleventh century (Stratum XI) finds were limited to Area B, the highest point on the acropolis. There, an unwalled Israelite village was built over the squatter remains that covered the destroyed and abandoned Canaanite settlement. The next occupation level at Hazor was Solomonic (Yadin 1972: 134; Beck 1989b: 361).

Room 3283, the Stratum XI cult structure, consisted of a 5 × 4 m room with benches lining its southern end. A jar filled with bronze votive objects was found under its floor. Two broken incense stands, beads and votive arrowheads were found in a paved area to the south. West of Room 3283, a row of four stone *maṣṣebôt* bordered another paved area. Small finds include a scarab, bone inlay, bronze needles and hematite weights. Another nearby room contained a millstone and fragments of two additional incense altars (Yadin 1972: 132–33, fig. 29).

The jar found under the floor in Room 3283 contained a bronze statue of a male figure in a cone-like helmet with a weapon in his left hand. It also held a sword, two javelin heads and butts, an arrowhead, a lugged axe and broken pieces of worked and alloy metal. According to Beck, the mix of LB II and Iron I objects, the combination of well-worn and new pieces, the inclusion of broken metal pieces and a lump of alloy and the disrupted condition of the floor around the jar suggest that the jar and its contents were a hoard hidden away for safekeeping (Beck 1989b: 358–62). The salvaged metal pieces suggest that the hoard might have supplied pieces for metalworking.[31]

At Hazor, an Iron I zoomorphic figurine was found in Area L, near the entrance to the water tunnel (Ben-Tor and Bonfil, eds. 1997: 220). Farther west in the Galilee, a *kernos* uncovered at Kibbutz Sasa may have originated in another Iron I cultic installation (Frankel 1994: 25, and references therein).

Dan

Although Judges 17–18 describes the establishment of a house shrine at Dan, officiated over by a Levitical priest, no Iron I sanctuary has been uncovered at Tel Dan. However, an unusual assemblage of objects was found in Room 7082, a small room associated with the late twelfth century (Stratum V) metal workshops. It contained a chalice, a krater and a clay "snake house" or model shrine. Metalworking implements were also uncovered in this cult corner (Biran 1994a: 147–53). The metalworkers operated a small-scale workshop in recycled metals, meeting local needs and supplying a circumscribed region with tools, weapons and more (Shalev 1993: 65). The traditional link between metalworking and cult is supported by reference to a Danite ancestor named Aholiab, who is said to have overseen craft production for Tabernacle construction (Exod 31:6; 35:34–36:2; 38:23) (Biran 1994a: 151). In the story of Micah and his move from Ephraim to Dan (Judg 17–18), metal images and a silversmith also played a prominent role.

Megiddo

Area CC in Iron I Megiddo was a residential neighborhood. An interesting assemblage of ceramic cult stands, together with chalices, goblets, zoomorphic vessels, a *kernos* and a bird bowl were discovered in Stratum VIA loci (Loud 1948: 113, 149–53). Gilmour relates this ceramic assemblage to a number of bronze objects found nearby (1995: 64). They include spearheads, adzes, jugs, bowls, strainers, a double axe and metal fragments (Loud 1948: 150). The area in which these objects were recovered was primarily residential, but it included a setting for metal production and for worship. Whether worship took place in a domestic shrine (A. Mazar 1980: 84) or in a workshop is uncertain, but the relationship between cult and metalworking seems clear.

Tell el-Wawiyat

The Iron I occupation (Stratum III) at Tell el-Wawiyat displayed continuity with that of the Canaanite LB IIB (Stratum IV). The twelfth century settlement contained two large buildings, used for a variety of domestic activities and for small-scale industry. In the K-L Building, an unusual installation in a particularly well-built room combined a jarstand, a low column base and a *tabun*, and suggests cultic usage. Another room in the same building contained a tripod basalt bowl, a mold for making jewelry, bits of gold jewelry and a broken female figurine, while the partially articulated skeleton of a cow lay elsewhere in the building (Nakhai, Dessel and Wisthoff 1993: 1501).

'Ai

Room 65 at 'Ai was identified by its excavator, Marquet-Krause, as a cult room (1949: 23). It was somewhat larger than others at the site, and was the only benched room in this early twelfth–mid-eleventh century village. Its cultic use is demonstrated not only by architectural features, but also by its unique contents. They include an unusually tall fenestrated ceramic stand with lions' feet at its base, specialized ceramic vessels including a funnel-based chalice designed to fit into a cult stand, two animal figurines and jewelry (Callaway 1993a: 45).

Khirbet Raddana

Khirbet Raddana was a Central Highlands village settled from the early twelfth–mid-eleventh centuries B.C.E. Four-room houses clustered into compounds were typical of this farming settlement. Evidence for metalworking was also uncovered. Variations in house size and configuration suggest a social hierarchy within the village (Callaway 1988: 82; 1993b: 1253; Cooley 1997: 402).

Two housing compounds, Site T and Site R, contained evidence for religious practice. Offering stands and stone-paved platforms for presenting offerings were found in several houses. Their discovery "suggests a cultic use in some form of family worship" (Callaway 1993b: 1253). A multi-handled *kernos*-style krater with bullhead spouts was used for cultic activities. Its unique hybrid style contained local and Hittite elements (Beck 1994: 376–79).

Tel Qiri

At Tel Qiri, a village on the slopes of Mt. Carmel, cultic material from the eleventh century (Stratum VIII) settlement was uncovered (Ben-Tor and Portugali 1987: plan 62). An interesting cultic assemblage was found in a building in the residential Area D (Ben-Tor and Portugali 1987: plans 627–34). This building, with three architectural phases, consisted of two main rooms. The front room, benched in the earliest stratum, contained a *maṣṣebâ* and a stone basin. The rear room, in which assemblages of cultic materials were found, was subdivided into two small chambers (Ben-Tor and Portugali 1987: 82–89; plan 29). Cultic finds included an incense burner, beads, a faience figurine depicting the god Ptah-Sokar, a double libation vessel and more. Five piles of bones were almost exclusively those of sheep and goats. They were mainly right forelegs, indicating specialized sacrificial practices similar to those in the Late Bronze Age Fosse Temple and later adopted by Israelites (Exod 29:22; Lev 7:32) (Ben-Tor and Portugali 1987: 89).

An unusual Stratum VIII/IX building was excavated in Area A_2 (Ben-Tor and Portugali 1987: plans 52–53). The Area A_2 building, the only four-room building at Tel Qiri, contained chalices, votive bowls and a cup-and-saucer (Ben-Tor and Portugali 1987: 90). While its size and contents indicate that it had a special place in eleventh century Tel Qiri, its function as a temple is uncertain (Gilmour 1995: 52).

Tel Qiri's poor state of preservation precludes full knowledge of its Iron I occupation. Several factors including the site's proximity to the long-sacred Mt. Carmel (B. Mazar in Ben-Tor and Portugali 1987: 90 n. 10) and the high percentage of chalices in the cultic assemblage (70+ chalices = 1%; Ben-Tor and Portugali 1987: 90) suggest that this village originally included more cultic places than are currently known.

Shechem

The story of Abimelech ben Jerubaal recounted in Judges 9 attests to the presence of a Canaanite sanctuary in twelfth century Shechem. The Temple of Baal-berith/El-berith (Judg 9:4, 27, 46–49) destroyed by Abimelech and his supporters has been identified with the Canaanite Fortress Temple 2b of Temenos 9/Stratum XI (Toombs and Wright 1963: 29; Toombs 1976: 59; 1979: 73). The large scale of this Canaanite sanctuary, known from archaeological excavations and biblical descriptions, is impressive, especially when contrasted with the typically rather small contemporary places of Iron I worship.

Tell el-ʿUmeiri

Several Iron I cultic sites were uncovered in Jordan. At Tell el-ʿUmeiri, two buildings were discovered inside the inner casemate wall. In one, the eastern room was used for food preparation and the other for domestic activities. The western room was paved with large unworked flagstones. A standing stone had been erected against the inner casemate wall, and a flat-topped boulder was set on the floor in front of it (Clark 1994: 146).

Tell es-Saʿidiyeh

A gap of a century followed the destruction of the LB IIB settlement at Tell es-Saʿidiyeh. In the mid-11th century B.C.E., a small bipartite building with well-made mudbrick floors was constructed in Area AA on the upper mound. A plastered offering bench with an inset niche stood along its rear wall (Tubb 1993: 1298).

Tell Irbid

Tell Irbid (Beth Arbel) was a walled site that spanned the transition from the LB IIB into the Iron I (Phase II). At this time, a public complex in Area C included a number of multistory buildings. One room contained storage vessels filled with food products. In another, Room 1, cultic objects included an incense burner, goblets, cup-and-saucers, lamps and a basalt stand. They were found on shelves along the rear wall of this cultic storeroom. The Area C complex was destroyed by a fire that left the rest of the tel untouched (Ji 1995: 127; Lenzen 1997: 181).

Summary: Iron I

The sacred places of the Iron I were eclectic. A pilgrimage sanctuary with buildings used for storage and safekeeping was used by settlers in the Central Highlands (Shiloh), but they or others also worshipped at another pilgrimage sanctuary, this one open-air (Bull Site). Worship also took place at a number of village sanctuaries (Hazor, Dan, ʿAi, Khirbet Raddana, Tel Qiri, Megiddo, Tell el-Wawiyat, Tell Irbid, Tell es-Saʿidiyeh, Tell ʿUmeiri). In most instances, a full description of the village sanctuaries is not possible, but several generalizations can be made.

Often, a cultic installation or sanctuary stood among domestic structures (Megiddo, Tell el-Wawiyat, ʿAi, Khirbet Raddana, Tel Qiri, Tell es-Saʿidiyeh), but in some cases was distinguished from them by its larger size or unique architectural elements. The cultic installation at Tell el-ʿUmeiri may be related to gateway sanctuaries, known from the Late Bronze Age and earlier. The association between cult and metalworking (Hazor, Dan, Megiddo, Tell el-Wawiyat[?]) is also interesting. The type of sacred places at which the Iron I settlers worshipped—small and simple—stands in contrast to the single large fortified Canaanite sanctuary (Shechem) of the same period.

IRON II: THE UNITED MONARCHY

Once a king was installed in Jerusalem, the constellation of sacred places at which Israelites worshipped began to change. Sanctuaries from the tenth century, the period of the United Monarchy, display an increasing uniformity as reflected in their architecture, in the cultic artifacts that they contain and in the choice of locations in which they were situated. The town sanctuary became the predominant place of worship in Israel but it also increasingly became a political tool of the monarchy.[32]

Jerusalem

No remains of the Solomonic Temple in Jerusalem have been found, but its existence, luxuriantly described in the Hebrew Bible, is undisputed. See, among others, Busink 1970; Fritz 1987; Meyers 1992; Bloch-Smith 1994; Keel and Uehlinger 1996: 167–73; Dever in press.

Megiddo

Two tenth century sanctuaries were constructed at Megiddo as part of a massive Solomonic building project (Stratum VA–IVB). Shrines 338 and 2081, like the two contemporary palace complexes (Palace 1723 and Palace 6000), were built of ashlar masonry, decorated with proto-Ionic capitals and situated so that their rear façades marked the periphery of the site (Ussishkin 1989: 170–72; 1993a: 78–79). In addition, domestic shrines with small stone altars were uncovered in residential structures on the east side of the city (May 1935: 12–13, pl. 12; Shiloh 1979: 149; Shiloh 1993: 1017).

Shrine 2081 was the forecourt or entrance hall in a large and solidly constructed building. Cultic objects carved from limestone include two portable horned altars, an offering table, a tall round stand and a tripod mortar and pestles made of basalt. Ceramic objects include a stand, chalices, juglets and other vessels. Burned grain and a bowl of sheep or goat astragali were found in a niche in the southwest corner. A doorway in the northern wall of Room 2081 led to a narrow stone-paved chamber, its entryway flanked by two *maṣṣebôt* (May 1935: 4–9; Loud 1948: 45–46, figs. 100–102). A large horned altar, similar to those found at Beersheba and Dan, evidently once stood in the courtyard in front of this sacred building. The thickness of the building's walls, the possibility that the ashlar doorway was capped with a proto-Ionic capital, the large horned altar in the courtyard and the building's location indicate that Shrine 2081's function was public rather than domestic (Ussishkin 1989: 170–72).[33]

Shrine 338, first excavated by G. Schumacher at the beginning of the twentieth century, was recently retrieved from archaeological anonymity (Ussishkin 1989; 1993a).[34] The shrine was located in the southern part of a larger structure. It contained an offering table and bench, and six cultic *stelae*, two of which were positioned so as to form the religious focus of the room. Its artifactual assemblage included basalt three-legged mortars with pestles, small juglets, square ceramic model shrines and a primitive male figure. Horned and round stone altars and a stone basin once stood in the courtyard. After the shrine went out of use, it was carefully filled in (Ussishkin 1989: 154–66, fig. 5; 1993a).[35]

Megiddo was the capital of an important Solomonic administrative district and therefore it was crucial that its royally appointed cultic personnel work toward national goals and provide supervision over religious practice. Shrine 2081 and Shrine 338 were built in conjunction with other Solomonic construction, as part of the royal strategy intended to create centralized Israelite worship in areas critical to the success of the monarchy. Private worship at Megiddo also took place in a number of domestic shrines.

Ta'anach

Like Megiddo, Ta'anach was first home to a small Israelite community in the decades of the Davidic monarchy. Occupation during the Solomonic period (Stratum IIB) was on a larger scale (Rast 1978: 21, 26–27). The architectural features of the Ta'anach Cult Structure were poorly preserved (Rast 1978: fig. 97a). However, its scale and contents, the good quality of its construction and its location near an oil installation suggest some kind of public usage, perhaps as a work area for the manufacture, storage and repair of cultic objects, by priests or by artisans working for them (Rast 1994: 361).

Among the objects associated with this subsidiary cultic room were iron knives, astragali, a figurine mold and ceramic vessels including some with specialized cultic functions. Two unique ceramic stands decorated with elaborate cultic motifs were also uncovered (Lapp 1964: 26–39; 1969a: 42–44; Rast 1978: 26–39). The iconography of the stand excavated by P. Lapp in 1968 has been the subject of much discussion. That it indicates the worship of a goddess is clear. Hestrin (1987a) and Dever (1990: 135–36) have identified her with Asherah, Smith (1990: 19–20) with Astarte (and perhaps Asherah, as well), and Keel and Uehlinger with Anat-Astarte (1996: 160). Whether the worship of Yahweh (Taylor 1988) or Baal (Hestrin 1987a) is also indicated has been a matter of some debate (see Smith 1990: 19–20; Keel and Uehlinger 1996: 159–60). Beck (1994) notes both local (Canaanite/ Phoenician) and northern (Anatolian/Hittite and north Syrian/Neo-Hittite) affinities in these two stands.

Lachish

Cult Room 49 was part of Stratum V, the tenth century Solomonic occupation at Lachish (Ussishkin 1993b: 905). It consisted of one small room with a low bench along its walls, elevated in one corner to form an altar. Small and simply constructed, Cult Room 49 was nonetheless outstanding as the finest building in this United Monarchy settlement.

As might be expected, the assemblage of sacred objects resembled those from contemporary sacred structures. A limestone four-horned altar and a basalt *maṣṣebâ* lay on the sanctuary floor. Other artifacts include ceramic cult stands and domestic pottery (Aharoni 1975c: 26–32). The pottery and faunal remains found in the sanctuary demonstrate that ritual there included making animal sacrifices, presenting food offerings and sharing sacral meals. The four-horned altar suggests that the offering of incense (Gitin 1989) was the only other cultic elaboration in Iron Age Lachish.

Although much smaller and less complex, Cult Room 49 retained the essential features of the traditional Canaanite "bench temple," such as that at Late Bronze Age Tel Mevorakh. A significant difference, however, was the absence of the *favissae* and refuse pits so common at the earlier Lachish Fosse Temples and at other sanctuaries of the Canaanite Late Bronze Age. This may reflect the economic priorities of the Israelite worshippers, who could not afford to discard containers in the rather profligate manner of their Canaanite predecessors.

Tel Reḥov

Tel Reḥov, south of Beth Shean in the Jordan Valley, was important during the time of the monarchy. The tenth century city was the first Israelite occupation of the site. The cause of its destruction late in the century is uncertain (Mazar and Camp 2000: 51). An open-air sanctuary stood on the edge of a spacious courtyard in the lower city. It contained an altar installation, made of a 1 m^2 platform of unworked stone, set atop a 3 × 3.55 m mudbrick platform. Four unhewn *maṣṣebôt*, similar to those from Divided Monarchy Tel Dan, stood on one side of the smaller stone platform. A limestone slab measuring 0.7 × 0.5 m and supported by five smaller stones may have been an offering table, set up in front of the mudbrick platform. A square ceramic cult stand with triangular windows, once probably four-horned, was found next to the mudbrick platform. It resembles two found at contemporary Pella. Chalices, a Phoenician-style painted storejar, an animal figurine and two female figurines, several seals and the head of a bronze bull figurine lay nearby (A. Mazar 1999b: 25–27; Mazar and Camp 2000: 44–45).

The courtyard contained ovens and other installations used for preparing sacred meals. A large quantity of animal bones, many of which were from wild goats, was found near the mudbrick platform. Elsewhere at Iron II Rehov, domesticated rather than wild goats were represented in the faunal assemblage, together with sheep and cattle. This simple open-air cultic center may have served the needs of a small community, perhaps an extended family living in that neighborhood (A. Mazar 1999b: 28; Mazar and Camp 2000: 44–45).

Tel Qasile

The destruction of Stratum X, the last independent Philistine city at Tel Qasile, early in the tenth century B.C.E., has been attributed to an invasion by David. Strata IX–VIII represent the settlement of the United Monarchy (first half of the tenth century-Shishak's destruction), during which time the Stratum X sanctuary was partially reconstructed. No cultic objects were found in Temple 118 (A. Mazar 1997b: 376). This poorly preserved structure was surrounded on three sides by a large plastered courtyard that covered the buildings of the previous era and functioned as a public piazza. The round stone altar and two ovens found in it were used for ritual purposes (A. Mazar 1980: 47–56, figs. 51–52; 1993c: 1211).

At this time, Qasile served as a port for the kings of the United Monarchy. The Stratum IX–Stratum VIII rebuilding of the earlier sanctuary indicates its continuing importance for the indigenous Philistine inhabitants of the city, some of whom worked for the new nation of Israel, which required their maritime expertise (A. Mazar 1980: 47–49; 1985: 127–28; 1990a: 389). Israelites also resided in Qasile at this time. Since nothing about the Stratum IX–VII sanctuary was incompatible with Israelite worship, it is possible that Temple 118, or at least its courtyard installations, were used by Qasile's new inhabitants as well.

Tell el-Ḥammah

Tell el-Ḥammah (ancient Hamath) is located at the southern entrance to the Beth Shean Valley. Excavations revealed evidence for a tenth century settlement, destroyed perhaps during Shishak's Judaean campaign. Two building complexes separated by a courtyard were uncovered on the L Terrace. The eastern building was used primarily as a center for textile production. It was found filled with beads, stone weights, wood spindles and whorls, bone spatulae, clay loom weights, textile remains, and seals and sealings. Room 406 in the western building contained a number of cultic objects including a *kernos*, a zoomorphic vessel, a multi-handled krater with four-legged animals in relief, a female plaque figurine, a faience amulet, astragali and a stamp seal. Some similar objects were found in the eastern building, as well (Cahill, Lipovitz and Tarler 1987; 1988; Cahill and Tarler 1993; Tarler, Lipovitz and Cahill 1986; 1991). While no actual sanctuary was uncovered on the L Terrace, cultic worship related to the textile industry has been suggested (Gilmour 1995: 95).

Tel ʿAmal

Tel ʿAmal, an Israelite farming village and textile center, was located in the Jezreel Valley not far from Beth Shean. Founded during David's reign (Stratum IV), it was incorporated by Solomon (Stratum III) into his twentieth administrative district. A three-room building with residential, textile and cultic activity areas remained in use throughout the United Monarchy. Religious artifacts found in it include votive vessels, a decorated bowl, chalices, a tambourine-playing figurine, a fenestrated ceramic stand, a cup-and-saucer lamp and stone cultic stands. A stone tripod was decorated with zoomorphic and botanical motifs (Levy and Edelstein 1972: 331–44, pl. 20).

Tell el-Mazar Mound A

The site of Tell el-Mazar is located in the Jordan Valley 3 km north of Tell Deir ʿAlla. Badly eroded remains of a late eleventh to late tenth century B.C.E. cultic site were discovered outside the bounds of the tel itself, on Mound A. It included at least three contiguous chambers bordered on the south by a large courtyard.[36] A stone bench lined two walls of the easternmost chamber, which also contained an embedded stone basin and a deep bell-shaped pit. Numerous late tenth century vessels, including two chalices and a fenestrated ceramic stand, were found in the eastern room, while several ovens and a stone table were set into the enclosed courtyard to its south (Yassine 1984).

Taken together, the installations, pottery and thick deposit of ashy refuse suggest that the courtyard was used for long-term public participation in religious ritual (Yassine 1988b: 120). While cultic artifacts suggest religious activities, the structure itself seems to have served multiple functions. Yassine, the excavator, suggests that the site may have fulfilled an economic role in food processing. A. Mazar notes the Mound A building's resemblance to the Solomonic Palace 6000 at Megiddo. In his opinion, if it was a public structure, it should be considered part of royal construction associated with the "official metal-processing activity" in the Jordan Valley. Related sites included Succoth (probably Tell Deir 'Alla) and Zarethan (probably Tell es-Sa'idiyeh), as suggested by 1 Kgs 7:46 (1990a: 390, 401 n. 21).[37] If so, then the Mound A cultic materials might be related to industrial production.

Beth Shean

Beth Shean remained under 20th Dynasty Egyptian control late into the twelfth century, perhaps as late as the reign of Rameses VIII (Stratum Lower VI). In the eleventh century the site, now returned to a "purely Canaanite" occupation, was renovated (Stratum Upper VI). It is to this era that the "Twin" or "Northern" and "Southern" Temples should be dated. As a tribute to the past (A. Mazar 1993a: 217–18; 1997a: 73), Egyptian *stelae* dedicated to Seti I and Rameses II, and a statue of Rameses III, were set up in the courtyard (James 1966: 152–53). Numerous cultic remains, including an extraordinary assemblage of cult stands, were found on the floor, while storerooms contained a number of large vessels (James 1966: 110–18; Ottosson 1980: 71–73). These cultic objects should be dated to the Stratum Upper VI occupation (A. Mazar 1993a: 221).[38]

After the destruction of the eleventh century Canaanite town, Beth Shean fell under the control of David and then Solomon (Stratum Lower V). During this period, the temples may have no longer served a cultic function, but instead met the administrative needs of the tenth century monarchy (A. Mazar 1993a: 222).

Summary: United Monarchy

A number of important United Monarchy era sites including Ta'anach, Megiddo and Lachish display a relative homogeneity of cultic artifacts, including similar limestone altars and ritual ceramic vessels. This suggests "the management of cult and religion by the emerging state society of the tenth century, whose integrating power also brought this aspect of social life under strong national influence, if not direct control" (Rast 1994: 361). Centralized authority over religious worship, and efforts to organize priestly groups or guilds (Boling 1992a: 1013; van der Toorn 1995: 2049), were outcomes of increasing monarchical control throughout the tenth century. While many sites continued to display a great deal of cultic variability, the occasional correspondence between their ritual objects and those at sites with greater monarchic or priestly control should not be considered coincidental.

Most cultic places of the United Monarchy (Megiddo, Taʿanach, Tel Reḥov, Tell el-Mazar Mound A, Tel Qasile, Lachish, Tell el-Ḥammah, Tel ʿAmal) other than the Solomonic Temple were destroyed late in the tenth century. The Egyptian pharaoh Shishak (1 Kgs 14:25) was the perpetrator at many if not all these sites. The destruction of those sites with significance for the Jerusalem monarchy (such as Lachish and Megiddo) is to be expected, but additionally Shishak may have targeted sites of lesser religious significance because they too were important for the royalty and were home to burgeoning priestly groups and skilled artisans.

Taken as a whole, the admixture of sacred places in the era of the United Monarchy underscores the complex interplay between religion and industry, between the "state," professional communities and private citizens, which was typical of religion in many phases of the Bronze and Iron Ages. The state sanctioned religious practice at some important sites, and therefore a certain degree of uniformity in structure and content is evident. Priestly control at these sites is likewise indicated. However, sacred objects from homes and graves (Bloch-Smith 1992) support what is intimated by rural cult sites; not all religious activities during the era of the United Monarchy took place in those sanctuaries that operated under royal sanction. Still, for the first time in the history of this region, an attempt to utilize religion in the service of the state occurred on a wide-scale basis and the consequence of this religious reorganization was wide-ranging.

IRON II: THE DIVIDED MONARCHY

Despite many biblical illusions to worship at *bāmôt* during the Divided Monarchy, only a few sacred sites from Israel and Judah from that era have been excavated. As during the United Monarchy, evidence exists for public and private worship, as well as for worship associated with industrial production.

Dan

There is no archaeological evidence for the late tenth century B.C.E. royal cult center which Jeroboam I is said to have built at Bethel (1 Kgs 12:29). His *temenos* at Dan was located near the spring at the northern edge of the mound (Area T).[39] Subsequent construction took place in the mid-ninth and early eighth centuries (Biran 1994a: 184–206).

In Stratum IV, an enormous raised platform constructed in several stages may originally have supported a sanctuary.[40] The ashlar platform (Bamah A), originally 18.5 × 9.0 m and later expanded, was surrounded on three sides by a beaten earth floor. Finds associated with this platform include seven-spouted lamps, an Astarte figurine, a four-horned altar, an incense stand, and three *pithoi* with snakes curling around them in high relief. An unusual installation containing a small rectangular pool and a large terracotta tub with a seat lay at the southern end of the complex (Biran 1974: 40–43; 1981: 144–45; 1994a: 162–74).

A second part of the 27 × 17 m *temenos* included a complex of rooms and an open area. It was there that the main sacrificial altar, measuring 7.5 × 5.0 m, was located. A decorated stand, the head of a male figurine and a bowl containing animal bones were found on the adjacent cobbled paving (Biran 1994a: 168–73). The small rooms near the altar, identified as the biblical לשכות (*lišākôt*), were used for religious, administrative and storage purposes (Biran 1985: 187–89; A. Mazar 1990a: 492–95).

An unusual installation, consisting of a large sunken basin flanked by two basalt slabs and two plastered jars, was found in the northern part of the sacred complex. The basalt slabs tilt in the direction of the jars and contain grooves designed to channel liquids into them. Nearby lay a group of stones with perforated ends. Four green faience figurines decorated with black dots and bands were found, one in each jar, one north of the basin and one a few meters to its southwest. According to the excavator, this installation was used for water libations (Biran 1980: 91–95; 1994a: 174–81), although others have suggested that it was a press for the preparation of olive oil for ritual purposes.[41]

In the mid-ninth century (Stratum III; reign of Ahab), the central structure was renovated and greatly enlarged. The beautifully constructed Bamah B measured over 18 × 18 m and was fronted by a courtyard paved in crushed yellow travertine. Additional construction took place over the area of the Stratum IV pool installations (Biran 1994a: 184–91).

In the early eighth century (Stratum II; reign of Jeroboam II–Tiglath-pileser III destruction), a monumental staircase was constructed on the southern side of the still-imposing Bamah B. The *temenos* wall was enhanced and a central altar was constructed south of Bamah C. The horn of a large ashlar altar that originally stood 3 m high, as well as a smaller horned limestone altar, was also uncovered.

Another small altar, this one made of five limestone blocks, stood in one room within the sacred complex. A bronze and silver scepter head was discovered beneath it. Nearby, a carinated bronze bowl, three iron shovels, a sunken jar filled with ashes and two travertine altars were also found. Another room along the courtyard contained a faience die, presumably used for priestly divination. Although the handle stamped with the name "ImmadiYo" was found just outside the *temenos* complex, its presence attests to the worship of Yahweh at the eighth century sanctuary at Dan (Biran 1994a: 191–210; Ilan 1997: 109–10).

Other interesting cultic finds were attributed to Stratum II. Not far from a beautifully constructed royal throne mount in the gateway area were "groups of small *maṣṣebôt* in small 'chapels,' altars, groups of complete pottery vessels presumed to have a cultic function, and more" (Ilan 1997: 110). One such shrine consisted of five unhewn stones set upright behind a bench or table, to the right of the outer gate to the city near the royal throne dais. Three similar shrines were uncovered, one by the inner gate and two along the wall outside the outer gate (Biran 1998: 41–45). The pottery found associated with these *maṣṣebôt*, both whole and fragmentary, included seven-spouted lamps, small bowls and incense cups. These gateway shrines (see 2 Kgs 23:8) were part of a well-planned path of entry into the city (Biran 1994a: 245; 1994b: 11), one that afforded the opportunity to make offerings to the city's god and to pay obeisance to its earthly rulers. The shrines outside the outer gate may have been used by people occupying the temporary shelters (חוצות; *hûṣôt*) just outside of the city (Biran 1998: 45, 70; 1999).

The royal sanctuary at Dan provided the apex, visually and spiritually, of worship in this ancient religious center. Indoor and outdoor rituals were enacted at the Bamah, within the *temenos* area, at the inner and outer gateways, and in more private locations. A priesthood with deep local roots, one closely allied with Israel's monarchy, officiated over the Dan cult.

Arad

At Arad, a tripartite-style sanctuary was constructed in the northwestern corner of the Iron II royal fortress. A large altar of unhewn stones topped by a flint slab with plastered channels stood in the center of its 10 × 10 m courtyard. This courtyard opened into a narrow bench-lined chamber, the first of its two covered rooms.

The second, interior room was approached by two steps. Two small limestone incense altars bearing residue from animal fat and two stone pillars flanked its entrance. A single smooth *stele* decorated with red paint stood on a small platform within the holy-of-holies. It was later replaced by two crude flint slabs.[42] Over time, the building underwent structural changes, including the addition of storerooms (Aharoni 1968: 19; Herzog, Aharoni and Rainey 1987: 28–29). The altars, and perhaps the *stele* in the interior room, seem to have been deliberately covered over (Dever in press).

Cultic paraphernalia including an eighth century ceramic stand decorated with a tree motif, a stone basin and the small bronze figurine of a lion were found in and around the sanctuary and its courtyard.[43] Two shallow bowls inscribed with the Hebrew letters *qop* and *kap* (an abbreviation for קדש כהנים [*qōdeš kōhanîm*], "set apart for [or holy to] the priests") were found at the foot of the stone altar. These late eighth century bowls were used to receive those portions of the offerings that were dedicated to the temple priesthood. Kilns found near the entrance to the sanctuary were part of the pottery workshop that supplied its sacred vessels (Aharoni 1968: 21–30).

A number of ostraca were found in the temple storerooms and in the associated debris layers. They bore the names of members of priestly families known in Jerusalem at the time of Jeremiah and Ezra,[44] as well as Yahwistic names including Eshiyahu and Netanyahu. They may have been used for assigning temple duties. Other ostraca bore administrative entries, noting payments made to or by the priestly families of Korah (also known from Num 16, 26:9–11) and Bezal[el] (also known from Exod 31:2; Herzog, Aharoni and Rainey 1987: 34–35).

All this evidence combines to depict a Yahwistic sanctuary in the royal fortress at Arad during the Divided Monarchy. In this, it finds a parallel with the roughly contemporary shrine in the Aramaean fortress at ʿEn Gev (Mazar et al. 1964; Kochavi et al. 1992; B. Mazar 1993). The Elyashib archive, including the reference to *byt yhwh* (the house/

temple of Yahweh) in Letter 18, should be understood to refer to the sanctuary at Arad rather than to the temple in Jerusalem (Ussishkin 1988: 155).

Unfortunately, the date of the Arad temple is uncertain. The tenth to late-seventh centuries B.C.E. date suggested by its excavators (Herzog et al. 1984: 4, and references therein; Holladay 1987: 257; Dever 1990: 20) has been questioned. One recent analysis suggests that the sanctuary was constructed early in the seventh century and destroyed a century later (see Ussishkin 1988 and references therein, particularly n. 45). More likely, the temple was, at minimum, used throughout the seventh century (Stratum VII–VI) and destroyed either late in the seventh (by Josiah) or early in the sixth century (by Nebuchadnezzar; Dever in press). Ultimately, "one can only state ... that a shrine had been allowed to be built and used in the peripheral fort of Arad during the later part of the Judaean kingdom till its final destruction" (Ussishkin 1988: 156).[45]

Beersheba

A number of cultic objects found at Beersheba indicate that a religious structure was an important part of this Iron II city. A large ashlar horned altar found in a secondary context (Stratum II) had evidently been used during the first centuries of the Divided Monarchy (Stratum III).[46] Its dismantling has been attributed to the reforms of Hezekiah (2 Kgs 18:4), although it is not possible to substantiate this archaeologically.

The original setting of the Beersheba sanctuary, including the courtyard in which the altar would have stood, is subject to debate (Aharoni 1975b: 154–56). One suggestion places the sanctuary on the spot of the later Building 32, the only building at Beersheba that was oriented east–west (Aharoni 1975b: 162; Herzog, Rainey and Moshkovitz 1977: 56–58). Another associates the altar with Building 430, southwest of the city gate (Yadin 1976a: 8). Zoomorphic vessels, animal figurines and a krater bearing the inscription קדש (holy) were found in several houses at Beersheba (Aharoni 1975a: 126).

Vered Jericho

An unusual and well-planned building at Vered Jericho was a late seventh–early sixth century B.C.E. fortress that guarded the road between

Jericho and the Dead Sea. The well-constructed building, built with a solid fortress-like exterior wall, was symmetrical. Beyond its well-fortified entryway lay an enclosed courtyard and two four-room houses (Eitan 1984). The presence of a cult place in the courtyard area is suggested by two unusual stepped installations (Shanks 1986: 30–34). Vered Jericho's strategic location and fortress-like plan underscore its official function for the Judaean monarchy.

Tel Kedesh

Tel Kedesh (Tell Abu Qudeis), located between Megiddo and Ta'anach, may have been the Kedesh of the Deborah story in Judges 4. After a period of abandonment, it was resettled in the tenth century B.C.E. Early in the ninth century (Stratum IV), Kedesh was reconstructed along a completely new plan. Protected by a defensive wall, the settlement now covered only the peak of the tel (Stern and Beit Arieh 1979: 5–6).

A single building with one large room was excavated. Its size and contents suggest sacred functions. Many jar bases were set into the floor near a four-horned limestone altar. A crude limestone figure was found nearby, while a stone paved courtyard extended south of the main hall (Stern and Beit Arieh 1973: xiv, 96; 1979: 4–6, 9; Stern 1993: 860).

Tell es-Sa'idiyeh

The late ninth to early eighth century B.C.E. walled town of Tell es-Sa'idiyeh in the central Jordan Valley may have been linked to Jeroboam II's renewed activity in Transjordan (Tubb 1993: 1296–97). Most houses were small and two-roomed, haphazardly set along narrow streets (Stratum VII). In contrast, Building 64 was a three-roomed house, the contents and installations of which suggest both domestic and cultic activities.

In one room, two basins were set into a plastered platform. An arrowhead lay on the platform and a ceramic tripod incense burner surrounded by ash and charcoal lay in one of the basins. Other finds include additional tripod incense burners, nine shells and the only four lamps found in this stratum (Pritchard 1985: 8–9, 77–80, fig. 177; Tubb 1993: 1296).

Objects typically associated with Iron Age sanctuaries, including portable limestone altars, ceramic stands and figurines were absent from

Tell es-Saʿidiyeh, complicating the identification of Building 64 as a sacred structure. According to its excavator, when Stratum VII Saʿidiyeh was abandoned its residents took most of their household possessions with them (Pritchard 1985: 10). The priests, too, would have saved the most valuable sacred objects by taking them from the sanctuary. Given its unique plastered platform and remaining cultic contents, it seems certain that one activity within Building 64 was the celebration of religious rites.

Kuntillet ʿAjrud

Kuntillet ʿAjrud was a mid-ninth to mid-eighth century B.C.E. caravanserai located about 50 km south of Kadesh Barnea. The site's location at the juncture of desert crossroads and the number of nearby wells explain its importance in antiquity. Two buildings stood on the top of the site. One was small, once "splendid" but poorly preserved and the other, large and well preserved. The larger (15 × 25 m) building was not a typical Judaean fortress but rather a well-defended hostel with an entryway sanctuary. It was small and consisted of two rooms, complete with plastered benches and side repositories. Its plastered walls were decorated with religious motifs and it contained a number of inscribed vessels (Meshel 1978). The religious expression attested in these drawings and inscriptions is marked by its syncretistic nature, including the worship of Yahweh of Samaria, of Baal and of Asherah (Beck 1982; Dever 1990: 140–49; Keel and Uehlinger 1998: 210–39 and references therein).

Hazor

Geva claims that in the eighth century, "the inhabitants of Hazor were simply not religiously inclined, and did not observe religious practices on a regular basis or in an institutionalized form" (1989: 110). However, an interesting assemblage of cultic objects was discovered there. These objects, including human and animal figurines and an ivory pyxis showing a man at a sacred tree, were found inside and in front of House 3067a in Area B. The location and nature of these materials led to the suggestion that the worship observed there was somewhat public, if unofficial, rather than an expression of private or domestic cult (Willett 1999: 205).

Jerusalem Cave 1

Jerusalem Cave 1, a man-made cave located on the eastern slope of the Ophel outside the walled city, was used ca. 700 B.C.E. (Kenyon 1974: 143). According to the excavators, this cave and a similar one in Squares A 11–12 "were most likely repositories or *favissae* for the sanctuary or possibly two sanctuaries in Area A" (Holland 1977: 154). According to Holladay, Cave 1 (and, presumably, the Square A cave) was used for religious rituals not in conformity with the nearby official Jerusalem cult. They were therefore physically removed from its sight. The difference between state and private religion is emphasized by the caves' cultic paraphernalia, which differ significantly from those found in sanctioned sanctuaries (Holladay 1987: 265, 274).

Samaria Locus E 207

At Samaria, Locus E 207 refers to a trench located some 635 m southeast of the city gate. It was dug to form and encircle a trapezoidal rock "island" which remained attached to the land by a narrow bridge on its western side (Holladay 1987: 257). The trench, 4–6 m wide and 2–5 m deep, covered an area of some 30 × 26 m (Avigad 1978: 1046). Partially cleared, it was found filled with pottery and cultic objects similar to those in the Jerusalem caves (Holladay 1987: 258) and dated to the eighth century B.C.E. (Avigad 1978: 1046).[47]

Holladay highlights the importance of Jerusalem Cave 1 and Samaria Locus E 207 for understanding folk religion in Israel and Judah. Both sites, and caves at Tell en-Nasbeh and Tell Beit Mirsim, were used intensively over short periods of time (1987: 280). Keel and Uehlinger elaborate further. Noting the "underworld type of milieu" suggested by the caves and the "massive use of cooking, eating, and drinking utensils," they postulate that the Jerusalem and Samaria caves were used for מרזח (*marzēaḥ*) meals, sacral meals related to the cult of the dead (1996: 348–49).

Household Shrines

Albertz comments upon the two "foci of identity" within Israelite religion, one official and one family-based. In his opinion, "both strata always stand in a historically changing relationship, but are distinct in terms of content, function and the degree of their institutionalization"

(1994: 19). This insight helps explain the dichotomy we have observed between royal and informal places of worship. However one further religious arena, that of domestic piety, remains to be explored. Worship within the home can generally be associated with the world of Israelite and Judaean women.

In her recent doctoral dissertation, Willett investigates *Women and Household Shrines in Ancient Israel* (1999). She documents enduring Near Eastern traditions related to personal gods and to their worship in household shrines. In particular, she demonstrates the importance of Asherah as a protective goddess whose worship by Israelite women was believed to invoke blessing and prevent harm.

Willett isolates domestic shrines in Israelite and Judaean houses at Tel Masos, Tell el-Farʿah (N), Beersheba and Tell Halif. These date from the tenth to the early sixth centuries B.C.E. These prayer corners contained special assemblages of ritual implements and furnishings, including incense altars and female figurines (1999: 101–65).

The documentation of these domestic shrines makes it clear that for the people, or at least the women of Israel and Judah, religion had important personal components (Albertz 1994; van der Toorn 1994). The state-sanctioned religion of the Jerusalem Temple and the *bāmôt*, and even the somewhat public but unofficial religion practiced in some locations, only met certain needs. Other significant concerns were allayed through the use of private shrines in people's own homes.

Summary: Divided Monarchy

The absence of standardization among places of worship in the Divided Monarchy highlights the fact that despite royal and priestly efforts, religion in Judah and Israel was not fully organized or imposed from above. Indeed both textual and archaeological evidence point to the eclectic forms of worship practiced by Israelites and Judaeans in the tenth through early sixth centuries B.C.E. Worship took place in officially sanctioned sites such as the Jerusalem Temple, Dan and Bethel, Arad, Beersheba, Vered Jericho, at less formal sites with some degree of public access such as Kedesh, Hazor, Tell es-Saʿidiyeh, Kuntillet ʿAjrud, Samaria Locus E 207, and the Jerusalem, Tell en-Nasbeh and Tell Beit Mirsim caves and in private, domestic locations.

Yahweh was worshipped,[48] sometimes together with Asherah. At the same time, people also engaged in numerous religious practices excoriated by the various biblical authors, such as child sacrifice, *bāmôt* offerings, incubation, necromancy and cults of the dead (Smith 1990: 124–38; Ackerman 1992; Albertz 1994: 186–95; Ackerman 1998; Bloch-Smith 1992: 147–51).

SUMMARY: THE IRON AGE

Befitting the amalgam of clans and ethnic communities that would soon coalesce into the nation of Israel, religion—and places of worship—in the Iron I were somewhat idiosyncratic, tailored to meet the customs and needs of individual worshipping groups. The testimony of 1 Sam 9:11–25 and 1 Sam 10:5 suggests that in this era, the word *bāmâ* referred to specific sacred places or structures either within or outside of settlements.

My examination of the remains of Iron I sacred sites has revealed the breadth of religious experience typical to the period. Pilgrimage sites could incorporate structures (Shiloh) or be little more than open-air sanctuaries (Bull Site). Small village shrines and cultic installations (Dan, Hazor, ʿAi, Khirbet Raddana, Tel Qiri, Megiddo, Tell el-Wawiyat, Tell Irbid, Tell es-Saʿidiyeh, Tell el-ʿUmeiri) point the way toward the sort of local religious practice that would come to typify the Iron II Israelite nation.

Continuity with the Late Bronze Age is apparent at some sites, in the continued use of earlier structures at Shechem and of traditional materials at Hazor, and Bull Site and others. While there is some evidence for the accumulation of wealth at the Shiloh storerooms, and of specialized religious groups such as the Shiloh and Dan priesthoods and cultic craftsmen, for the most part the simplicity of the Iron I settlements is mirrored in its sacred sites.

Extensive editing by the Deuteronomistic Historians has obscured the United Monarchy's policy of sanctuary construction, but such a policy actually fits well with what is known about David's and Solomon's empire-building stratagems. The tenth century sanctuaries excavated throughout Israel were located at sites with Israelite occupation during the Davidic era, even though sanctuary construction may not have taken place until Solomon's reign. The fact that these sanctuaries were often located in regions at some distance from the early Israelite core, regions which had only decades earlier been populated by non-Israelites, underscores the importance of the *bāmâ* sanctuary as a tool in Israelite nation-building.

During the United Monarchy, the sanctuary of the Iron I was reformulated into an institution of social and religious control, a means of forging national unification from the disparate elements of Israelite clans, other ethnic groups and the local conquered populations. The tenth century *bāmôt* were constructed as part of a well-conceived policy designed to place religious practice in logistically vital centers under the scrutiny of the royal administration, and to foster solidarity among the diverse elements which comprised the newly formed nation-state of Israel.

Given the Hebrew Bible's attestation to the legitimacy of the monarchical *bāmâ* in Yahwistic religion, to Solomon's construction of *bāmôt* in Jerusalem, to the role of the *bāmâ* as a place of service for otherwise disenfranchised priestly groups and to its function in meeting the needs of non-Jerusalemites, the description of the tenth century sanctuaries at Megiddo, Taʻanach, and Lachish as *bāmôt* seems appropriate. At these sites, standardization of cultic objects more than architectural conformity suggests the growing authority of priestly groups who operated with monarchical support. At the same time, people continued their traditional practice of congregating and worshipping at less official public venues (Tel Reḥov, Tel Qasile). The link between economic subsistence, small-scale production and the development of religious elites can be seen at some sites (Tell el-Ḥammah, Tel ʻAmal, Tell el-Mazar Mound A).

During the Divided Monarchy, Jeroboam I in the north and various rulers in the south, in pursuit of similar goals, continued to implement this earlier and very legitimate policy. *Bāmôt*, long since recognized as an institution of the state, were constructed at sites of special importance to the monarchy (Dan, Bethel, Samaria[?], Arad, Beersheba, and Vered Jericho). At the same time, worship took place in village sites (Kedesh, Tell es-Saʻidiyeh), along trade routes (Kuntillet ʻAjrud) and in alternative settings (Jerusalem Caves, Samaria Locus E 207, Tell Beit Mirsim, Tell en-Nasbeh, and the witness of numerous biblical passages). In addition, domestic worship was important, particularly for the women of Israel and Judah. In this way, the rather eclectic traditions of the premonarchical period merged with those of the monarchy, highlighting the texture and variety of the Israelite religious experience.

NOTES

[1] Since the completion of my doctoral dissertation in 1993, some material in this chapter was revised for publication (Nakhai 1994; 1999). It has been reworked for this monograph and is published with permission.

[2] Gleis echoes this perspective. In his recent book, *Die Bamah*, he identifies the *bāmâ* as an explicitly Iron Age phenomenon (cited in Barrick 1999).

[3] Note Torczyner's comment: "I have tried to show that 'bamot' are not 'high places' but sacred *buildings* erected, both on high as in low places." He suggested that the term *bāmâ* referred to a cultic building and to all the ritual objects found within it (1938: 30).

[4] See, for example, Macalister's interpretation of the Gezer High Place (1912: 381–406). His presentation of the standing stone installation at MB IIC Gezer as a Canaanite precursor of the biblical *bāmâ*, implicit in his very use of the term "High Place," was of lasting influence.

[5] See, for example, Biran 1981: 142–45. Here, he discussed the enormous stone platform from Divided Monarchy Tel Dan. P. Miller's description of the *bāmâ* as, minimally, "a raised elevation, platform, or mound often alongside or near a sanctuary and set up primarily for the purpose of sacrifices" incorporated the idea of platform with several others (1985: 228). Vaughan specifies two types of *bāmôt* or "cultic platforms." They are "truncated cones of some height; and low oblong ones which may also have had an altar standing on them" (1974: 55).

[6] See Yadin 1976a: 8; Haran 1981: 33; 1988.

[7] See, e.g., Albright 1957; 1969: 102; and *contra* Barrick 1975.

[8] See Dever 1994 and references therein.

[9] Kittel, a pioneer in the study of Israelite religion, considered the *bāmâ* to have been *the* place for the enactment of Canaanite cult. The later tendency of Israel to revert to Canaanite religious practices he likened to the allure of Catholicism ("pleasing both to the senses and to the imagination") over and against the "sternly ethical" Protestantism of the Reformed Churches. The latter, in Kittel's opinion, was closely aligned to the "serious form of worship" offered by the prophets (1925: 34–35, 146).

[10] Note the fascinating story of the transformation of W. F. Albright's "Conway High Place" at Petra into a round tower, following its re-excavation by P. Parr (Vaughan 1974: 37–39). Conventional wisdom has it that the large stone altar from Early Bronze Age Megiddo was a Canaanite high place, as were the small Middle Bronze Age sanctuary in Nahariya, the Area C Stelae Temple from Late Bronze Age Hazor and any number of other Canaanite-era sacred installations.

[11] See Catron 1995 for the suggestion that *bāmâ* and temple were synonymous. Thus, in her opinion, *any* Bronze or Iron Age sacred building could be described as a *bāmâ*.

[12] See Hurvitz 1993 for a discussion of similar terms such as אוֹצָר (*'oṣār*) and בֵּית־(הָ)אוֹצָר (*bêt [ha] 'oṣār*). He attributes the former to biblical Hebrew and the latter, construct form to the influence of Imperial Aramaic in the late biblical period.

[13] Berlinerblau's recent comment is helpful: "I would suggest that it would be best to structure future investigations around 'adjectived' Israelites—bearers of precise economic, social, sexual and geographic attributes" (1993: 17).

[14] Note, e.g., Aharoni's useful description of the Arad and other *bāmôt* temples as institutions "at the royal administrative and military centers dominating the [Israelite and Judaean] borders" (1968: 28–30).

[15] The following comments of Dever are appropriate:

> There seems to be a great deal of unnecessary confusion, not to mention skepticism, in our discipline about the use of social science "models" in archaeology. Yet a model is simply a heuristic device, an aid in interpretation and understanding the basic evidence. It is, if you wish, a hypothesis to be tested against the evidence, and if necessary replaced by one that is more useful as new evidence becomes available. A model is simply a way of framing appropriate questions. And without doing that *explicitly*, I would argue that we can never hope to convert so-called archaeological "facts" into true and meaningful data, data that can elucidate the complex cultural process in ancient Palestine (1993b: 107–8).

See also Yoffee 1982: 347–48.

[16] Two previous references are found in Priestly passages, in Lev 26:30 (in which Yahweh threatened to destroy Israelite *bāmôt*) and Num 33:52 (in which the Israelites were instructed to destroy Canaanite *bāmôt* as they took control of the Promised Land). However, there is no reason to assume the accuracy of P's claim that the *bāmâ* was an originally Canaanite institution since the Priestly authors wrote some half-millennium after the Settlement period that Num 33:52 allegedly describes. This verse is part of a polemical document that intentionally constructed its condemnation of Judaean religious practice by reference to the alleged religious apostasies of the Canaanites. In doing this, P either shared, or borrowed, DH's perspective. Either way, these references to *bāmôt* should be understood as anachronistic.

[17] See E. Mazar (1997) for a discussion of David's construction of a Jerusalem palace.

[18] See also Ahlström 1982: 15, 47–74. Boling suggests that the Levites, with their Mushite affiliation, were banished to Israel's north during the time of Solomon, as the Aaronite Zadokites established their own control over the Jerusalem Temple (1992a: 1013).

[19] The reference to the *bāmôt* of Baal in the Transjordanian Balaam story (Num 22:41) comes from the Elohist's text although the story may be derived from earlier epic material (Hackett 1987: 128). From this perspective, the mention of a *bāmâ* (or *bt bmt*) in the Mesha Inscription is interesting. This Transjordanian text described the mid-ninth century victory of Mesha, king of Moab, over Israel. To give thanks to Chemosh for recent victories, Mesha built (or rebuilt) a new royal quarter in his capital, Dibon. It contained a *bmt* for Chemosh, a palace, a walled acropolis and housing. Mesha set up his victory *stele*, presumably in the *bt bmt*, at which site the *stele* was discovered in the nineteenth century. The *bt bmt* itself has not been discovered, but it may lie under the later Nabatean temple (Pritchard, ed. 1969: 320–21; Dahood 1986: 437; Lemaire 1994: 33; Pardee 1997: 39; Tushingham 1997: 157).

The eighth-century prophet Isaiah also mentions worship at *bāmôt* in Moab (Isa 15:2; 16:12). Biran notes the close (although not necessarily amicable) relationship between Moab and Israel during these centuries (1981: 143) and this relationship may have extended to shared modes of worship.

[20] 1 Kgs 12:25 notes that Jeroboam rebuilt Shechem, making it his royal capital. Although Shechem of the early Divided Monarchy is known from archaeological excavations, Jeroboam's palace has not been discovered (Toombs 1976: 59). While Dan and Bethel served as the religious centers of Jeroboam's kingdom, a royal chapel inside his palace in Shechem should be expected, as well.

[21] The migration of the tribe of Dan to the Canaanite city of Laish is recounted in Judg 18:27–31. Judges 17–18 describes the Danites' theft of a פסל, a מסכה, an אפוד and תרפים. These objects, made of silver consecrated to Yahweh, were used in a sanctuary (בית אלהים) that had been set up in the home of an Ephraimite named Micah. A Levite priest (כהן) from Bethlehem, a member of the clan of Judah who had officiated over Micah's sanctuary, joined the Danites in their expedition of conquest. Once Laish was conquered and renamed, the Danites established a religious center there, setting up the פסל and establishing the Levite priest and his descendants as its cultic officiants.

[22] The Levites' alienation from northern religious institutions and from the monarchy is suggested by 2 Chr 11:13–17. This passage claims that some years into Rehoboam's reign, the Levites and their followers gave the Judaean king their support as an expression of their anger at Jeroboam for his rejection of them.

[23] For further discussion of the authenticity of the religious practices described in this passage see Dever 1994.

[24] The prophet Amos articulated this when he described Bethel as a king's sanctuary and a royal palace (מקדש־מלך הוא ובית ממלכה הוא) (Amos 7:13).
[25] The Deuteronomistic Historians linked the *bāmôt* of Josiah's reform (2 Kgs 23) with the forbidden cult "places" (המקמות אשר עבדו־שם) of Deut 12:2–3 (Barrick 1992: 198).
[26] A number of non-Israelite temples and sanctuaries dating to the Iron Age have been excavated. They include those of the Phoenicians (Tell Abu Hawam [Hamilton 1934; 1935; Balensi 1985], Tel Michal and its hilltop sites, Makmish and Area C [Avigad 1961; Herzog 1993; 1997], Tel Sippor [Negbi 1966: 8; Biran 1976; A. Mazar 1990a]; see also Stern 1990a: 32), the Philistines (Ashdod [M. Dothan 1993; Dever 1997b], Tel Miqne/Ekron [Iron I, T. Dothan 1990, Dothan and Dothan 1992; Iron II, Gitin 1993], Tel Qasile [especially Iron I; A. Mazar 1980; 1985], Beit Afula [Beck 1994: 352, 360 n. 25], Sarepta [Pritchard 1978; Markoe 1997]; and generally, Dothan and Dothan 1992; T. Dothan 1997), the Edomites (Ḥorvat Qitmit [Beit-Arieh 1991; 1993; 1997; Beit-Arieh, ed. 1995]), Geshurites (Beitsaida [Arav et al. 2000]), and the Aramaeans ('En Gev [B. Mazar et al. 1964; Kochavi et al. 1992; B. Mazar 1993], Tel Tayinat [McEwan 1937; Ussishkin 1966], 'Ain Dara [Abu Assaf 1990; Monson 2000]). The Iron I Canaanite sanctuaries at Shechem and Beth Shean are discussed within the body of this chapter.
[27] Many recent treatments of the Iron Age are available. For a discussion of the Iron I in Israel and Jordan, see Bloch-Smith and Nakhai 1999 and Finkelstein 1999; for Iron II Israel and Jordan, see Herr 1997b; for Syria, see Pitard 1987 and Dion 1995; for Phoenicia, see Lipiński 1995; for Philistia, see Dothan and Dothan 1992.
[28] *Contra*, see Fritz 1993: 185–86. Coogan suggests that the site may not have been exclusively cultic in function and was certainly not Israelite in proprietorship (1987b). According to Ahlström, the Bull Site may have been the cult place for a group of newly settled non-Canaanite people with northern, possibly Anatolian, origins (1990b).
[29] Zertal, the excavator of a twelfth century hilltop site on Mt. Ebal, describes the site as cultic. A number of installations, including what may have been the remains of a stone altar, were encircled by a stone wall. Among the artifacts recovered were animal bones. These, as well as biblical references to Joshua's altar on Mt. Ebal (Deut 11:29; 27: 4–8; Josh 8:30–32) have led some to conclude that this was a open-air cultic site, perhaps an altar sacred to the early Israelites (Zertal 1986/1987; A. Mazar 1990b: 348–50). Kempinski suggested that the search for Joshua's altar should instead take place on Mt. Gerizim, in the vicinity of the Samaritan Temple (1993: 237*). Finkelstein agrees that the Mt. Ebal site was cultic but dates it to an earlier period, since he identifies ninety percent of the potsherds as Middle Bronze Age (1995: 359). Others disagree with the cultic identification, suggesting that its central stone

installation was the foundation of a farmhouse or fortress and not an altar (Kempinski 1986; Dever 1992b: 32–34; Fritz 1993: 185). According to Coogan, the site was cultic in function, but may not have been Israelite, let alone the location of Joshua's altar (1990: 25–26). For a discussion of the difficulties in explaining the artifactual and architectural evidence on Mt. Ebal, see Gilmour 1995: 108–20. See Zertal 1993: 377 for a brief summary of the controversy.

[30] For an alternative location for the sanctuary, together with the suggestion that the sacred area was comprised of an enclosed courtyard with a tented tabernacle and outdoor sacrificial paraphernalia, see Kaufman 1988.

[31] According to its excavator, the figurine, a god, and the bronze pieces buried with it comprised a foundation deposit buried under the sanctuary floor at the time of its construction (Yadin 1972: 132–33; 1975: 257; so too Ahlström 1990a: 93). The figurine, originally Canaanite, may have originated in the debris of one of the Late Bronze Age temples at Hazor, been brought by Hazor's new settlers from their Canaanite homes, or acquired by Israelites from their Canaanite neighbors in the Galilee, or in the nearby Esdraelon or Jordan Valleys.

[32] According to van der Toorn, "Palace and temple were in many ways connected. So intricate were their links that it is often difficult to say where religion stops and politics begins and visa versa" (1995: 2049).

[33] Some have interpreted Room 2081 as a cult room in a domestic structure (Dever 1990: 134; A. Mazar 1990a: 499), while Kempinski suggests that the building housed a high-ranking government official (1989a: 187). In a much different reconstruction, Herzog suggests that the 2081 cultic materials originated in a gateway sanctuary, and were placed in this building for safekeeping when Megiddo was under military threat (1992: 251).

[34] Stern has refuted Ussishkin's reconstruction of Shrine 338. He suggests that Building 338 may have been a cult corner in an Israelite palace (1990b: 106), a suggestion with which Kempinski (1989a: 188) and some others (Ussishkin 1993a: 84) agree. Some place this building later in the Iron II, no earlier than Stratum IVA (Kempinski 1989a: 188; Shiloh 1993: 1012).

[35] Three stone altars and two clay cult stands attributed to Shrine 338 were found to its south, south of Building 10 (Fisher's "Astarte Temple"; May 1935: 4–11, pl. 1; Lamon and Shipton 1939: fig. 6; Ussishkin 1993a: 70; Rast 1994: 356). Originally attributed to the later Stratum IV (May 1935: 4–5; and see Kempinski 1989a: 92, 188), recent studies have demonstrated its setting in the Solomonic Stratum VA–IVB (Rast 1978: 25). Rast's suggestion that Building 10 was used for the manufacture, repair and storage of cultic materials supports Ussishkin's association of these cultic materials with Shrine 338. For a comparison of the materials from Buildings 10 and 2081 with the Taʿanach

Cult Structure, see Rast 1978: 25, 35, Table 1.

[36] A separate sanctuary has been reported, located within the city on the mound of Tell el-Mazar (Yassine 1988b: 120).

[37] The Aramaic Balaam inscription uncovered in Stratum IX (mid-late eighth century) at Tell Deir ʿAlla was found in a building that was otherwise used for textile work and domestic activities. Some architectural features and rare, luxury goods, as well as the inscription itself, suggest that special cultic activities took place there. As at Tell el-Mazar Mound A, they may have been related to industrial production.

[38] Alternatively, these *stelae* may all have stood in a Stratum VIa–Vb (Upper VI–Lower V) Egyptian complex. This complex, which included the temples, was probably constructed during the reign of Rameses III (Yannai 1996: 190–94, fig. 2).

[39] Egyptian New Kingdom cultic fragments suggest that Jeroboam I constructed his sacred complex on the site of a Late Bronze Age sanctuary (Biran 1998: 40).

[40] A. Mazar 1990a: 493; Stager and Wolff 1981: 99. The excavator suggests that Jeroboam's golden calf stood atop the platform (Biran 1998: 40). Alternatively, the podium may have been a raised platform upon which sacrifices were made. Holladay notes Bull's interpretation of a similar platform from Samaritan period Tell er-Ras as a sacrificial altar. Following Ahlström, he also cites *temenos* platforms depicted upon Phoenician coins (1987: 255 and references therein).

[41] The preparation of olive oil for ritual purposes was required by its use in anointing ceremonies, as fuel for sanctuary lamps and for offerings. It was one of a number of small-scale "industries" which typically took place within temple precincts (Stager and Wolff 1981; see also Ilan 1997: 109). Other such workshop activities included the casting of metal figurines, the preparation of ceramic vessels and figurines, and the weaving of sacred garments (Stager and Wolff 1981: 95–98). According to some archaeologists, the stone basin and large stone pillar located in an open area inside the city gate at Tell el-Farʿah (N) (biblical Tirzah) was part of a gateway temple (de Vaux 1976: 401–4; A. Mazar 1990a: 500). However, Stager and Wolff's study of the basin/pillar configuration suggests that it too should be understood as an olive oil installation (1981: 99–100; see also Dever 1990: 136).

[42] Noting the disparity in size between the two standing stones within the innermost room and the similar disparity between the pillars flanking its entrance, A. Mazar suggested that the large and small stones reflected Yahweh and Asherah respectively (1990a: 497; Dever in press).

[43] This lion was originally a zoomorphic weight. The imagery of Asherah as the "Lion Lady" has been well documented (Cross 1967: 13; Willett 1999: 251 and references therein; Dever in press).

44 These include Meremoth from Ezra 8:33 and 1 Chr 9:12, and Pashhur from Jer 20:1.
45 Given the uncertainty, it is not possible to link occupational strata at Arad to biblical narratives about Solomon, Hezekiah and Josiah.
46 Similar horns, once part of large ashlar masonry altars, were also found at Dan and Megiddo.
47 Two other Divided Monarchy cave sites, the extramural Cave 193 at Tell en-Nasbeh and a cave opening into Tell Beit Mirsim Courtyard NW32-12, also contained cultic artifacts (Holladay 1987: 274–75).
48 See Tigay 1987; Albertz 1994; Keel and Uehlinger 1996.

CHAPTER SEVEN
CONCLUSIONS

The goal of this monograph has been the study of Canaanite and Israelite religions. Archaeological evidence has been fundamental for this investigation. At the same time, the voices of the ancient texts and insights from the social sciences have been critically important.

This approach reverses that of the past century, during which time studies of Canaanite and Israelite religions have relied heavily upon written sources, in particular the texts from Ugarit and the Hebrew Bible. The growing corpus of archaeological data has often served as documentation for the texts rather than as an independent witness to Bronze and Iron Age religious practice.

Traditionally, studies have focussed upon religion as religion rather than viewing it as one aspect of culture as a complete entity. Indeed, "the conceptualization of religion as an integral and integrative part of society rather than as a discrete cultural expression, and as a component of sociocultural identity rather than as its sole foundation, has been slow to penetrate the scholarship of biblical religion" (Meyers 1988: 22). Here, the insistence of anthropologists and sociologists that the organization and practice of religion reflect multiple dimensions of society at-large has enriched our study. It has led us to focus our attention on sacrifice, which for Canaanites and Israelites was *the* primary religious rite, one well attested in Ugaritic texts and in the HB. Its importance surpassed that of an arcane series of ritual enactments, for sacrifice was "an institutional way in which ... social and religious life ... was both conceived and ordered" (Davies 1985: 161). Through its study, social structure and socio-political relationships can be seen. Our study of texts from Ugarit and the HB likewise underscored the multiplicity of worship experiences in Canaan and Israel as it validated the anthropological insistence upon viewing sacrifice as the quintessential religious ritual.

The importance of sacrifice was twofold. First, it provided the essential metaphor for expressing the relationship between the community at-large, its ruler and its god(s). As king and priest cared for their god(s) through offering sacrifices, so too did people provide for their leaders, both human and divine. These relationships had spiritual dimensions, but at the same time, their economic and psychological implications were not forgotten. In addition, sacrifice and the sharing of sacral meals provided the forum for the convening of the social group, at annual festivals or at special one-time events. Tribal or clan ties were solidified, covenants ratified, and kingship acclaimed and celebrated.

The role of religion in the Chalcolithic and Early Bronze Ages was noted. In the fourth–third millennia B.C.E., elite groups attained and maintained authority in part through capitalizing upon the importance of religion as a means of ordering society. In Early Bronze Age and Middle Bronze Age Syria, relationships were reflected in city planning. Evidence for royal cult and small-scale community worship was found in the layout of its many large cities and in their religious architecture.

In Canaan, the regeneration and development of the urban phenomenon subsequent to the pastoral interlude of the EB IV was a slow process. Religion in the MB IIA was characterized by its regional quality, as sacred sites were typically countryside pilgrimage sites rather than urban structures. The growth of these regional sacred centers was an important factor in the development of new tribal elites. These elites used religion to develop and maintain the social order by deploying local resources and providing symbols that assured the loyalty of local clan groups. Two religious traditions, that of the obelisk/*maṣṣebôt* open-air sanctuary and that of the fortress temple, both crystallized in the MB IIA.

Even in the MB IIB, the locus for organized religion was primarily rural. Eventually, however, those clan groups with Syrian connections that had dominated the Jordan Valley and its environs earlier in the Middle Bronze Age consolidated their position within the growing cities of the MB IIC. The alignment of fortress temples with palaces during this last phase of the Middle Bronze Age underscores this complex socio-political process.

Despite the military instability of the LB IA, the practice of religion continued along traditional lines. As Canaan began its process of recovery in the LB IB–LB IIA, new sanctuaries were built along trade routes and, even more commonly, within cities. The relatively swift regeneration of urban religious traditions suggests the increased solidity of the urban tradition as well as the entrenched power of the Canaanite royalty and priesthood and their firm control over religious matters.

As Egypt consolidated its authority over Canaan in the LB IIB, it usurped indigenous religious traditions in support of its own imperial demands. It is impossible to gauge the degree of cooperation supplied by various Canaanite kings, but the facile way in which Egyptians used native religion suggests complicity. This must have increased the alienation between kings and priest on the one hand and local clan groups on the other, and must have been in part responsible for the collapse of the Canaanite socio-political infrastructure at the end of the Late Bronze Age.

In the Iron I, much of Canaanite society reverted to its tribal components. In the absence of cities, worship took place at pilgrimage sites and in small villages. The wide variety of sacred sites highlights the individuation of many clan groups that would eventually join together to form the nation of Israel. The process of their consolidation was slow, however. Even united, these communities did not graciously submit to royal authority and to the centralization of worship required by the establishment of national sanctuaries in Jerusalem, Bethel and Dan.

In order to ensure clan loyalty, systems of *bāmôt* sanctuaries designed to control regional worship were established during the United and Divided Monarchies. They served to forge the nation of Israel from disparate tribal elements and ethnic groups, to involve local cultic leaders in the national religion and to provide sanctioned places of worship for people living outside the capital cities. At the same time, alternate forms of community and private worship took place at sacred places in cities and rural locations alike. All are appropriate for a region in which tension between clan and royalty was endemic and in which control over sacred sites and forms of worship had often provided the means for resolving this recurring conflict.

REFERENCES

Abu-Assaf, A.
1990 Der Tempel von ʿAin Dara. *Damaszener Forschungen* 3. Mainz am Rhein: Philipp von Zabern.

Ackerman, S.
1992 *Under Every Green Tree: Popular Religion in Sixth-Century Judah*. Harvard Semitic Monographs 46. Atlanta: Scholars.
1998 *Warrior, Dancer, Seductress, Queen: Women in Judges and Biblical Israel*. New York: Doubleday.

Ackroyd, P. R.
1985 The Historical Literature. Pp. 297–323 in *The Hebrew Bible and Its Modern Interpreters*, eds. D. A. Knight and G. M. Tucker. Minneapolis: Fortress and Atlanta: Scholars.

Aharoni, Y.
1957 Problem of the Israelite Conquest in Light of Archaeological Discoveries. *Antiquity and Survival* 2: 131–50.
1967 *The Land of the Bible: A Historical Geography*. Philadelphia: Westminster.
1968 Arad: Its Inscriptions and Temple. *Biblical Archaeologist* 31: 2–32.
1970 New Aspects of the Israelite Occupation of the North. Pp. 254–67 in *Near Eastern Archaeology in the Twentieth Century: Essays in Honor of Nelson Glueck*, ed. J. A. Sanders. Garden City, NY: Doubleday.
1975a Tel Beersheba. Pp. 160–68 in *Encyclopedia of Archaeological Excavations in the Holy Land*, Vol. 1, ed. M. Avi-Yonah. Englewood Cliffs, NJ: Prentice-Hall.
1975b Excavations at Tel Beer-sheba: Preliminary Report of the Fifth and Sixth Seasons, 1973–1974. *Tel Aviv* 2: 146–68.
1975c *Investigations at Lachish: The Sanctuary and the Residency (Lachish V)*. Tel Aviv: Gateway.

Ahituv, S.
1978 Economic Factors in the Egyptian Conquest of Canaan. *Israel Exploration Journal* 28: 93–105.

Ahlström, G. W.
1975 Heaven on Earth—At Hazor and Arad. Pp. 67–83 in *Religious Syncretism in Antiquity: Essays in Conversation with Geo*

　　　　　　　Widengren, ed. B. A. Pearson. Missoula, MT: Scholars.
1982　　　*Royal Administration and National Religion in Ancient Palestine.* Leiden: Brill.
1985　　　The Cultroom at ʿEn Gev. *Tel Aviv* 12: 93–95.
1990a　　Diffusion in Iron Age Palestine: Some Aspects. *Scandinavian Journal of the Old Testament* 1: 81–105.
1990b　　The Bull Figurine from Dhahrat et-Tawileh. *Bulletin of the American Schools of Oriental Research* 280: 77–82.

Albertz, R.
1994　　　*A History of Israelite Religion in the Old Testament Period, Volume I: From the Beginnings to the End of the Monarchy.* Trans. J. Bowden. Louisville, KY: Westminster/John Knox.

Albright, W. F.
1940　　　*From the Stone Age to Christianity:Monotheism and the Historical Process.* Baltimore: Johns Hopkins University.
1942　　　*Archaeology and the Religion of Israel.* Baltimore: Johns Hopkins University.
1943　　　*The Excavation of Tell Beit Mirsim: Vol. III, The Iron Age.* American Schools of Oriental Research Annual 21–22. New Haven: American Schools of Oriental Research.
1954　　　*The Bible after Twenty Years of Archaeology (1932–1952).* Pittsburgh: Biblical Colloquium.
1957　　　*The High Place in Ancient Palestine.* Supplement to Vetus Testamentum 4. Leiden: Brill.
1960　　　*The Archaeology of Palestine*, rev. ed. Baltimore: Penguin.
1963　　　*The Biblical Period from Abraham to Ezra: An Historical Survey*, rev. ed. New York: Harper and Row.
1966　　　Remarks on the Chronology of the Early Bronze IV—Middle Bronze II A in Phoenicia and Syria-Palestine. *Bulletin of the American Schools of Oriental Research* 184: 26–35.
1968　　　*Yahweh and the Gods of Canaan: An Historical Analysis of Two Contrasting Faiths.* Garden City, NY: Doubleday.
1969　　　*Archaeology and the Religion of Israel.* Garden City, NY: Doubleday.

Aldred, C.
1987　　　*The Egyptians.* London: Thames and Hudson.

Alon, D. and Levy, T. E.
1989　　　The Archaeology of Cult and the Chalcolithic Sanctuary at Gilat. *Journal of Mediterranean Archaeology* 2: 163–221.

Alter, R.
1981　　　*The Art of Biblical Narrative.* New York: Basic Books.

Amiet, P.
1980   *Art of the Ancient Near East*. New York: Abrams.

Amiran, R.
1981   Some Observations on Chalcolithic and Early Bronze Age Sanctuaries and Religion. Pp. 47–53 in *Temples and High Places in Biblical Times*, ed. A. Biran. Jerusalem: Hebrew Union College–Jewish Institute of Religion.
1989   Re-examination of a Cult—and—Art Object from Beth Yerah. Pp. 31–33 in *Essays in Ancient Civilization Presented to Helene J. Kantor*, eds. A. Leonard Jr. and B. B. Williams. Studies in Ancient Civilization 47. Chicago: The Oriental Institute of the University of Chicago.

Anderson, G. A.
1987   *Sacrifices and Offerings in Ancient Israel: Studies in Their Social and Political Importance*. Harvard Semitic Monographs 41. Atlanta: Scholars.
1992a   The Interpretation of the Purification Offering (חטאת) in the *Temple Scroll* (11QTemple) and Rabbinic Literature. *Journal of Biblical Literature* 111: 17–35.
1992b   Sacrifice and Sacrificial Offerings (OT). Pp. 870–86 in *The Anchor Bible Dictionary*, Vol. 5, ed. D. N. Freedman. New York: Doubleday.

Arav, R., Freund, R. A. and Shroder, J. E., Jr.
2000   Bethsaida Rediscovered: Long-Lost City Found North of Galilee Shore. *Biblical Archaeology Review* 26/1: 45–56.

Artzy, M.
1993a   The Bronze Age Anchorage Site of Tel Nami. Pp. 632–39 in *Biblical Archaeology Today, 1990: Proceedings of the Second International Congress on Biblical Archaeology, Jerusalem, June–July 1990*, eds. A. Biran and J. Aviram. Jerusalem: Israel Exploration Society and Israel Academy of Sciences and Humanities.
1993b   Nami, Tel. Pp. 1095–98 in *The New Encyclopedia of Archaeological Excavation in the Holy Land*, Vol. 3, ed. E. Stern. Jerusalem: Israel Exploration Society and Carta.
1997   Nami, Tel. Pp. 96–97 in *The Oxford Encyclopedia of Archaeology in the Near East*, Vol. 3, ed. E. M. Meyers. Oxford: Oxford University.

Asad, T.
1983   Anthropological Conceptions of Religion: Reflections on Geertz. *Man* 18: 237–59.

Astour, M. C.
1981   Ugarit and the Great Powers. Pp. 3–29 in *Ugarit in Retrospect: Fifty Years of Ugarit and Ugaritic*, ed. G. D. Young. Winona Lake, IN: Eisenbrauns.

Avigad, N.
1961   Excavations at Makmish, 1960: Preliminary Report. *Israel Exploration Journal* 11: 97–100.
1978   Samaria. Pp. 1032–50 in *Encyclopedia of Archaeological Excavations in the Holy Land*, Vol. 4, eds. M. Avi-Yonah and E. Stern. Englewood Cliffs, NJ: Prentice–Hall.

Avner, U.
1984   Ancient Cult Sites in the Negev and Sinai Deserts. *Tel Aviv* 11: 115–31.
1990   Ancient Agricultural Settlement and Religion in the Uvda Valley in Southern Israel. *Biblical Archaeologist* 53: 125–41.
1993   *Mazzebot* Sites in the Negev and Sinai and Their Significance. Pp. 166–81 in *Biblical Archaeology Today, 1990: Proceedings of the Second International Congress on Biblical Archaeology, Jerusalem, June–July 1990*, eds. A. Biran and J. Aviram. Jerusalem: Israel Exploration Society and Israel Academy of Sciences and Humanities.

Baaren, T. P., van
1964   Theoretical Speculations on Sacrifice. *Numen* 11: 1–12.

Bahat, D.
1978   Did the Patriarchs Live at Givat Sharett? *Biblical Archaeology Review* 4/3: 8–11.

Balensi, J.
1985   Revising *Tell Abu Hawam*. *Bulletin of the American Schools of Oriental Research* 257: 65–74.

Balensi, J., Herrera, M. D., Artzy, M.
1993   Abu Hawam, Tell. Pp. 7–14 in *The New Encyclopedia of Archaeological Excavation in the Holy Land*, Vol. 1, ed. E. Stern. Jerusalem: Israel Exploration Society and Carta.

Barkay, G.
1990   A Late Bronze Age Egyptian Temple in Jerusalem? *Eretz-Israel* 21 (R. Amiran volume): 94–106 (Hebrew), 104* (English summary).
1996   A Late Bronze Age Egyptian Temple in Jerusalem? *Israel Exploration Journal* 46: 23–43.
2000   What's an Egyptian Temple Doing in Jerusalem? *Biblical Archaeology Review* 26/3: 48–57, 67.

Barrick, W. B.
1975 The Funerary Character of "High Places" in Ancient Palestine: A Reassessment. *Vetus Testamentum* 25: 565–95.
1980 What Do We Really Know About "High-places"? *Svensk Exegetisk Arsbok* 45: 50–57.
1992 High Place. Pp. 196–200 in *The Anchor Bible Dictionary*, Vol. 3, ed. D. N. Freeedman. New York: Doubleday.
1996 On the Meaning of בית־ה/במות and בתי־הבמות and the Composition of the King's History. *Journal of Biblical Literature* 115: 621–42.
1999 Review of M. Gleis, *Die Bamah*. *Journal of Biblical Literature* 118: 532–34.

Barton, J.
1992 Source Criticism (OT). Pp. 162–65 in *The Anchor Bible Dictionary*, Vol. 6, ed. D. N. Freedman. New York: Doubleday.

Beattie, J. H. M.
1980 On Understanding Sacrifice. Pp. 29–44 in *Sacrifice*, eds. M. F. C. Bourdillon and M. Fortes. New York: Academic.

Beck, P.
1982 The Drawings from Ḥorvat Teiman (Kuntillet ʿAjrud). *Tel Aviv* 9: 3–68.
1989a Cylinder Seals from the Temple in Area H. Pp. 310–21 in Y. Yadin, et al., *Hazor III–IV: An Account of the Third and Fourth Seasons of Excavations, 1957–1958, Text,* ed. A. Ben-Tor. Jerusalem: Israel Exploration Society.
1989b The Metal Figures. Pp. 348–62 in Y. Yadin, et al., *Hazor III–IV: An Account of the Third and Fourth Seasons of Excavation, 1957–1958, Text,* ed. A. Ben-Tor. Jerusalem: Israel Exploration Society.
1989c Stone Ritual Artifacts and Statues from Areas A and H. Pp. 322–38 in Y. Yadin, et al., *Hazor III–IV: An Account of the Third and Fourth Seasons of Excavations, 1957–1958, Text,* ed. A. Ben-Tor. Jerusalem: Israel Exploration Society.
1990 A Note on the "Schematic Statues" from the Stelae Temple at Hazor. *Tel Aviv* 17: 91–95.
1994 The Cult–Stands from Taanach: Aspects of the Iconographic Tradition of Early Iron Age Cult Objects in Palestine. Pp. 352–81 in *From Nomadism to Monarchy: Archaeological and Historical Aspects of Early Israel*, eds. I. Finkelstein and N. Na'aman. Jerusalem: Yad Izhak Ben-Zvi and Israel Exploration Society and Washington, DC: Biblical Archaeology Society.

Beidelman, T. O.
1974 *W. Robertson Smith and the Sociological Study of Religion.* Chicago: University of Chicago.

1987 Sacrifice and Sacred Rule in Africa. *American Ethnologist* 14: 542–51

Beit-Arieh, I.
1987 Canaanites and Egyptians at Serabit el-Khadim. Pp. 57–67 in *Israel, Egypt, Sinai: Archaeological and Historical Relationships in the Biblical Period*, ed. A. Rainey. Tel Aviv: Institute of Archaeology, Tel Aviv University.
1991 The Edomite Shrine at Horvat Qitmit in the Judean Negev: Preliminary Excavation Report. *Tel Aviv* 18: 93–116.
1993 Qitmit, Ḥorvat. Pp. 1230–33 in *The New Encyclopedia of Archaeological Excavation in the Holy Land*, Vol. 4, ed. E. Stern. Jerusalem: Israel Exploration Society and Carta.
1997 Qitmit, Ḥorvat. Pp. 390–91 in *The Oxford Encyclopedia of Archaeology in the Near East*, Vol. 4, ed. E. M. Meyers. Oxford: Oxford University.

Beit-Arieh, I., ed.
1995 *Ḥorvat Qitmit: An Edomite Shrine in the Biblical Negev*. Monograph Series of the Institute of Archaeology, Tel Aviv University 11. Tel Aviv: Institute of Archaeology, Tel Aviv University.

Ben-Tor, A.
1992 The Early Bronze Age. Pp. 81–125 in *The Archaeology of Ancient Israel*, ed. A. Ben-Tor. Trans. R. Greenberg. New Haven: Yale University and London: Open University of Israel.
1997a Hazor. Pp. 1–5 in in *The Oxford Encyclopedia of Archaeology in the Near East*, Vol. 3, ed. E. M. Meyers. Oxford: Oxford University.
1997b Introduction. Pp. 1–14 in *Hazor V: An Account of the Fifth Season of Excavation, 1968*, A. Ben-Tor and R. Bonfil, eds. Jerusalem: Israel Exploration Society and The Hebrew University.
1997c The Yigael Yadin Memorial Excavations at Hazor, 1990–93: Aims and Preliminary Results. Pp. 107–27 in *The Archaeology of Israel: Constructing the Past, Interpreting the Present*, eds. N. A. Silberman and D. Small. Journal for the Study of the Old Testament Supplement Series 237. Sheffield: Sheffield Academic.
1999a Tel Ḥazor—1996. *Excavations and Surveys in Israel* 19: 2*–3*.
1999b Tel Ḥazor—1998. *Hadashot Arkheologiyot: Excavations and Surveys in Israel* 110: 4*–5*.
1999c Tel Ḥazor, 1999. *Israel Exploration Journal* 49: 269–74.

Ben-Tor, A. and Bonfil, R., eds.
1997 *Hazor V: An Account of the Fifth Season of Excavation, 1968*.

Jerusalem: Israel Exploration Society and The Hebrew University.

Ben-Tor, A. and Portugali, Y.
1987 *Tell Qiri: A Village of the Jezreel Valley, Report of the Archaeological Excavations 1975–1977*. Qedem 24. Jerusalem: Institute of Archaeology, Hebrew University of Jerusalem.

Berlinerblau, J.
1993 The "Popular Religion" Paradigm in Old Testament Research: A Sociological Critique. *Journal for the Study of the Old Testament* 60: 3–26.

Bienkowski, P.
1986 *Jericho in the Late Bronze Age*. Warminster: Aris and Phillips.
1987 The Role of Hazor in the Late Bronze Age. *Palestine Exploration Quarterly* 119: 50–61.

Bietak, M.
1979 Avaris and Piramesse: Archaeological Exploration in the Eastern Nile Delta. *Proceedings of the British Academy* 65: 225–89.

Biran, A.
1974 Tel Dan. *Biblical Archaeologist* 37: 26–51.
1976 Tel Sippor. Pp. 1111–13 in *Encyclopedia of Archaeological Excavations in the Holy Land*, Vol. 4, ed. M. Avi-Yonah. Englewood Cliffs, NJ: Prentice-Hall.
1980 Two Discoveries at Tel Dan. *Israel Exploration Journal* 30: 89–98.
1981 "To the God Who Is in Dan." Pp. 142–51 in *Temples and High Places*, ed. A. Biran. Jerusalem: Hebrew Union College–Jewish Institute of Religion.
1985 Notes and News: Tel Dan, 1984. *Israel Exploration Journal* 35: 186–89.
1994a *Biblical Dan*. Jerusalem: Israel Exploration Society and Hebrew Union College/Jewish Institute of Religion.
1994b Tel Dan: Biblical Texts and Archaeological Data. Pp. 1–17 in *Scripture and Other Artifacts: Essays on the Bible and Archaeology in Honor of Philip J. King*, eds. M. D. Coogan, J. C. Exum and L. E. Stager. Louisville: Westminster/John Knox.
1998 Sacred Spaces: Of Standing Stones, High Places and Cult Issues and Tel Dan. *Biblical Archaeology Review* 24/5: 38–45, 70.
1999 Two Bronze Plaques and the *Hussot* of Dan. Israel Exploration Journal 49: 43–54.

Bloch-Smith, E.
1992 *Judahite Burial Practices and Beliefs about the Dead*. Journal for the Study of the Old Testament/American Schools of Oriental

Research, Monograph Series 7. Sheffield: Sheffield Academic.
1994   "Who is the King of Glory?" Solomon's Temple and Its Symbolism. Pp. 18–31 in *Scripture and Other Artifacts: Essays on the Bible and Archaeology in Honor of Philip J. King*, eds. M. D. Coogan, J. C. Exum and L. E. Stager. Louisville: Westminster/John Knox.

Bloch-Smith, E. and Nakhai, B. Alpert
1999   A Landscape Comes to Life: The Iron Age I. *Near Eastern Archaeology* 62: 62–92, 101–27.

Boadt, L.
1992   Ezekiel, Book of. Pp. 711–22 in *The Anchor Bible Dictionary*, Vol. 2, D. N. Freedman, ed. New York: Doubleday.

Bolle, K. W.
1983   A World of Sacrifice. *History of Religions* 23: 37–63.

Boling, R. G.
1969   Bronze Age Buildings at the Shechem High Place: ASOR Excavations at Tananir. *Biblical Archaeologist* 32: 82–103.
1975   *The Anchor Bible: Judges*. Garden City, NY: Doubleday.
1982   *The Anchor Bible: Joshua*. Garden City, NY: Doubleday.
1992a Joshua, Book of. Pp. 1002–15 in *The Anchor Bible Dictionary*, Vol. 3, ed. D. N. Freedman. New York: Doubleday.
1992b Judges, Book of. Pp. 1107–17 in *The Anchor Bible Dictionary*, Vol. 3, ed. D. N. Freedman. New York: Doubleday.

Bonfil, R.
1997   Area A: Analysis of the Temple. Pp. 85–101 in *Hazor V: An Account of the Fifth Season of Excavation, 1968*, eds. A. Ben-Tor and R. Bonfil. Jerusalem: Israel Exploration Society and The Hebrew University.

Bourdillon, M. F. C.
1980   Introduction. Pp. 1–27 in *Sacrifice*, eds. M. F. C. Bourdillon and M. Fortes. New York: Academic.

Bourke, S.
1999   The New Pella Bronze Age Temple: The Largest "Migdol" Ever Found. *Occident & Orient* 192/4: 57–58.

Bourke, S. J., Sparks, R. T., Sowada, K. N., McLaren, P. B., Mairs, L. D.
1998   Preliminary Report on the University of Sydney's Sixteenth and Seventeenth Seasons of Excavations at Pella (Ṭabaqat Faḥl) in 1994/95. *Annual of the Department of Antiquities of Jordan* 42: 179–211.

Bright, J.
1972   *A History of Israel*, 2nd ed. Philadelphia: Westminster.

Brongers, H. A.
1977   Fasting in Israel in Biblical an Post–Biblical Times. Pp. 1–21 in

Instruction and Interpretation: Studies in Hebrew Language, Palestinian Archaeology and Biblical Exegesis, Papers Read at the Joint British–Dutch Old Testament Conference Held at Louvain, 1976, ed. H. A. Brongers. Leiden: Brill.

Brueggemann, W.
1992 Samuel, Book of 1–2: Narrative and Theology. Pp. 965–73 in *The Anchor Bible Dictionary*, Vol. 5, ed. D. N. Freeedman. New York: Doubleday.

Bull, R. J.
1960 A Re–examination of the Shechem Temple. *Biblical Archaeologist* 23: 110–19.

Bull, R. J., Callaway, J. A., Campbell, E. F., Jr., Ross, J. F., Wright, G. E.
1965 The Fifth Campaign at Balâtah (Shechem). *Bulletin of the American Schools of Oriental Research* 180: 7–41.

Bunimovitz, S.
1993a The Study of Complex Societies: The Material Culture of Late Bronze Age Canaan as a Case Study. Pp. 443–51 in *Biblical Archaeology Today, 1990: Proceedings of the Second International Congress on Biblical Archaeology, Jerusalem, June–July 1990*, eds. A. Biran and J. Aviram. Jerusalem: Israel Exploration Society and Israel Academy of Sciences and Humanities.

1993b The Changing Shape of Power in Bronze Age Canaan. Pp. 142–49 in *Biblical Archaeology Today, 1990: Proceedings of the Second International Congress on Biblical Archaeology: Pre-Congress Symposium: Population, Production and Power, Jerusalem, June 1990, Supplement*, eds. A. Biran and J. Aviram. Jerusalem: Israel Exploration Society.

1995 On the Edge of Empires—Late Bronze Age (1500–1200 BCE). Pp. 320–29 in *The Archaeology of Society in the Holy Land*, ed. T. E. Levy. London: Leicester University.

Burkert, W.
1983 *Homo Necans: The Anthropology of Ancient Greek Sacrificial Ritual and Myth*. Berkeley: University of California.

Burrows, M.
1941 *What Mean These Stones? The Significance of Archaeology for Biblical Studies*. New Haven: American Schools of Oriental Research.

Busink, T. A.
1970 *Der Tempel von Jerusalem: Von Salomo bis Herodes, Vol. 1, Der Tempel Salomo*. Leiden: Brill.

Cahill, J. and Tarler, D.
1993 Ḥammah, Tell el-. Pp. 561–62 in *The New Encyclopedia of*

Archaeological Excavation in the Holy Land, Vol. 2, ed. E. Stern. Jerusalem: Israel Exploration Society and Carta.

Cahill, J., Lipovich, G. and Tarler, D.
1987   Tell el-Ḥammah, 1985–1987. *Israel Exploration Journal* 37: 280–83.
1988   Tell el-Ḥammah, 1988. *Israel Exploration Journal* 38: 191–94.

Callaway, J. A.
1966   The Emerging Role of Biblical Archaeology. *Review and Expositor* 63: 199–209.
1988   The Settlement in Canaan: The Period of the Judges. Pp. 53–84 in *Ancient Israel: A Short History from Abraham to the Roman Destruction of the Temple*, ed. H. Shanks. Englewood Cliffs, NJ: Prentice–Hall and Washington, DC: Biblical Archaeology Society.
1993a   Ai. Pp. 39–45 *The New Encyclopedia of Archaeological Excavation in the Holy Land*, Vol. 1, ed. E. Stern. Jerusalem: Israel Exploration Society and Carta.
1993b   Raddana, Khirbet. Pp. 1253–54 in *The New Encyclopedia of Archaeological Excavation in the Holy Land*, Vol. 4, ed. E. Stern. Jerusalem: Israel Exploration Society and Carta.

Callot, O.
1983   *Une maison à Ougarit: Etude d'architecture domestique*. Paris: Editions Recherche sur les Civilisations.

Campbell, E. F.
1993   Shechem: Tell Balatâh. Pp. 1345–54 in *The New Encyclopedia of Archaeological Excavation in the Holy Land*, Vol. 4, ed. E. Stern. Jerusalem: Israel Exploration Society and Carta.

Campbell, E. F., Jr. and Wright, G. E.
1969   Tribal League Shrines in Amman and Shechem. *Biblical Archaeologist* 32: 104–16.

Carroll, M. P.
1985   One More Time: Leviticus Revisited. Pp. 117–26 in *Anthropological Approaches to the Old Testament*, ed. B. Lang. Issues in Religion and Theology 8. Philadelphia: Fortress.

Carter, C. E.
1996   A Discipline in Transition: The Contribution of the Social Sciences to the Study of the Hebrew Bible. Pp. 3–36 in *Community, Identity, and Ideology: Social Sciences Approaches to the Hebrew Bible*, eds. C. E. Carter and C. L. Meyers. Sources for Biblical and Theological Study 6. Winona Lake, IN: Eisenbrauns.

Carter, C. E. and Meyers, C. L., eds.
1996   *Community, Identity, and Ideology: Social Sciences Approaches*

to the Hebrew Bible. Sources for Biblical and Theological Study 6. Winona Lake, IN: Eisenbrauns.

Catron, J. E.
1995 Temple and *bāmāh*: Some Considerations. Pp. 150–65 in *The Pitcher Is Broken: Memorial Essays for Gösta W. Ahlström*, eds. S. W. Holloway and L. K. Handy. Journal for the Study of the Old Testament Supplement Series 190. Sheffield: JSOT.

Chambon, A.
1984 *Tell el-Far'ah I: L'âge du fer.* Paris: Editions Recherche sur les Civilisations.

Childs, B.
1986 *Old Testament Theology in a Canonical Context.* Philadelphia: Fortress.

Clamer, C.
1980 A Gold Plaque from Tel Lachish. *Tel Aviv* 7: 152–62.

Clark, D. R.
1994 The Iron I Western Defense System at Tell el-'Umeiri, Jordan. *Biblical Archaeologist* 57: 138–48.

Clarke, D. L.
1968 *Analytical Archaeology.* London: Methuen.

Cole, D. P.
1984 *Shechem I: The Middle Bronze IIB Pottery.* Winona Lake, IN: American Schools of Oriental Research/Eisenbrauns.

Cole, S. G.
1985 Archaeology and Religion. Pp. 49–59 in *Contributions to Aegean Archaeology: Studies in Honor of William A. McDonald*, eds. N. C. Wilkie and W. D. E. Coulson. Publications in Ancient Studies. Minneapolis: Center for Ancient Studies, University of Minnesota.

Coogan, M.
1978 *Stories from Ancient Canaan.* Philadelphia: Westminster.
1987a Canaanite Origins and Lineage: Reflections on the Religion of Ancient Israel. Pp. 115–24 in *Ancient Israelite Religion: Essays in Honor of Frank Moore Cross*, eds. P. D. Miller, Jr., P. D. Hanson and S. D. McBride. Philadelphia: Fortress.
1987b Of Cults and Cultures: Reflections on the Interpretation of Archaeological Evidence. *Palestine Exploration Quarterly* 119: 1–8.
1990 Archaeology and Biblical Studies: The Book of Joshua. Pp. 19–32 in *The Hebrew Bible and Its Interpreters*, eds. W. H. Propp and D. N. Freedman. Biblical and Judaic Studies from The University of California, San Diego 1. Winona Lake, IN: Eisenbrauns.

Cook, S. A.
1908 *The Religion of Ancient Palestine in the Second Millennium B.C. in the Light of Archaeology and the Inscriptions*. London: Constable.
1930 *The Religion of Ancient Palestine in the Light of Archaeology*. London: British Academy.

Cooley, R. E.
1997 Radannah. Pp. 401–2 in *The Oxford Encyclopedia of Archaeology in the Near East*, Vol. 4, ed. E. M. Meyers. Oxford: Oxford University.

Cross, F. M.
1967 The Origin and Early Evolution of the Alphabet. *Eretz-Israel* 8 (E. Sukenik volume): 8*–24* (English).
1973 *Canaanite Myth and Hebrew Epic: Essays in the History of the Religion of Israel*. Cambridge, MA: Harvard University.
1984 An Old Canaanite Inscription Recently Found at Lachish. *Tel Aviv* 11: 71–76.
1998 *From Epic to Canon: History and Literature in Ancient Israel*. Baltimore: Johns Hopkins University.

Cross, F. M. and Milik, J. T.
1954 Inscribed Javelin–Heads from the Period of the Judges: A Recent Discovery in Palestine. *Bulletin of the American Schools of Oriental Research* 134: 5–15.

Dahood, M.
1986 The Moabite Stone and Northwest Semitic Philology. Pp. 429–41 in *The Archaeology of Jordan and Other Studies*, eds. L. T. Geraty and L. G. Herr. Berrien Springs, MI: Andrews University.

Daviau, P. M. M.
1993 *Houses and Their Furnishings in Bronze Age Palestine: Domestic Activity Areas and Artefact Distribution in the Middle and Late Bronze Ages*. Sheffield: Sheffield Academic/JSOT.

Davies, D.
1985 An Interpretation of Sacrifice in Leviticus. Pp. 151–62 in *Anthropological Approaches to the Old Testament*, ed. B. Lang. Issues in Religion and Theology 8. Philadelphia: Fortress.

Davies, G. I.
1986 *Megiddo*. Cities of the Biblical World. Cambridge: Lutterworth.

Day, John
1992 Canaan, Religion of. Pp. 831–37 in *The Anchor Bible Dictionary*, Vol. 1, ed. D. N. Freedman. New York: Doubleday.

Detienne, M.
1989 Culinary Practices and the Spirit of Sacrifice. Pp. 1–20 in *The*

Cuisine of Sacrifice among the Greeks, eds. M. Detienne and J.-P. Vernant. Chicago: University of Chicago.

Dever, W. G.

1971   Archaeological Methods and Results: A Review of Two Recent Publications. *Orientalia* 40: 459–71.

1973   The Gezer Fortifications and the "High Place": An Illustration of Stratigraphic Methods and Problems. *Palestine Exploration Quarterly* 61–70.

1974   *Archaeology and Biblical Studies: Retrospects and Prospects.* Evanston, IL: Seabury Western Theological Seminary.

1976a Gezer. Pp. 428–43 in *Encyclopedia of Archaeological Excavations in the Holy Land*, Vol. 2, ed. M. Avi-Yonah. Englewood Cliffs, NJ: Prentice–Hall.

1976b The Beginning of the Middle Bronze Age in Syria-Palestine. Pp. 3–38 in *Magnalia Dei, The Mighty Acts of God: Essays on the Bible and Archaeology in Memory of G. Ernest Wright*, eds. F. M. Cross, W. E. Lemke and P. D. Miller. Garden City, NY: Doubleday.

1977   The Patriarchal Traditions. Pp. 70–120 in *Israelite and Judaean History*, eds. J. H. Hayes and M. J. Miller. London: SCM.

1980   New Vistas on the EB IV ("MB I") Horizon in Syria-Palestine. *Bulletin of the American Schools of Oriental Research* 237: 35–64.

1983   Material Remains and the Cult in Ancient Israel: An Essay in Archaeological Systematics. Pp. 571–87 in *The Word of the Lord Shall Go Forth: Essays in Honor of David Noel Freedman in Celebration of His Sixtieth Birthday*, eds. C. L. Meyers and M. O'Connor. Winona Lake, IN: American Schools of Oriental Research/Eisenbrauns.

1984   Asherah, Consort of Yahweh? New Evidence from Kuntillet ʿAjrud. *Bulletin of the American Schools of Oriental Research* 255: 21–37.

1985a Relations Between Syria-Palestine and Egypt in the "Hyksos" Period. Pp. 69–87 in *Palestine in the Bronze and Iron Ages: Papers in Honour of Olga Tufnell*, ed. J. N. Tubb. London: Institute of Archaeology.

1985b Syro–Palestinian and Biblical Archaeology. Pp. 31–74 in *The Hebrew Bible and Its Modern Interpreters*, eds. D. A. Knight and G. M. Tucker. Philadelphia: Fortress and Atlanta: Scholars.

1987a The Contribution of Archaeology to the Study of Canaanite and Early Israelite Religion. Pp. 209–47 in *Ancient Israelite Religion*, eds. P. D. Miller, Jr., P. D. Hanson and S. D. McBride. Philadelphia: Fortress.

1987b	The Middle Bronze Age: The Zenith of the Urban Canaanite Era. *Biblical Archaeologist* 50: 148–77.
1988	The Impact of the "New Archaeology." Pp. 337–57 in *Benchmarks in Time and Culture: An Introduction to Biblical Archaeology*, eds. J. F. Drinkard, G. L. Mattingly and J. M. Miller. Atlanta: Scholars.
1989	Review of J. Mallet, *Tell el-Far'ah II, 1; 2: Le Bronze Moyen. Paleorient* 15/2: 146.
1990	*Recent Archaeological Discoveries and Biblical Research.* Seattle and London: University of Washington.
1991	Archaeology, Ideology, and the Quest for an "Ancient" or "Biblical" Israel. *Near Eastern Archaeology* 61: 39–52.
1992a	The Chronology of Syria-Palestine in the Second Millennium B.C.E.: A Review of Current Issues. *Bulletin of the American Schools of Oriental Research* 288: 1–25.
1992b	How to Tell a Canaanite from an Israelite. Pp. 27–60 in *The Rise of Ancient Israel*, eds. H. Shanks, W. G. Dever, B. Halpern, P. K. McCarter, Jr. Washington, DC: Biblical Archaeology Society.
1992c	Palaces and Temples in Canaan and Ancient Israel. Pp. 605–14 in *Civilizations of the Ancient Near East*, Vol. 1, ed. J. M. Sasson. New York: Scribner's.
1993a	Biblical Archaeology: Death and Rebirth. Pp. 706–22 in *Biblical Archaeology Today, 1990: Proceedings of the Second International Congress on Biblical Archaeology, Jerusalem, June–July 1990*, eds. A. Biran and J. Aviram. Jerusalem: Israel Exploration Society and Israel Academy of Sciences and Humanities.
1993b	The Rise of Complexity in Palestine in the Early Second Millennium B.C.E. Pp. 98–109 in *Biblical Archaeology Today, 1990: Proceedings of the Second International* Congress *on Biblical Archaeology: Pre-Congress Symposium: Population, Production and Power, Jerusalem, June 1990, Supplement*, eds. A. Biran and J. Aviram. Jerusalem: Israel Exploration Society.
1994	The Silence of the Text: An Archaeological Commentary on 2 Kings 23. Pp. 143–68 in *Scripture and Other Artifacts: Essays on the Bible and Archaeology in Honor of Philip J. King*, eds. M. D. Coogan, J. C. Exum and L. E. Stager. Louisville: Westminster/ John Knox.
1995	Social Structure in the Early Bronze IV Period in Palestine. Pp. 282–96 in *The Archaeology of Society in the Holy Land*, ed. T. E. Levy. London: Leicester University.
1997a	Abu Hawam, Tel. P. 9 in *The Oxford Encyclopedia of*

	Archaeology in the Near East, Vol. 1, ed. E. M. Meyers. Oxford: Oxford University.
1997b	Ashdod. Pp. 219–20 in *The Oxford Encyclopedia of Archaeology in the Near East*, Vol. 1, ed. E. M. Meyers. Oxford: Oxford University.
1997c	Gezer. Pp. 396–400 in *The Oxford Encyclopedia of Archaeology in the Near East*, Vol. 2, ed. E. M. Meyers. Oxford: Oxford University.
1998	What Did the Biblical Writers Know, and When Did They Know It? Pp. 241–57 in *Hesed ve–Emet: Studies in Honor of Ernest S. Frerichs*, eds. J. Magness and S. Gitin. Atlanta: Scholars.
in press	Were There Temples in Ancient Israel? The Archaeological Evidence. *Text, Artifact and Image: Revealing Ancient Israelite Religion*, ed. T. J. Lewis. Philadelphia: University of Pennsylvania.

Dion, P. E.

1995	Aramaean Tribes and Nations of First–Millennium Westren Asia. Pp. 1281–94 in *Civilizations of the Ancient Near East*, Vol. 2, ed. J. M. Sasson. New York: Scribner's.

Dornemann, R.

1981	The Excavations at Ras Shamra and Their Place in the Current Archaeological Picture of Ancient Syria. Pp. 59–69 in *Ugarit in Retrospect: Fifty Years of Ugarit and Ugaritic*, ed. G. D. Young. Winona Lake, IN: Eisenbrauns.

Dothan, M.

1957	Some Aspects of Religious Life in Palestine during the Hyksos Rule. Pp. 121–30 in *The Holy Land: New Light on the Prehistory and Early History of Israel*. Antiquity and Survival 2: 2–3. The Hague and Jerusalem: Hebrew University and Israel Exploration Society.
1959	Tel Mor (Tell Kheidar). *Israel Exploration Journal* 9: 271–72.
1960	Tel Mor (Tell Kheidar). *Israel Exploration Journal* 10: 123–25.
1977a	Mor, Tel. Pp. 889–90 in *Encyclopedia of Archaeological Excavations in the Holy Land*, Vol. 3, eds. M. Avi-Yonah and E. Stern. Englewood Cliffs, NJ: Prentice–Hall.
1977b	Nahariya. Pp. 908–12 in *Encyclopedia of Archaeological Excavations in the Holy Land*, Vol. 3, eds. M. Avi-Yonah and E. Stern. Englewood Cliffs, NJ: Prentice–Hall.
1979	Ashdod at the End of the Late Bronze Age and the Beginning of the Iron Age. Pp. 125–34 in *Symposia Celebrating the Seventy-Fifth Anniversary of the Founding of the American Schools of Oriental Research (1900–1975)*, ed. F. M. Cross. Cambridge,

MA: American Schools of Oriental Research.
1981 Sanctuaries along the Coast of Canaan in the MB Period: Nahariyah. Pp. 74–81 in *Temples and High Places in Biblical Times*, ed. A. Biran. Jerusalem: Hebrew Union College-Jewish Institute of Religion.
1993 Ashdod. Pp. 93–102 in *The New Encyclopedia of Archaeological Excavation in the Holy Land*, Vol. 1, ed. E. Stern. Jerusalem: Israel Exploration Society and Carta.

Dothan, T.
1990 Ekron of the Philistines, Part I: Where They Came From, How They Settled Down, and the Place They Worshipped In. *Biblical Archaeology Review* 16/1: 26–36.
1997 Philistines: Early Philistines. Pp. 310–11 in *The Oxford Encyclopedia of Archaeology in the Near East*, Vol. 4, ed. E. M. Meyers. Oxford: Oxford University.

Dothan, T. and Dothan, M.
1992 *People of the Sea: The Search for the Philistines*. New York: Macmillan.

Douglas, M.
1969 *Purity and Danger: An Analysis of Concepts of Pollution and Taboo*, 2nd ed. London: Routledge and Kegan Paul.
1975 *Implicit Meanings: Essays in Anthropology*. London: Routledge and Kegan Paul.

Driver, S. R.
1909 *Modern Research as Illustrating the Bible*. London: Oxford University.

Dunand, M.
1982 Byblos et ses temples après la pénétration amorite. Pp. 195–201 in *Mesopotamien und seine Nachbarn*, Vol. 1, *XXV Rencontre Assyriologique Internationale Berlin, 1978*, eds. H.-J. Nissen and J. Renger. Berlin: Dietrich Reimer.

Durkheim, E.
1915 *Elementary Forms of Religious Life*. London: George Allen and Unwin.

Eisenberg, E.
1977 The Temples at Tell Kittan. *Biblical Archaeologist* 40: 77–81.
1981 The Middle and Late Bronze Age Temples at Tel Kittan. P. 159 in *Temples and High Places in Biblical Times*, ed. A. Biran. Jerusalem: Hebrew Union College–Jewish Institute of Religion.
1993 Kitan, Tel. Pp. 878–81 in *The New Encyclopedia of Archaeological Excavation in the Holy Land*, Vol. 3, ed. E. Stern. Jerusalem: Israel Exploration Society and Carta.

Eissfeldt, O.
1976   *The Old Testament: An Introduction.* Trans. Peter R. Ackroyd. New York: Harper and Row. Original 1934.
Eitan, A.
1984   Vered Yeriḥo. *Excavations and Surveys in Israel 1983* 2: 106–7.
Emerton, J. A.
1997   The Biblical High Place in the Light of Recent Study. *Palestine Exploration Quarterly* 129: 116–32.
Epstein, C.
1965   An Interpretation of the Megiddo Sacred Area During the Middle Bronze II. *Israel Exploration Journal* 15: 204–21.
1985   Laden Animal Figurines from the Chalcolithic Period in Palestine. *Bulletin of the American Schools of Oriental Research* 258: 53–62.
Evans-Pritchard, E. E.
1956   *Nuer Religion.* Oxford: Clarendon.
Faherty, R. L.
1974   Sacrifice. Pp. 128–35 in *The New Encyclopaedia Britannica*, Vol. 16, 15th ed. Chicago: Benton.
Falconer, S. E. and Magness–Gardiner, B.
1989   Bronze Age Village Life in the Jordan Valley: Archaeological Investigations at Tell el-Hayyat and Tell Abu en-Niʿaj. *National Geographic Research* 5/3: 335–47.
Finkelstein, I.
1988   *The Archaeology of the Israelite Settlement.* Jerusalem: Israel Exploration Society.
1993   Shiloh: Renewed Excavations. Pp. 1366–70 in *The New Encyclopedia of Archaeological Excavation in the Holy Land*, Vol. 4, ed. E. Stern. Jerusalem: Israel Exploration Society and Carta.
1995   The Great Transformation: The "Conquest" of the Highlands Frontiers and the Rise of the Territorial States. Pp. 349–65 in *The Archaeology of Society in the Holy Land*, ed. T. E. Levy. London: Leicester University.
1998   Two Notes on Northern Samaria: The "'Einun Pottery" and the Date of the "Bull Site." *Palestine Exploration Quarterly* 130: 94–98.
1999   State Formation in Israel and Judah: A Contrast in Context, A Contrast in Trajectory. *Near Eastern Archaeology* 62: 35–52.
Firth, R.
1972   Offering and Sacrifice: Problems of Organization. Pp. 324–33 in *Reader in Comparative Religion: An Anthropological Approach*,

eds. W. A. Lessa and E. Z. Vogt. New York: Harper and Row.
Fischer, P. M.
1991a A Possible Late Bronze Age Sanctuary at Tell Abū al-Kharaz, Transjordan. *Journal of Prehistoric Religion* 5: 42–47.
1991b Tall Abū al–Kharaz: The Swedish Jordan Expedition 1989, First Season Preliminary Report from Trial Soundings. *Annual of the Department of Antiquities of Jordan* 35: 67–104.
1996 Tall Abū al–Kharaz: The Swedish Jordan Expedition 1994, Fifth Season Preliminary Excavation Report. *Annual of the Department of Antiquities of Jordan* 40: 101–10.
1997 Tall Abū al–Kharaz: The Swedish Jordan Expedition 1995–1996, Sixth and Seventh Season Preliminary Excavation Report. *Annual of the Department of Antiquities of Jordan* 41: 129–44.
1998 Tall Abū al–Kharaz: The Swedish Jordan Expedition 1997, Eighth Season Preliminary Excavation Report. *Annual of the Department of Antiquities of Jordan* 42: 213 23.
1999 Chocolate–on–White Ware: Typology, Chronology, and Provenance: The Evidence from Tell Abu al–Kharaz, Jordan Valley. *Bulletin of the American Schools of Oriental Research* 313: 1–29.

Fishbane, M. A.
1985 *Biblical Interpretation in Ancient Israel*. New York: Clarendon and Oxford: Oxford University.
1998 Substitutes for Sacrifice in Judaism. Pp. 123–35 in *The Exegetical Imagination: On Jewish Thought and Theology*, essays by M. A. Fishbane. Cambridge, MA and London: Harvard University.

Flanagan, J. W.
1992 Samuel, Book of 1–2: Text, Composition, and Context. Pp. 957–65 in *The Anchor Bible Dictionary*, Vol. 5, ed. D. N. Freeedman. New York: Doubleday.

Fohrer, G.
1972 *History of Israelite Religion*. New York: Abingdon.

Franke, D.
1995 The Middle Kingdom in Egypt. Pp. 735–48 in *Civilizations of the Ancient Near East*, Vol. 2, ed. J. M. Sasson. New York: Scribner's.

Frankel, R.
1994 Upper Galilee in the Late Bronze–Iron I Transition. Pp. 18–34 in *From Nomadism to Monarchy: Archaeological and Historical Aspects of Early Israel*, eds. I. Finkelstein and N. Na'aman. Jerusalem: Yad Izhak Ben-Zvi and Israel Exploration Society and Washington, DC: Biblical Archaeology Society.

Franken, H. J.
1969 *Excavations at Tell Deir 'Alla*. Leiden: Brill.

1975 Tell Deir ʿAlla. Pp. 321–24 in *Encyclopedia of Archaeological Excavations in the Holy Land*, Vol. 1, ed. M. Avi-Yonah. Englewood Cliffs, NJ: Prentice–Hall.
1997 Deir ʿAlla, Tell. Pp. 137–38 in *The Oxford Encyclopedia of Archaeology in the Near East*, Vol. 1, ed. E. M. Meyers. Oxford: Oxford University.

Franken, H. J. and Franken–Battershill, C. A.
1963 *A Primer of Old Testament Archaeology*. Leiden: Brill.

Frazer, J. G.
1919 *Folk–Lore in the Old Testament: Studies in Comparative Religion, Legend and Law*, 3 vols. London: Macmillan.
1925 *The Golden Bough: A Study in Magic and Religion*, abr. ed. New York: Macmillan.

Freedman, D. N.
1965 Archaeology and the Future of Biblical Studies: The Biblical Languages. Pp. 294–312 in *The Bible in Modern Scholarship*, ed. J. P. Hyatt. Nashville and New York: Abingdon.
1985 The Relationship of Archaeology to the Bible. *Biblical Archaeology Review* 9: 6–8.

Freedman, D. N., ed.
1992 *The Anchor Bible Dictionary*. 6 vols. New York: Doubleday.

Friedman, R. E.
1981 *The Exile and Biblical Narrative: The Formation of the Deuteronomistic and Priestly Works*. Harvard Semitic Monographs 22. Chico, CA: Scholars.
1987 *Who Wrote the Bible?* Englewood Cliffs, NJ: Prentice– Hall.

Fritz, V.
1987 Temple Architecture: What Can Archaeology Tell Us about Solomon's Temple? *Biblical Archaeology Review* 13/4: 38–49.
1993 Open Cult Places in Israel in the Light of Parallels from Prehistoric Europe and Pre-Classical Greece. Pp. 182–87 in *Biblical Archaeology Today, 1990: Proceedings of the Second International Congress on Biblical Archaeology, Jerusalem, June–July 1990*, eds. A. Biran and J. Aviram. Jerusalem: Israel Exploration Society and Israel Academy of Sciences and Humanities.

Gamble, C.
1985 Formation Processes and the Animal Bones from the Sanctuary at Phylakopi. Pp. 479–83 in *The Archaeology of Cult: The Sanctuary at Phylakopi* by C. Renfrew. The British School of Archaeology at Athens Supplementary Volume 18. London: Thames and Hudson.

Gardiner, A.
1964 *Egypt of the Pharaohs: An Introduction.* London: Oxford University.

Gaster, T. H.
1950 *Thespis: Ritual, Myth and Drama in the Ancient Near East.* New York: Schuman.
1969 *Myth, Legend and Custom in the Old Testament: A Comparative Study with Chapters from Sir James G. Frazer's Folklore in the Old Testament.* New York: Harper and Row.

Gathercole, P.
1984 A Consideration of Ideology. Pp. 149–54 in *Marxist Perspectives in Archaeology*, ed. M. Spriggs. New Directions in Archaeology. Cambridge: Cambridge University.

Geertz, C.
1969 Religion as a Cultural System. Pp. 1–46 in *Anthropological Approaches to the Study of Religion*, 2nd ed., ed. M. Banton. London: Tavistock.

Georgoudi, S.
1989 Sanctified Slaughter in Modern Greece: The "*Kourbánia*" of the Saints. Pp. 183–203 in *The Cuisine of Sacrifice among the Greeks*, eds. M. Detienne and J.-P. Vernant. Chicago: University of Chicago.

Gershuny, L.
1981 Stratum V at Tell Abu Hawam. *Zeitschrift des deutschen Palästina–Vereins* 97: 36–44.

Geva, S.
1989 *Hazor, Israel: An Urban Community of the 8th Century* B.C.E. BAR International Series 543. Oxford: B.A.R.

Gibson, T.
1986 *Sacrifice and Sharing in the Philippine Highlands: Religion and Society among the Buid of Mindoro.* London School of Economics Monographs on Social Anthropology 57. London: Athlone.

Gilmour, G. H.
1995 *The Archaeology of Cult in the Southern Levant in the Early Iron Age: An Analytical and Comparative Approach.* Unpublished Ph.D. dissertation, University of Oxford, St. Cross College.

Gilula, M.
1976 An Inscription in Egyptian Hieratic from Lachish. *Tel Aviv* 3: 107–8.

Ginsberg, H. L.
1982 *The Israelian Heritage of Judaism.* New York: Jewish Theological Seminary.

Gitin, S.
1989 Incense Altars from Ekron, Israel and Judah: Context and Typology. *Eretz-Israel* 20 (Y. Yadin volume): 52*–67* (English).
1993 Seventh Century BCE Cultic Elements at Ekron. Pp. 248–58 in Biblical Archaeology Today, 1990: Proceedings of the Second International Congress on Biblical Archaeology, Jerusalem, June–July 1990, eds. A. Biran and J. Aviram. Jerusalem: Israel Exploration Society and Israel Academy of Sciences and Humanities.

Gittlen, B. M.
1982 Form and Function in the New Late Bronze Age Temple at Lachish. *Eretz-Israel* 16 (H. Orlinsky volume): 67*–69* (English).

Giveon, R.
1978 *The Impact of Egypt on Canaan: Iconographical and Related Studies*. Orbis Biblicus et Orientalis 20. Göttingen: Biblical Institute of the University of Fribourg, Switzerland.

Glueck, N.
1960 *Rivers in the Desert: A History of the Negev*. New York: Grove.

Gnuse, R. K.
2000 Redefining the Elohist? *Journal of Biblical Literature* 119: 201–20.

Goldwasser, O. and Wimmer, S.
1999 Hieratic Fragments from Tell el-Farʿah (South). *Bulletin of the American Schools of Oriental Research* 313: 39–42.

Gonen, R.
1984 Urban Canaan in the Late Bronze Period. *Bulletin of the American Schools of Oriental Research* 253: 61–73.
1987 Megiddo in the Late Bronze Age—Another Reassessment. *Levant* 19: 83–100.
1992 The Chalcolithic Period. Pp. 40–80 in *The Archaeology of Ancient Israel*, ed. A. Ben-Tor. Trans. R. Greenberg. New Haven: Yale University and London: Open University of Israel.

Gophna, R.
1979 A Middle Bronze Age II Village in the Jordan Valley. *Tel Aviv* 6: 28–33.

Gophna, R. and Beck, P.
1981 The Rural Aspect of the Settlement Pattern of the Coastal Plain in the Middle Bronze Age II. *Tel Aviv* 8: 45–80.

Gordon, C. H.
1953 *Introduction to Old Testament Times*. Ventnor, NJ: Ventnor.
1965 *Ugaritic Textbook*. Rome: Pontifical Biblical Institute.

Graesser, C. F.
1972   Standing Stones in Ancient Palestine. *Biblical Archaeologist* 35: 34–63.
Graham, M. P.
1989   The Discovery and Reconstruction of the Mesha Inscription. Pp. 41–92 in *Studies in the Mesha Inscription and Moab*, ed. J. A. Dearman. Archaeological and Biblical Studies 2. Atlanta: Scholars.
Graham, W. C. and May, H. G.
1936   *Culture and Conscience: An Archaeological Study of the New Religious Past in Ancient Palestine*. Chicago: University of Chicago.
Gray, J.
1962   *Archaeology and the Old Testament World*. New York: Harper and Row.
Ha, J.
1989   *Genesis 15: A Theological Compendium of Pentateuchal History*. Berlin: de Gruyter.
Habel, N. C.
1964   *Yahweh versus Baal, a Conflict of Religious Cultures: A Study in the Relevance of Ugaritic Materials for the Early Faith of Israel*. New York: Bookman.
Hackett, J. A.
1987   Religious Traditions in Israelite Transjordan. Pp. 125–36 in *Ancient Israelite Religion: Essays in Honor of Frank Moore Cross*, eds. P. D. Miller, Jr., P. D. Hanson and S. D. McBride. Philadelphia: Fortress.
1997a   Canaan. Pp. 408–9 in *The Oxford Encyclopedia of Archaeology in the Near East*, Vol. 1, ed. E. M. Meyers. Oxford: Oxford University.
1997b   Canaanites. Pp. 409–14 in *The Oxford Encyclopedia of Archaeology in the Near East*, Vol. 1, ed. E. M. Meyers. Oxford: Oxford University.
Hahn, H. F.
1966   *The Old Testament in Modern Research*, 2nd ed. Philadelphia: Fortress.
Hallo, W. W.
1987   The Origins of the Sacrificial Cult: New Evidence from Mesopotamia and Israel. Pp. 3–13 in *Ancient Israelite Religion: Essays in Honor of Frank Moore Cross*, eds. P. D. Miller, Jr., P. D. Hanson and S. D. McBride. Philadelphia: Fortress.
Halpern, B.
1981   Sacred History and Ideology: Chronicles' Thematic Structure—

Indications of an Earlier Source. Pp. 35–54 in *The Creation of Sacred Literature*, ed. R.E. Friedman. Near Eastern Studies 22. Berkeley and Los Angeles: University of California.
1983   *The Emergence of Israel in Canaan*. Society for Biblical Literature Monograph Series 29. Chico, CA: Scholars.
1992   Shiloh. Pp. 1213–15 in *The Anchor Bible Dictionary*, Vol. 5, ed. D. N. Freedman. New York: Doubleday.

Hamilton, R. W.
1934   Tell Abu Hawam: Interim Report. *Quarterly of the Department of Antiquities in Palestine* 3: 74–80.
1935   Excavations at Tell Abu Hawam. *Quarterly of the Department of Antiquities of Palestine* 4: 1–69.

Handcock, P. S. P.
1916   *The Archaeology of the Holy Land*. London: Unwin.

Haran, M.
1969   *Zebah Hayyamim. Vetus Testamentum* 19: 11–22.
1978   *Temples and Temple-Service in Ancient Israel: An Inquiry into the Character of Cult Phenomena and the Historical Setting of the Priestly School*. Oxford: Clarendon.
1981   Temples and Cultic Open Areas as Reflected in the Bible. Pp. 31–37 in *Temples and High Places in Biblical Times*, ed. A. Biran. Jerusalem: Hebrew Union College–Jewish Institute of Religion.
1988   Temple and Community in Ancient Israel. Pp. 17–25 in *Temple in Society*, ed. M. Fox. Winona Lake, IN: Eisenbrauns.

Harif, A.
1978   Middle Kingdom Architectural Elements in Middle Bronze Age Megiddo. *Zeitschrift des deutschen Palästina–Vereins* 94: 24–31.

Harris, M.
1968   *The Rise of Anthropological Theory*. New York: Crowell.

Hartog, F.
1989   Self-cooking Beef and the Drinks of Ares. Pp. 170–82 in *The Cuisine of Sacrifice among the Greeks*, eds. M. Detienne and J.-P. Vernant. Chicago: University of Chicago.

Heidel, A.
1963   *The Babylonian Genesis: The Story of Creation*, 2nd ed. Chicago: University of Chicago.

Heltzer, M.
1976   *The Rural Community in Ancient Ugarit*. Wiesbaden: Ludwig Reichert.
1978   *Goods, Prices and the Organization of Trade in Ugarit (Marketing and Transportation in the Eastern Mediterranean in the Second Half of the II Millennium B.C.E.)*. Weisbaden: Ludwig Reichert.

1982   *The Internal Organization of the Kingdom of Ugarit (Royal Service–System, Taxes, Royal Economy, Army and Administration)*. Wiesbaden: Ludwig Reichert.
1989   The Royal Economy of King David Compared with the Royal Economy in Ugarit. *Eretz-Israel* 20 (Y. Yadin volume): 175–80 (Hebrew), 200* (English summary).

Hennessy, J. B.
1966   Excavations of a Late Bronze Age Temple at Amman. *Palestine Exploration Quarterly* 108: 155–62.

Hennessy, J. B. and Smith, R. H.
1997   Pella. Pp. 256–59 in *The Oxford Encyclopedia of Archaeology in the Near East*, Vol. 4, ed. E. M. Meyers. New York and London: Oxford University.

Herr, L. G.
1997a   Amman Airport Temple. Pp. 102–3 in *The Oxford Encyclopedia of Archaeology in the Near East*, Vol. 1, ed. E. M. Meyers. Oxford: Oxford University.
1997b   The Iron Age II Period: Emerging Nations. *Biblical Archaeologist* 60: 114–83.

Herr, L. G., ed.
1983   *The Amman Airport Excavations, 1976*. Annual of the American Schools of Oriental Research 48. Winona Lake, IN: American Schools of Oriental Research.

Herzog, Z.
1980   A Functional Interpretation of the Broadroom and Longroom House Types. *Tel Aviv* 7: 82–89.
1992   Settlement and Fortification Planning in the Iron Age. Pp. 231–74 in *The Architecture of Ancient Israel: From the Prehistoric to the Persian Periods*, eds. A. Kempinski and R. Reich. Jerusalem: Israel Exploration Society.
1993   Michal, Tel. Pp. 1036–41 in *The New Encyclopedia of Archaeological Excavation in the Holy Land*, Vol. 3, ed. E. Stern. Jerusalem: Israel Exploration Society and Carta.
1997   Michal, Tel. Pp. 20–22 in *The Oxford Encyclopedia of Archaeology in the Near East*, Vol. 4, ed. E. M. Meyers. Oxford: Oxford University.

Herzog, Z., Aharoni, M. and Rainey, A. F.
1987   Arad—An Ancient Israelite Fortress with a Temple to Yahweh. *Biblical Archaeology Review* 13/2: 16–35.

Herzog, Z., Aharoni, M., Rainey, A. F. and Moshkovitz, S.
1984   The Israelite Fortress at Arad. *Bulletin of the American Schools of Oriental Research* 254: 1–34.

Herzog, Z., Rainey, A. F. and Moshkovitz, S.
1977 The Stratigraphy at Beer–sheba and the Location of the Sanctuary. *Bulletin of the American Schools of Oriental Research* 225: 49–58.

Hestrin, R.
1987a The Cult Stand from Taʿanach and Its Religious Background. *Studia Phoenicia* 5: 61–77.
1987b The Lachish Ewer and the ʾAsherah. *Israel Exploration Journal* 37: 212–23.

Heusch, L., de
1985 *Sacrifice in Africa: A Structuralist Approach*. Manchester: Manchester University.

Higginbotham, C.
1996 Elite Emulation and Egyptian Governance in Ramesside Canaan. *Tel Aviv* 23: 154–69.

Hoffmeier, J. K.
1996 *Israel in Egypt: The Evidence for the Authenticity of the Exodus Tradition*. Oxford: Oxford University.

Holladay, J. S., Jr.
1987 Religion in Israel and Judah under the Monarchy: An Explicitly Archaeological Approach. Pp. 249–99 in *Ancient Israelite Religion: Essays in Honor of Frank Moore Cross*, eds. P. D. Miller, Jr., P. D. Hanson and S. D. McBride. Philadelphia: Fortress.

Holland, T. A.
1977 A Study of Palestinian Iron Age Baked Clay Figurines, with Special Reference to Jerusalem: Cave 1. *Levant* 9: 121–55.

Holloway, S. W.
1992 Kings, Book of 1–2. Pp. 69–83 in *The Anchor Bible Dictionary*, Vol. 4, ed. D. N. Freeedman. New York: Doubleday.

Hooke, S. H., ed.
1933 *Myth and Ritual: Essays on the Myth and Ritual of the Hebrews in Relation to the Culture Patterns of the Ancient East*. London: Oxford University.

Hooke, S. H.
1938 *The Origins of Early Semitic Ritual*. London: Oxford University.

Hubert, H. and Mauss, M.
1964 *Sacrifice, Its Nature and Function*. London: Cohen and West. Orig. 1899.

Hurvitz, A.
1993 בית (ה)אוצר—The History of a Biblical Administrative–Economic Term. *Eretz-Israel* 24 (A. Malamat volume): 74–78 (Hebrew), 234* (English summary).

Ilan, D.
1992a   A Middle Bronze Age Offering Deposit from Tel Dan and the Politics of Cultic Giving. *Tel Aviv* 19: 247–66.
1992b   A Middle Bronze Age Cache from Tel Dan. *Eretz-Israel* 23 (A. Biran volume): 9–20 (Hebrew), 145* (English summary).
1995   The Dawn of Internationalism—The Middle Bronze Age. Pp. 297–319 in *The Archaeology of Society in the Holy Land*, ed. T. E. Levy. London: Leicester University.
1997   Dan. Pp. 107–12 in *The Oxford Encyclopedia of Archaeology in the Near East*, Vol. 2, ed. E. M. Meyers. Oxford: Oxford University.

James, F.
1966   *The Iron Age at Beth Shan: A Study of Levels VI–IV*. Philadelphia: University Museum.

James, F. and Kempinski, A.
1975   Beth Shean. Pp. 207–25 in *Encyclopedia of Archaeological Excavations in the Holy Land*, Vol. 1, ed. M. Avi-Yonah. Englewood Cliffs, NJ: Prentice–Hall.

James, T. G. H.
1979   *An Introduction to Ancient Egypt*. New York: Farrar Straus Giroux.

Jameson, M. H.
1988   Sacrifice and Ritual: Greece. Pp. 959–79 in *Civilization and the Ancient Mediterranean World 2*, eds. M. Grant and R. Kitzinger. New York: Charles Scribner's Sons.

Jenks, A. W.
1977   *The Elohist and North Israelite Traditions*. Society for Biblical Literature Monograph Series 22. Missoula, MT: Scholars.
1992   Elohist. Pp. 478–82 in *The Anchor Bible Dictionary*, Vol. 2, ed. D. N. Freedman. New York: Doubleday.

Ji, C–H. C.
1995   Iron Age I in Central and Northern Transjordan: An Interim Summary of Archaeological Data. *Palestine Exploration Quarterly* 127: 122–40.

Jidejian, N.
1968   *Byblos through the Ages*. Beirut: Dar el-Machreq.

Joffe, A. H.
1993   *Settlement and Society in the Early Bronze I & II Southern Levant: Complementarity and Contradiction in a Small–scale Complex Society*. Monographs in Mediterranean Archaeology 4. Sheffield: Sheffield Academic.

Kallai, Z.
1997   The Patriarchal Boundaries, Canaan and the Land of Israel:

Patterns and Application in Biblical Historiography. *Israel Exploration Journal* 47: 69–82.

Kaplan, J.
1971 Mesopotamian Elements in the Middle Bronze II Culture of Palestine. *Journal of Near Eastern Studies* 30: 293–307.
1972 The Archaeology and History of Tel Aviv-Jaffa. *Biblical Archaeologist* 35: 66–95.

Kaplan, J. and Kaplan, H.
1976 Jaffa. Pp. 531–41 in in *Encyclopedia of Archaeological Excavations in the Holy Land*, Vol. 2, ed. M. Avi-Yonah. Englewood Cliffs, NJ: Prentice-Hall.

Kaplan, J. and Ritter–Kaplan, H.
1993 Jaffa. Pp. 655–59 in *The New Encyclopedia of Archaeological Excavation in the Holy Land*, Vol. 2, ed. E. Stern. Jerusalem: Israel Exploration Society and Carta.

Katzenstein, H. J.
1982 Gaza in the Egyptian Texts of the New Kingdom. *Journal of the American Oriental Society* 102: 111–13.

Kaufman, A. S.
1988 Fixing the Site of the Tabernacle at Shiloh. *Biblical Archaeology Review* 14/6: 46–52.

Kaufmann, Y.
1960 *The Religion of Israel: From Its Beginnings to the Babylonian Exile*. Chicago: University of Chicago.

Keel, O. and Uehlinger, C.
1998 *Gods, Goddesses, and Images of God in Ancient Israel*. Trans. T. H. Trapp. Minneapolis: Fortress.

Kelso, J. L.
1948 *The Ceramic Vocabulary of the Old Testament*. Bulletin of the American Schools of Oriental Research Supplement 5–6. New Haven: American Schools of Oriental Research.

Kempinski, A.
1986 Joshua's Altar—An Iron Age I Watchtower. *Biblical Archaeology Review* 12/1: 42.
1989a *Megiddo: A City-State and Royal Centre in North Israel*. Materialien zur Allgemeinen und Vergleichenden Archäologie 40. Munich: Beck.
1989b Reconstructing the Canaanite Tower–Temple. *Eretz-Israel* 20 (Y. Yadin volume): 82–85 (Hebrew), 196*–97* (English summary).
1992 The Middle Bronze Age. Pp. 159–210 in *The Archaeology of Ancient Israel*, ed. A. Ben-Tor. Trans. R. Greenberg. New Haven: Yale University and London: Open University of Israel.

1993 "When History Sleeps, Theology Arises": A Note on Joshua 8:30–35 and the Archaeology of the Settlement Period. *Eretz-Israel* 24 (A. Malamat volume): 175–83 (Hebrew), 237* (English summary).

Kenyon, K. M.
1963 Preface to *A Primer of Old Testament Archaeology*, by H. J. Franken and C. A. Franken–Battershill. Leiden: Brill.
1974 *Digging up Jerusalem*. London: Ernest Benn.
1978 *The Bible and Recent Archaeology*. London: British Museum.

Kimbrough, S. T., Jr.
1978 *Israelite Religion in Sociological Perspective: The Work of Antonin Causse*. Wiesbaden: Harrassowitz.

Kittel, R.
1895 *A History of the Hebrews, Vol. I: Sources of Information and History of the Period up to the Death of Joshua*. London: Williams and Norgate.
1896 *A History of the Hebrews, Vol. II: Sources of Information and History of the Period down to the Babylonian Exile*. London: Williams and Norgate.
1925 *The Religion of the People of Israel*. New York: Macmillan.

Knapp, A. B.
1988 *The History and Culture of Ancient Western Asia and Egypt*. Belmont, CA: Wadsworth.
1989 Response: Independence, Imperialism, and the Egyptian Factor. *Bulletin of the American Schools of Oriental Research* 275: 64–68.

Knight, D. A.
1985 The Pentateuch. Pp. 263–96 in *The Hebrew Bible and Its Modern Interpreters*, eds. D. A. Knight and G. M. Tucker. Minneapolis: Fortress and Atlanta: Scholars.

Knight, D. A. and Tucker, G. M., eds.
1985 *The Hebrew Bible and Its Modern Interpreters*. Minneapolis: Fortress and Atlanta: Scholars.

Kochavi, M.
1978 Canaanite Aphek: Its Acropolis and Inscriptions. *Expedition* 20: 12–17.

Kochavi, M., Beck, P. and Gophna, R.
1979 Aphek–Antipatris, *Tel Poleg, Tel Zeror* and *Tel Burga*: Four Fortified Sites of the Middle Bronze Age IIA in the Sharon Plain. *Zeitschrift des deutschen Palästina–Vereins* 95: 121–65.

Kochavi, M., Renner, T., Spar, I. and Yadin, E.
1992 Rediscovered! The Land of Geshur. *Biblical Archaeology Review* 18/4: 30–44, 84–85.

Kooij, G., van der
1993   Deir ʿAlla, Tell. Pp. 338–42 in *The New Encyclopedia of Archaeological Excavation in the Holy Land*, Vol. 1, ed. E. Stern. Jerusalem: Israel Exploration Society and Carta.

Kraus, H.-J.
1966   *Worship in Israel: A Cultic History of the Old Testament.* Richmond, VA: John Knox.

Lamon, R. S. and Shipton, G. M.
1939   *Megiddo I: Seasons of 1925–34, Strata I–V.* Oriental Institute Publications 42. Chicago: The Oriental Institute of the University of Chicago.

Lang, B.
1985   Introduction: Anthropology as a New Model for Biblical Studies. Pp. 1–20 in *Anthropological Approaches to the Old Testament*, ed. B. Lang. Issues in Religion and Theology 8. Philadelphia: Fortress.

Lapp, P. W.
1964   The 1963 Excavation at Taʿannek. *Bulletin of the American Schools of Oriental Research* 173: 4–44.
1969   *Biblical Archaeology and History.* Cleveland: World Publishing.

Leach, E.
1985   The Logic of Sacrifice. Pp. 136–50 in *Anthropological Approaches to the Old Testament*, ed. B. Lang. Issues in Religion and Theology 8. Philadelphia: Fortress.

Lemaire, A.
1994   "House of David" Restored in Moabite Inscription. *Biblical Archaeology Review* 20/3: 30–37.

Lemche, N. P.
1991   *The Canaanites in Their Land: The Tradition of the Canaanites.* Journal for the Study of the Old Testament Supplement Series 110. Sheffield: JSOT.

Lenzen, C. J.
1997   Irbid. P. 181 in *The Oxford Encyclopedia of Archaeology in the Near East*, Vol. 3, ed. E. M. Meyers. Oxford: Oxford University.

Leonard, A., Jr.
1987   The Significance of the Mycenaean Pottery found East of the Jordan River. Pp. 261–66 in *Studies in the History and Archaeology of Jordan III*, ed. A. Hadidi. London: Routledge and Kegan Paul.
1989   Archaeological Sources for the History of Palestine: The Late Bronze Age. *Biblical Archaeologist* 52: 4–39.

Levine, B. A.
1963 Ugaritic Descriptive Rituals. *Journal of Cuneiform Studies* 17: 105–11.
1965 The Descriptive Tabernacle Texts of the Pentateuch. *Journal of the American Oriental Society* 85: 307–18.
1971 Prolegomenon to *Sacrifice in the Old Testament: Its Theory and Practice*, by G. B. Gray. New York: Ktav.
1983 The Descriptive Ritual Texts from Ugarit: Some Formal and Functional Features of the Genre. Pp. 467–75 in *The Word of the Lord Shall Go Forth: Essays in Honor of David Noel Freedman in Celebration of His Sixtieth Birthday*, eds. C. L. Meyers and M. O'Connor. Philadelphia: American Schools of Oriental Research.
1992 Leviticus, Book of. Pp. 311–21 in *The Anchor Bible Dictionary*, Vol. 4, ed. D. N. Freedman. New York: Doubleday.

Levinson, B. M.
2000 The Hermeneutics of Tradition in Deuteronomy: A Reply to J. D. McConville. *Journal of Biblical Literature* 119: 269–86.

Levy, S. and Edelstein, G.
1972 Cinq années de fouilles a Tel 'Amal (Nir David). *Revue biblique* 79: 325–67.

Levy, T. E.
1995 Cult, Metallurgy and Rank Societies—Chalcolithic Period (ca. 4500–3500 BCE). Pp. 226–43 in *The Archaeology of Society in the Holy Land*, ed. T. E. Levy. London: Leicester University.

Levy, T. E., ed.
1995 *The Archaeology of Society in the Holy Land*. London: Leicester University.

Lipiński, E.
1995 The Phoenicians. Pp. 1321–33 in *Civilizations of the Ancient Near East*, Vol. 2, ed. J. M. Sasson. New York: Scribner's.

Loud, G.
1939 *The Megiddo Ivories*. Chicago: The Oriental Institute of the University of Chicago.
1948 *Megiddo II, Seasons of 1935–1939, Text*. Oriental Institute Publications 62. Chicago: The Oriental Institute of the University of Chicago.

Macalister, R. A. S.
1912 *The Excavation of Gezer: 1902–1905 and 1907–1909*, Vol. 2. London: John Murray.
1925 *A Century of Excavation in Palestine*. London: Religious Tract Society.

Maeir, A. M.
1997   Tomb 1181: A Multiple–Interment Burial Cave of the Transitional Middle Bronze Age IIA–B. Pp. 295–340 in *Hazor V: An Account of the Fifth Season of Excavation, 1968*, eds. A. Ben-Tor and R. Bonfil. Jerusalem: Israel Exploration Society and The Hebrew University.

Malamat, A.
1984   The Monarchy of David and Solomon. Pp. 161–74 in *Recent Archaeology in the Land of Israel*, eds. H. Shanks and B. Mazar. Washington, D.C. and Jerusalem: Biblical Archaeology Society and Israel Exploration Journal.

Mallet, J.
1988   *Tell el-Far ʿah II, 2: Le Bronze Moyen*. Paris: Editions Recherche sur les Civilisations.

Marfoe, L.
1979   The Integrative Transformation: Patterns of Socio–political Organization in Southern Syria. *Bulletin of the American Schools of Oriental Research* 234: 1–42.

Markoe, G.
1997   Phoenicians. Pp. 324–31 in *The Oxford Encyclopedia of Archaeology in the Near East*, Vol. 4, ed. E. M. Meyers. Oxford: Oxford University.

Marquet–Krause, J.
1949   *Les fouilles de ʿAy (et-Tell), 1932–35*. Bibliothèque Archéologique et Historique 45. Paris: Guethner.

Marx, A.
1989   Sacrifice pour les péchés ou rite de passage? Quelques réflexions sur la fonction du *hattat*. *Revue biblique* 96: 27–48.

Matthiae, P.
1975   Unité et dévelopement du temple dans la Syria dur Bronze Moyen. Pp. 43–72 in *Le temple et le culte*. La Vingtième Rencontre Assyriologique Internationale. Istanbul: Nederlands Historisch–Archeologisch Instituut.

1980   *Ebla: An Empire Rediscovered*. London: Hodder and Stoughton.

May, H. G.
1935   *Material Remains of the Megiddo Cult*. The University of Chicago Oriental Institute Publications 26. Chicago: The Oriental Institute of the University of Chicago.

Mayes, A. D. H.
1983   *The Story of Israel between Settlement and Exile: A Redactional Study of the Deuteronomistic History*. London: SCM.

Mazar, A.
1980 *Excavations at Tel Qasile, Part One, The Philistine Sanctuary: Architecture and Cult Objects*. Qedem 12. Jerusalem: Institute of Archaeology, Hebrew University of Jerusalem.
1982 The "Bull Site": An Iron Age I Open Cult Place. *Bulletin of the American Schools of Oriental Research* 247: 27–42.
1985 *Excavations at Tel Qasile, Part Two, The Philistine Sanctuary: Various Finds, the Pottery, Conclusions, Appendixes.* Qedem 20. Jerusalem: Institute of Archaeology, Hebrew University of Jerusalem.
1990a *Archaeology of the Land of the Bible: 10,000–586* B.C.E. Anchor Bible Reference Library. New York: Doubleday.
1990b The Excavations at Tel Beth-Shean in 1989–1990. *Eretz-Israel* 21 (R. Amiran volume): 197–211 (Hebrew), 108* (English summary).
1992a Tel Bet She'an—1989/1990. *Excavations and Surveys in Israel 1991* 10: 5–9.
1992b Temples of the Middle and Late Bronze Ages and the Iron Age. Pp. 161–87 in *The Architecture of Ancient Israel: From the Prehistoric to the Persian Periods*, eds. A. Kempinski and R. Reich. Jerusalem: Israel Exploration Society.
1993a Beth-Shean: Tel Bet–Shean and the Northern Cemetery. Pp. 214–23 in *The New Encyclopedia of Archaeological Excavation in the Holy Land*, Vol. 1, ed. E. Stern. Jerusalem: Israel Exploration Society and Carta.
1993b "Bull" Site. Pp. 266–67 in *The New Encyclopedia of Archaeological Excavation in the Holy Land*, Vol. 1, ed. E. Stern. Jerusalem: Israel Exploration Society and Carta.
1993c Qasile, Tell. Pp. 1204–12 in *The New Encyclopedia of Archaeological Excavation in the Holy Land*, Vol. 4, ed. E. Stern. Jerusalem: Israel Exploration Society and Carta.
1997a Four Thousand Years of History at Tel Beth-Shean: An Account of the Renewed Excavations. *Biblical Archaeologist* 60: 62–76.
1997b Qasile, Tell. Pp. 373–76 in *The Oxford Encyclopedia of Archaeology in the Near East*, Vol. 4, ed. E. M. Meyers. Oxford: Oxford University.
1999a The "Bull Site" and the "'Einun Pottery" Reconsidered. *Palestine Exploration Quarterly* 131: 144–48.
1999b The 1997–1998 Excavations at Tel Reḥov: Preliminary Report. *Israel Exploration Journal* 49: 1–42.
Mazar, A. and Camp, J.
2000 Will Tel Rehov Save the United Monarchy? *Biblical Archaeology Review* 26/2: 38–51, 75.

Mazar, B.
1993 'En Gev, Excavation on the Mound. Pp. 409–11 in *The New Encyclopedia of Archaeological Excavation in the Holy Land*, Vol. 2, ed. E. Stern. Jerusalem: Israel Exploration Society and Carta.

Mazar, B., Biran, A., Dothan, M. and Dunayevsky, I.
1964 'En Gev: Excavations in 1961. *Israel Exploration Journal* 14: 1–49.

Mazar, E.
1997 King David's Palace—It's There. *Biblical Archaeology Review* 23/1: 50–57, 74.

McCarter, P. K., Jr.
1980 *The Anchor Bible: I Samuel*. Anchor Bible Commentary 8. Garden City, NY: Doubleday.
1984 *The Anchor Bible: II Samuel*. Anchor Bible Commentary 9. Garden City, NY: Doubleday.

McClellan, T. L.
1989 The Chronology and Ceramic Assemblages of Alalakh. Pp. 181–212 in *Essays in Ancient Civilization Presented to Helene J. Kantor*, eds. A. Leonard Jr. and B. B. Williams. Studies in Ancient Oriental Civilization 47. Chicago: Oriental Institute.

McCown, C. C.
1943 *The Ladder of Progress in Palestine: A Story of Archaeological Adventure*. New York: Harper.

McEwan, C. W.
1937 The Syrian Expedition of the Oriental Institute of Chicago. *American Journal of Archaeology* 41: 8–16.

McGovern, P. E.
1983 Test Sounding of Archaeological and Resistivity Survey Results at Rujm al–Henu. *Annual of the Department of Antiquities of Jordan* 27: 105–41.
1985 *Late Bronze Palestinian Pendants: Innovation in a Cosmopolitan Age*. JSOT/ASOR Monograph Series 1. Sheffield: JSOT.
1993 Baq'ah Valley. Pp. 144–47 in *The New Encyclopedia of Archaeological Excavation in the Holy Land*, Vol. 1, ed. E. Stern. Jerusalem: Israel Exploration Society and Carta.

McKenzie, S. L.
1992 Deuteronomistic History. Pp. 160–68 in *The Anchor Bible Dictionary*, Vol. 2, ed. D. N. Freedman. New York: Doubleday.

Meshel, Z.
1978 *Kuntillet 'Ajrud: A Religious Centre from the Time of the Judaean Monarchy on the Border of Sinai*. Israel Museum Catalogue 175. Jerusalem: Israel Museum.

Meyers, C. L.
1976 *The Tabernacle Menorah: A Synthetic Study of a Symbol from the Biblical Cult.* American Schools of Oriental Research Dissertation Series 2. Missoula, MT: Scholars.
1983 The Israelite Empire: In Defense of King Solomon. *Michigan Quarterly Review* 22: 412–28.
1987 David as Temple Builder. Pp. 357–76 in *Ancient Israelite Religion: Essays in Honor of Frank Moore Cross*, eds. P. D. Miller, Jr., P. D. Hanson and S. D. McBride. Philadelphia: Fortress.
1988 *Discovering Eve: Ancient Israelite Women in Context.* New York: Oxford University.
1992 Temple, Jerusalem. Pp. 350–69 in *The Anchor Bible Dictionary*, Vol. 6, ed. D. N. Freeedman. New York: Doubleday.

Meyers, C. L. and Meyers, E. M.
1989 Expanding the Frontiers of Biblical Archaeology. *Eretz-Israel* 20 (Y. Yadin volume): 140*–47* (English).

Meyers, E. M., ed.
1997 *The Oxford Encyclopedia of Archaeology in the Near East.* 5 vols. Oxford: Oxford University.

Milgrom, J.
1971 A Prolegomenon to Leviticus 17:11. *Journal of Biblical Literature* 90: 149–56.
1981 Sacrifices and Offerings, OT. Pp. 763–71 in *Interpreter's Dictionary of the Bible*, supp. vol. Nashville: Abingdon.
1992 Priestly ("P") Source. Pp. 454–61 in *The Anchor Bible Dictionary*, Vol. 5, ed. D. N. Freedman. New York: Doubleday.

Miller, D. and Tilley, C.
1984 Ideology, Power and Prehistory: An Introduction. Pp. 1–15 in *Ideology, Power and Prehistory*, eds. D. Miller and C. Tilley. New Directions in Archaeology. Cambridge: Cambridge University.

Miller, P. D.
1985 Israelite Religion. Pp. 201–37 in *The Hebrew Bible and Its Modern Interpreters*, eds. D. A. Knight and G. M. Tucker. Philadelphia: Fortress and Atlanta: Scholars.

Miller, P. D., Jr. and Roberts, J. J. M.
1977 *The Hand of the Lord: A Reassessment of the "Ark Narrative" of 1 Samuel.* Baltimore: Johns Hopkins University.

Monson, J.
2000 The New 'Ain Dara Temple: Closest Solomonic Parallel. *Biblical Archaeology Review* 26/3: 20–35, 67.

Morris, B.
1987 *Anthropological Studies of Religion: An Introductory Text*. Cambridge: Cambridge University.

Mowinckel, S.
1946 *Prophecy and Tradition: The Prophetic Books in the Light of the Study of the Growth and History of the Tradition*. Oslo: I Kommisjon Hos Jacob Dybwad.

Na'aman, N.
1981 Economic Aspects of the Egyptian Occupation of Canaan. *Israel Exploration Journal* 31: 172–85.
1994a The Canaanites and Their Land: A Rejoinder. *Ugarit-Forschungen* 26: 397–418.
1994b The "Conquest of Canaan" in the Book of Joshua and in History. Pp. 218–81 in *From Nomadism to Monarchy: Archaeological and Historical Aspects of Early Israel*, eds. I. Finkelstein and N. Na'aman. Jerusalem: Yad Izhak Ben-Zvi and Israel Exploration Society and Washington, DC: Biblical Archaeology Society.
1999 Four Notes on the Size of Late Bronze Age Canaan. *Bulletin of the American Schools of Oriental Research* 313: 31–37.

Nakhai, B. A.
1994 What's a Bamah? How Sacred Space Functioned in Ancient Israel. *Biblical Archaeology Review* 20/3: 18–29, 77–78.
1997 Temples: Syro–Palestinian Temples. Pp. 169–74 in *The Oxford Encyclopedia of Archaeology in the Near East*, Vol. 5, ed. E. M. Meyers. Oxford: Oxford University.
1999 Israelite Religion beyond the Temple: The Archaeological Witness. *The World of the Bible* 1: 38–48.

Nakhai, B. Alpert, Dessel, J. P., Wisthoff, B. L.
1993 Wawiyat, Tell el-. Pp. 1500–1501 *The New Encyclopedia of Archaeological Excavation in the Holy Land*, Vol. 4, ed. E. Stern. Jerusalem: Israel Exploration Society and Carta.

Negbi, O.
1966 A Deposit of Terracottas and Statuettes from Tel Sippor. *'Atiqot* 6.
1976 *Canaanite Gods in Metal: An Archaeological Study of Ancient Syro–Palestinian Figurines*. Tel Aviv: Institute of Archaeology, Tel Aviv University.
1989 The Metal Figurines. Pp. 348–62 in Y. Yadin, et al., *Hazor III–IV: An Account of the Third and Fourth Seasons of Excavations, 1957–1958, Text*, ed. A. Ben-Tor. Jerusalem: Israel Exploration Society.
1991 Were There Sea Peoples in the Central Jordan Valley at the Transition from the Bronze Age to the Iron Age? *Tel Aviv* 18: 205–43.

Neusner, J.
1979 *Method and Meaning in Ancient Judaism*. Brown Judaic Studies 10. Missoula, MT: Scholars.

Nicholson, E. W.
1967 *Deuteronomy and Tradition*. Philadelphia: Fortress.

Noth, M.
1972 *A History of Pentateuchal Traditions*. Trans. with an introduction by B. W. Anderson. Englewood Cliffs, NJ: Prentice–Hall 1972. Reprinted 1981. Chico, CA: Scholars. Orig. 1948.

Olyan, S. M.
1988 *Asherah and the Cult of Yahweh in Israel*. Society of Biblical Literature Monograph Series 34. Atlanta: Scholars.
1997 Cult. Pp. 79–86 in *The Oxford Encyclopedia of Archaeology in the Near East*, Vol. 2, ed. E. M. Meyers. Oxford: Oxford University.

Oren, E. D.
1984 "Governors' Residencies" in Canaan under the New Kingdom: A Case Study of Egyptian Administration. *Journal of the Society for the Study of Egyptian Antiquities* 14: 39–56.
1993 Haror, Tel. Pp. 580–84 in *The New Encyclopedia of Archaeological Excavation in the Holy Land*, Vol. 2, ed. E. Stern. Jerusalem: Israel Exploration Society and Carta.
1997 Haror, Tel. Pp. 474–76 in *The Oxford Encyclopedia of Archaeology in the Near East*, Vol. 2, ed. E. M. Meyers. Oxford: Oxford University.

Orlinsky, H. M.
1954 *Ancient Israel*. Ithaca, NY: Cornell University.
1972 *Understanding the Bible through History and Archaeology*. New York: Ktav.

Ottosson, M.
1980 *Temples and Cult Places in Palestine*. Boreas: Uppsala Studies in Ancient Mediterranean and Near Eastern Civilizations. Uppsala: Acta Universitatis Upsaliensis.

Owen, D. I.
1981 Ugarit, Canaan and Egypt: Some New Epigraphic Evidence from Tel Aphek in Israel. Pp. 49–53 in *Ugarit in Retrospect: Fifty Years of Ugarit and Ugaritic*, ed. G. D. Young. Winona Lake, IN: Eisenbrauns.

Pardee, D.
1997 Moabite Stone. Pp. 39–41 in *The Oxford Encyclopedia of Archaeology in the Near East*, Vol. 4, ed. E. M. Meyers. Oxford: Oxford University.

Patai, R.
1967   *The Hebrew Goddess*. New York: Ktav.
Peckham, B.
1985   *The Composition of the Deuteronomistic History*. Harvard Semitic Monographs 35. Atlanta: Scholars.
Pfeiffer, R. H.
1961   *Religion in the Old Testament: The History of a Spiritual Triumph*. New York: Harper.
Pitard, Wayne T.
1987   *Ancient Damascus: A Historical Study of the Syrian City-State from Earliest Times until Its Fall to the Assyrians in 732* B.C.E. Winona Lake, IN: Eisenbrauns.
1998   Before Israel: Syria-Palestine in the Bronze Age. Pp. 33–77 in *The Oxford History of the Biblical World*, ed. M. D. Coogan. Oxford: Oxford University.
Pritchard, J. B.
1943   *Palestinian Figurines in Relation to Certain Goddesses Known through Literature*. American Oriental Series 24. New Haven: American Oriental Society.
1965   Archaeology and the Future of Biblical Studies: Culture and History. Pp. 313–24 in *The Bible in Modern Scholarship*, ed. J. P. Hyatt. Nashville and New York: Abingdon.
1978   *Recovering Sarepta, A Phoenician City: Excavations at Sarafand, Lebanon, 1969–1974, by the University Museum of the University of Pennsylvania*. Princeton: Princeton University.
1985   *Tell es–Saʿidiyeh: Excavations on the Tell, 1964–1966*. University Museum Monography 60. Philadelphia: University of Pennsylvania.
Pritchard, J. B., ed.
1969   *Ancient Near Eastern Texts Relating to the Old Testament*, 3rd ed. with supp. Princeton: Princeton University.
Puech, E.
1986   The Canaanite Inscriptions of Lachish and Their Religious Background. *Tel Aviv* 13: 13–25.
Pury, A., de
1992   Yahwist ("J") Source. Pp. 1012–20 in *The Anchor Bible Dictionary*, Vol. 6, ed. D. N. Freedman. New York: Doubleday.
Rad, G., von
1966   *The Problem of the Hexateuch and Other Essays*. Edinburgh and London: Oliver and Boyd.
1972   *Genesis: A Commentary*, rev. ed. Philadelphia: Westminster.

Rainey, A. F.
1965   The Kingdom of Ugarit. *Biblical Archaeologist* 28: 102–25.
1970   The Order of Sacrifice in Old Testament Ritual Texts. *Biblica* 51: 485–98.
1996a   Who Is a Canaanite? A Review of the Textual Evidence. *Bulletin of the American Schools of Oriental Research* 304: 1–15.
1996b   Review Article: *Civilizations of the Ancient Near East. Biblical Archaeology Review* 22/6: 70–71, 76.
Rast, W.
1978   *Taanach I: Studies in the Iron Age Pottery*. Cambridge, MA: American Schools of Oriental Research.
1994   Priestly Families and the Cultic Structure at Taanach. Pp. 355–65 in *Scripture and Other Artifacts: Essays on the Bible and Archaeology in Honor of Philip J. King*, eds. M. D. Coogan, J. C. Exum and L. E. Stager. Louisville: Westminster/John Knox.
Raveh, K. and Kingsley, S. A.
1990   The Status of Dor in Late Antiquity: A Maritime Perspective. *Biblical Archaeologist* 54: 198–207.
Reed, W. L.
1949   *The Asherah in the Old Testament*. Fort Worth, TX: Texas Christian University.
Renfrew, C.
1982   *Toward an Archaeology of Mind*. Cambridge: Cambridge University.
1985   *The Archaeology of Cult: The Sanctuary at Phylakopi*. The British School of Archaeology at Athens Supplement 18. London: Thames and Hudson.
Reynolds, F. E.
1984   Introduction. Pp. 1–8 in *Anthropology and the Study of Religion*, eds. R. L. Moore and F. E. Reynolds. Chicago: Center for the Scientific Study of Religion.
Ringgren, H.
1966   *Israelite Religion*. Philadelphia: Fortress.
Robinson, T. H.
1932   *A History of Israel, Vol. I: From the Exodus to the Fall of Jerusalem, 586 B.C.* Reprinted 1955. Oxford: Clarendon.
Rogerson, J. W.
1978   *Anthropology and the Old Testament*. Oxford: Blackwell.
Rothenberg, B.
1988   *The Egyptian Mining Temple at Timna: Researches in the Arabah 1959–1984, Vol. I*. London: Institute of Archaeology.
Rowe, A.
1940   *The Four Canaanite Temples of Beth-Shan. Part I: The Temples*

and Cult Objects. Philadelphia: University of Pennsylvania.

Rowley, H. H.
1946   *The Rediscovery of the Old Testament.* Reprinted 1969. Freeport, NY: Books for Libraries.

Saghieh, M. S.
1983   *Byblos in the Third Millennium B.C.: A Reconstruction of the Stratigraphy and a Study of the Cultural Connections.* Warminster: Aris and Phillips.

Sarna, N. M.
1988   Israel in Egypt: The Egyptian Sojourn and the Exodus. Pp. 31–52 in *Ancient Israel: A Short History from Abraham to the Roman Destruction of the Temple*, ed. H. Shanks. Englewood Cliffs, NJ: Prentice–Hall and Washington, DC: Biblical Archaeology Society.

Sasson, J. M., ed.
1995   *Civilizations of the Ancient Near East.* 4 vols. New York: Scribner's.

Schaeffer, C. F. A.
1931   Les fouilles de Minet-el-Beida et de Ras Shamra, deuxième campaigne (printemps 1930), rapport sommaire. *Syria* 12: 1–14.
1935   Les fouilles de Ras Shamra-Ugarit, sixième campagne (printemps 1934), rapport sommaire. *Syria* 16: 141–76.
1939   *The Cuneiform Texts of Ras Shamra-Ugarit: The Schweich Lectures of the British Academy, 1936.* London: British Academy.

Schiemann, R.
1978   The Relevance of Archaeology to the Study of Ancient West Semitic Religions. *World Archaeology* 10: 129–38.

Seger, J. D.
1975   The MB II Fortifications at Shechem and Gezer: A Hyksos Retrospective. *Eretz-Israel* 12 (N. Glueck volume): 34*–45* (English).

Segert, S.
1967   Surviving of Canaanite Elements in Israelite Religion. Pp. 155–61 in *Studi Sull'Oriente e la Bibbia: Offerti al P. Giovanni Rinaldi.* Geneva: Editrice Studio e Vita.

Shalev, S.
1993   Metal Production and Society at Tel Dan. Pp. 57–65 in *Biblical Archaeology Today, 1990: Proceedings of the Second International* Congress *on Biblical Archaeology: Pre-Congress Symposium: Population, Production and Power, Jerusalem, June 1990, Supplement*, eds. A. Biran and J. Aviram. Jerusalem: Israel Exploration Society.

Shanks, H.
1986 BAR Interviews Avraham Eitan: Israel Antiquities Director Confronts Problems and Controversies. *Biblical Archaeology Review* 12/4: 30–38.

Sheehan, J. F. X.
1981 *Religion and Cult: A Translation of Sigmund Mowinckel's Religion og Kultus.* Orig. 1950. Milwaukee: Marquette University.

Shiloh, Y.
1979 Iron Age Sanctuaries and Cult Elements in Palestine. Pp. 147–57 in *Symposia Celebrating the Seventy-Fifth Anniversary of the Founding of the American Schools of Oriental Research (1900–1975)*, ed. F. M. Cross. Cambridge, MA: American Schools of Oriental Research.
1993 Megiddo. Pp. 1016–24 in *The New Encyclopedia of Archaeological Excavation in the Holy Land*, Vol. 3, ed. E. Stern. Jerusalem: Israel Exploration Society and Carta.

Singer, I.
1983 Takuhlinu and Haya: Two Governors in the Ugarit Letter from Tel Aphek. *Tel Aviv* 10: 3–25.
1988 Merneptah's Campaign to Canaan and the Egyptian Occupation of the Southern Coastal Plain of Palestine in the Ramesside Period. *Bulletin of the American Schools of Oriental Research* 269: 1–10.
1988/89 The Political Status of Megiddo VIIA. *Tel Aviv* 15: 101–12.

Smith, M. L.
1990 *The Early History of God: Yahweh and the Other Deities in Ancient Israel.* San Francisco: Harper and Row.

Speiser, E. A.
1964 *The Anchor Bible: Genesis.* Garden City, NY: Doubleday.

Spriggs, M.
1984 Another Way of Telling: Marxist Perspectives in Archaeology. Pp. 1–9 in *Marxist Perspectives in Archaeology*, ed. M. Spriggs. New Directions in Archaeology. Cambridge: Cambridge University.

Spriggs, M., ed.
1984 *Marxist Perspectives in Archaeology.* New Directions in Archaeology. Cambridge: Cambridge University.

Stager, L. E.
1991 When Canaanites and Philistines Ruled Ashkelon. *Biblical Archaeology Review* 17/2: 24–43.

Stager, L. E. and Wolff, S. R.
1981 Production and Commerce in Temple Courtyards: An Olive Press

in the Sacred Precinct at Tel Dan. *Bulletin of the American Schools of Oriental Research* 243: 95–102.

Stern, E.
1984   *Excavations at Tel Mevorakh (1973–1976), Part Two: The Bronze Age*. Qedem 18. Jerusalem: Institute of Archaeology, Hebrew University of Jerusalem.

1990a   New Evidence from Dor for the First Appearance of the Phoenicians along the Northern Coast of Israel. *Bulletin of the American Schools of Oriental Research* 279: 27–34.

1990b   Shumacher's Shrine in Building 338 at Megiddo: A Rejoinder. *Israel Exploration Journal* 40: 102–7.

1993   Kedesh, Tel (In Jezreel Valley). P. 860 *The New Encyclopedia of Archaeological Excavation in the Holy Land*, Vol. 3, ed. E. Stern. Jerusalem: Israel Exploration Society and Carta.

Stern, E., ed.
1993   *The New Encyclopedia of Archaeological Excavation in the Holy Land*. 4 vols. Jerusalem: Israel Exploration Society and Carta.

Stern, E. and Beit Arieh, I.
1973   Excavations at Tel Kedesh (Tell Abu Qudeis). Pp. xiv–xv (English) and 93–122 (Hebrew) in *Excavations and Studies: Essays in Honour of Professor Shemuel Yeivin*, ed. Y. Aharoni. Tel Aviv: Institute of Archaeology, Tel Aviv University.

1979   Excavations at Tel Kedesh (Tell Abu Qudeis). *Tel Aviv* 6: 1–25.

Tadmor, M.
1982   Female Cult Figurines in Late Canaan and Early Israel. Pp. 139–73 in *Studies in the Period of David and Solomon and Other Essays*, ed. T. Ishida. Winona Lake, IN: Eisenbrauns/Tokyo: Yamakawa–Shuppansha.

1989   The "Cult Standard" from Hazor in a New Light. *Eretz-Israel* 20 (Y. Yadin volume): 86–89 (Hebrew), 197* (English summary).

Tarler, D., Lipovitz, G. and Cahill, J.
1986   Tell el-Ḥammah—1985. *Excavations and Surveys in Israel 1985* 4: 41–42.

1991   Tell el-Ḥammah—1988. *Excavations and Surveys in Israel 1989/1990* 9: 134–35.

Tarragon, J.–M., de
1980   *Le culte à Ugarit: d'après les textes de la pratique en cunéiforme alphabétiques*. Cahiers de la Review Biblique 19. Paris: Gabalda.

Taylor, J. G.
1988   The Two Earliest Known Representations of Yahweh. Pp. 557–66 in *Ascribe to the Lord: Biblical and Other Studies in Memory of Peter C. Craigie*, eds. L. Eslinger and G. Taylor. Journal for the

Study of the Old Testament Supplement Series 67. Sheffield: Sheffield.

Teissier, B.
1990   The Seal Impression Alalakh 194: A New Aspect of Egypto–Levantine Relations in the Middle Kingdom. *Levant* 22: 65–73.

Thompson, R. J.
1963   *Penitence and Sacrifice in Early Israel outside the Levitical Law: An Examination of the Fellowship Theory of Early Israelite Sacrifice*. Leiden: Brill.

Tigay, J. H.
1987   Israelite Religion: The Onomastic and Epigraphic Evidence. Pp. 157–94 in *Ancient Israelite Religion: Essays in Honor of Frank Moore Cross*, eds. P. D. Miller, Jr., P. D. Hanson and S. D. McBride. Philadelphia: Fortress.

Toeg, A.
1973   Numbers 15:22–31—Midrash Halakha. *Tarbiz* 43: 1–10.

Toombs, L. E.
1976   The Stratification of Tell Balâtah (Shechem). *Bulletin of the American Schools of Oriental Research* 223: 57–59.
1979   Shechem: Problems of the Early Israelite Era. Pp. 69–83 in *Symposia Celebrating the Seventy–fifth Anniversary of the Founding of the American Schools of Oriental Research (1900–1975)*, ed. F. M. Cross. Cambridge, MA: ASOR.

Toombs, L. E. and Wright, G. E.
1963   The Fourth Campaign at Balâtah (Shechem). *Bulletin of the American Schools of Oriental Research* 169: 1–60.

Toorn, K. van der
1994   *From Her Cradle to Her Grave: The Role of Religion in the Life of the Israelite and the Babylonian Woman*. Trans. S. J. Denning–Bolle. Sheffield: Sheffield Academic/JSOT.
1995   Theology, Priests, and Worship in Canaan and Ancient Israel. Pp. 2043–58 in *Civilizations of the Ancient Near East*, Vol. 3, ed. J. M. Sasson. New York: Scribner's.

Torczyner (Tur–Sinai), H., et al.
1938   *Lachish I: Tel Lachish Letters*. London: Oxford University.

Tubb, J. N.
1983   The MBIIA Period in Palestine: Its Relationship with Syria and Its Origin. *Levant* 15: 49–62.
1993   Sa'idiyeh, Tell es: British Museum Excavations. Pp. 1297–1300 in *The New Encyclopedia of Archaeological Excavation in the Holy Land*, Vol. 4, ed. E. Stern. Jerusalem: Israel Exploration Society and Carta.

Tufnell, O., Inge, C. H. and Harding, L.
1940   *Lachish II (Tell ed Duweir): The Fosse Temple.* London: Oxford.
Tushingham, A. D.
1997   Dibon. Pp. 156–58 in *The Oxford Encyclopedia of Archaeology in the Near East*, Vol. 2, ed. E. M. Meyers. Oxford: Oxford University.
Ussishkin, D.
1966   Building IV in Hamah and the Temples of Solomon and Tell Tayinat. *Israel Exploration Journal* 16: 104–10.
1978a Lachish: Renewed Archaeological Excavations. *Expedition* 20: 18–28.
1978b Excavations at Tel Lachish—1973–1977: Preliminary Report. *Tel Aviv* 5: 1–97.
1983   Excavations at Tel Lachish—1978–1983: Second Preliminary Report. *Tel Aviv* 10: 97–175.
1985   Level VII and VI at Tel Lachish and the End of the Late Bronze Age in Canaan. Pp. 213–30 in *Palestine in the Bronze and Iron Ages: Papers in Honour of Olga Tufnell*, ed. J. N. Tubb. London: Institute of Archaeology.
1988   The Date of the Judaean Shrine at Arad. *Israel Exploration Journal* 38: 142–57.
1989   Shumacher's Shrine in Building 338 at Megiddo. *Israel Exploration Journal* 39: 149–72.
1993a Fresh Examination of Old Excavations: Sanctuaries of the First Temple Period. Pp. 67–85 in *Biblical Archaeology Today, 1990: Proceedings of the Second International Congress on Biblical Archaeology, Jerusalem, June–July 1990*, eds. A. Biran and J. Aviram. Jerusalem: Israel Exploration Society and Israel Academy of Sciences and Humanities.
1993b Lachish. Pp. 897–911 *The New Encyclopedia of Archaeological Excavation in the Holy Land*, Vol. 3, ed. E. Stern. Jerusalem: Israel Exploration Society and Carta.
1997a Lachish. Pp. 317–23 in *The Oxford Encyclopedia of Archaeology in the Near East*, Vol. 3, ed. E. M. Meyers. Oxford: Oxford University.
1997b Megiddo. Pp. 460–69 in *The Oxford Encyclopedia of Archaeology in the Near East*, Vol. 3, ed. E. M. Meyers. New York and London: Oxford University.
Van Seters, J.
1975   *Abraham in History and Tradition.* New Haven: Yale University.
1983   *In Search of History.* New Haven: Yale University.

Vaughan, P. H.
1974 *The Meaning of "Bama" in the Old Testament: A Study of Etymological, Textual and Archaeological Evidence*. Society for Old Testament Study Monograph Series 3. Cambridge: Cambridge University.

Vaux, R., de
1957 Les fouilles de Tell el-Farʿah près Naplouse. *Revue biblique* 64: 552–80.
1961 *Ancient Israel: Its Life and Institutions*. New York: McGraw-Hill.
1964 *Studies in Old Testament Sacrifice*. Cardiff: University of Wales.
1970 On Right and Wrong Uses of Archaeology. Pp. 64–80 in *Near Eastern Archaeology in the Twentieth Century: Essays in Honor of Nelson Glueck*, ed. J. A. Sanders. Garden City, NY: Doubleday.
1976 El–Farʿa, Tell, North. Pp. 395–404 in *Encyclopedia of Archaeological Excavations in the Holy Land*, Vol. 2, ed. M. Avi-Yonah. Englewood Cliffs, NJ: Prentice–Hall.

Vos, G. A., de and Suarez–Orozco, M. M.
1987 Sacrifice and the Experience of Power. *The Journal of Psychoanalytic Anthropology* 10: 309–40.

Vriezen, T. C.
1967 *The Religion of Ancient Israel*. London: Lutterworth.

Wachsman, S.
1996 *Seagoing Ships and Seamanship in the Bronze Age Levant*. College Station, TX: Texas A&M University and London: Chatham.

Weinfeld, M.
1992 Deuteronomy, Book of. Pp. 168–83 in *The Anchor Bible Dictionary*, Vol. 2, ed. D. N. Freedman. New York: Doubleday.

Weinstein, J. M.
1975 Egyptian Relations with Palestine in the Middle Kingdom. *Bulletin of the American Schools of Oriental Research* 217: 1–16.
1980 Was Tell Abu–Hawam a 19th–Century Egyptian Naval Base? *Bulletin of the American Schools of Oriental Research* 238: 43–46.
1981 The Egyptian Empire in Palestine: A Reassessment. *Bulletin of the American Schools of Oriental Research* 241: 1–28.
1992 The Chronology of Palestine in the Early Second Millennium B.C.E. *Bulletin of the American Schools of Oriental Research* 288: 27–46.

Wellhausen, J.
1957 *Prologomena to the History of Ancient Israel*, with Preface by W. Robertson Smith. Edinburgh: Adams and Charles Black, 1885.

Reprinted 1957. New York: Meridian Books. Orig. 1883.

Wheeler, R. E. M.
1954 *Archaeology from the Earth*. Oxford: Clarendon.

Whiting, R. M.
1995 Amorite Tribes and Nations of Second–Millennium Western Asia. Pp. 1231–42 in *Civilizations of the Ancient Near East*, Vol. 2, ed. J. M. Sasson. New York: Scribner's.

Whybray, N.
1987 *The Making of the Pentateuch*. Journal for the Study of the Old Testament Supplement Series 53. Sheffield: Sheffield Academic.

Willett, E. A. R.
1999 *Women and Household Shrines in Ancient Israel*. Unpublished Ph.D. dissertation, University of Arizona.

Wilson, R. R.
1984 *Sociological Approaches to the Old Testament*. Philadelphia: Fortress.

Wimmer, D.
1990 Egyptian Temples in Canaan and Sinai. Pp. 1065–1106 in *Studies in Egyptology Presented to Miriam Lichtheim, Vol. II*, ed. S. Israelit–Groll. Jerusalem: Magnes Press, Hebrew University of Jerusalem.
1997 Ṣafuṭ, Tell. Pp. 448–50 in *The Oxford Encyclopedia of Archaeology in the Near East*, Vol. 4, ed. E. M. Meyers. Oxford: Oxford University.

Woolley, L.
1955 *Alalakh: An Account of the Excavations at Tell Atchana in the Hatay, 1937–1939*. Oxford: Oxford University.

Wright, G. E.
1960 *Biblical Archaeology*, abr. ed. Philadelphia: Westminster.
1965 *Shechem: The Biography of a Biblical City*. New York: McGraw–Hill.
1971 Biblical Archaeology Today. Pp. 149–65 in *New Directions in Biblical Archaeology*, eds. D. N. Freedman and J. C. Greenfield. Garden City, NY: Doubleday.
1978 Shechem. Pp. 1083–94 in *Encyclopedia of Archaeological Excavations in the Holy Land*, Vol. 4, eds. M. Avi-Yonah and E. Stern. Englewood Cliffs, NJ: Prentice–Hall.

Wright, G. R. H.
1966 The Bronze Age Temple at Amman. *Zeitschrift für die Alttestamentliche Wissenschaft* 78: 351–57.
1971 Pre-Israelite Temples in the Land of Canaan. *Palestine Exploration Quarterly* 103: 17–32.

1975 Temples at Shechem—A Detail. *Zeitschrift für die Alttestamentliche Wissenschaft* 87: 56–64.

Yadin, Y.
1958 Solomon's City Wall and Gate at Gezer. *Israel Exploration Journal* 8: 80–86.
1969 The Fifth Season of Excavations at Hazor, 1968–1969. *Biblical Archaeologist* 32 (1969) 50–71.
1972 *Hazor, the Head of All Those Kingdoms.* London: Oxford University.
1975 *Hazor: The Rediscovery of a Great Citadel of the Bible.* London: Weidenfeld and Nicolson.
1976a Beer–sheba: The High Place Destroyed by King Josiah. *Bulletin of the American Schools of Oriental Research* 222: 5–17.
1976b Hazor. Pp. 474–95 in *Encyclopedia of Archaeological Excavations in the Holy Land*, Vol. 2, ed. M. Avi-Yonah. Englewood Cliffs, NJ: Prentice–Hall.
1978 The Nature of the Settlements During the Middle Bronze IIA Period in Israel. *Zeitschrift des deutschen Palästina–Vereins* 94: 1–23.

Yadin, Y., Aharoni, A., Amiran, R., Dothan, T., Dunayevsky, I. And Perrot, J.
1958 Hazor I: An Account of the First Season of Excavations, 1955. Jerusalem: Magnes.
1960 *Hazor II: An Account of the Second Season of Excavations, 1956.* Jerusalem: Magnes.

Yadin, Y., Aharoni, Y., Amiran, R., Dothan, M., Dothan, T., Dunayevsky, I., and Perrot, J.
1961 *Hazor III–IV: An Account of the Third and Fourth Seasons of Excavations, 1957–1958.* Jerusalem: Magnes.

Yadin, Y., Aharoni, Y., Amiran, R., Ben-Tor, A., Dothan, M., Dothan, T., Dunayevsky, I., Geva, S. and Stern, E.
1989 *Hazor III–IV: An Account of the Third and Fourth Seasons of Excavations, 1957–1958, Text*, ed. A. Ben-Tor. Jerusalem: Israel Exploration Society.

Yannai, E.
1996 A New Approach to Levels VI–V at Tel Beth-Shan. *Tel Aviv* 23: 185–94.

Yassine, K.
1984 The Open Court Sanctuary of the Iron Age I *Tell el-Mazar* Mound A. *Palestine Exploration Quarterly* 118: 108–18.
1988a El Mabrak: An Architectural Analogue of the Amman Airport Building. Pp. 61–64 in *Archaeology of Jordan: Essays and*

Reports. Amman: Department of Archaeology, University of Jordan.

1988b The Open Court Sanctuary of the Iron Age I *Tell El-Mazar* Mound A. Pp. 115–35 in *Archaeology of Jordan: Essays and Reports*. Amman: Department of Archaeology, University of Jordan.

Yeivan, S.

1966 On the Use and Misuse of Archaeology in Interpreting the Bible. *American Academy for Jewish Research Proceedings* 34: 141–54.

1973 Temples That Were Not. *Eretz-Israel* 11 (I. Dunayevsky volume): 28* (English summary), 163–75 (Hebrew).

Yoffee. N.

1978 Review of T. O. Beidelman, *W. Robertson Smith and the Sociological Study of Religion*. *Journal of the American Oriental Society* 93: 309–10.

1982 Social History and Historical Method in the Late Old Babylonian Period. *Journal of the American Oriental Society* 102: 347–53.

Yon, M.

1984 Sanctuaires d'Ougarit. Pp. 37–50 in *Temples et sanctuaires*, ed. G. Roux. Travaux de la Maison de l'Orient 7. Lyon: Maison de l'Orient Méditerranéen.

1992 Ugarit: The Urban Habitat—The Present State of the Archaeological Picture. *Bulletin of the American Schools of Oriental Research* 286: 19–34.

1997 Ugarit. Pp. 255–62 in *The Oxford Encyclopedia of Archaeology in the Near East*, Vol. 5, ed. E. M. Meyers. Oxford: Oxford University.

Zertal, A.

1986/87 An Early Iron Age Cultic Site on Mt. Ebal: Excavation Seasons 1982–1987. *Tel Aviv* 13–14: 105–65.

1993 Ebal, Mount. Pp. 375–77 in *The New Encyclopedia of Archaeological Excavation in the Holy Land*, Vol. 1, ed. E. Stern. Jerusalem: Israel Exploration Society and Carta.

INDEX

A

Abraham, 7
Acropolis, 88–89, 124–25, 136, 155, 171, 196
Aegean, 35
Ahab, 59, 77, 184
Ahaz, 63
Ahimelech, 56
'Ai, 47, 173, 176, 192
'Ain Dara, 197
Alalakh, 6, 8, 84, 87, 90, 92, 107–8, 110, 112, 114, 116–17, 123, 127
Aleppo, 117, 127
Altar, 40, 43–44, 47–50, 52–54, 57, 59–61, 64, 66–67, 70, 74, 81–82, 88, 93–95, 98, 100, 103, 117, 124–29, 136–38, 140–41, 144–45, 147, 151, 153, 162, 170–71, 177–80, 182, 184–88, 191, 194, 197–200
Amenophis II, 6, 151
Amenophis III, 151, 157
Amenophis IV, 157
Amman, 154
Amman Airport, 117–18, 140, 156–59
Ammon, 58, 164–65, 168
Amon, 121
    temple of, 149
Amorites, 7, 8, 82
Amos, 57, 62, 64, 197
Anat, 146, 178
Anatolia, 123

Animal bones, 43, 94–96, 99–100, 102, 105–6, 126, 129, 138, 140–42, 147, 149, 151, 170, 174, 179, 184, 197
Animals. *See also* Birds; Cattle; Goats; Sheep
    dog, 106, 148
    domestic, 32, 37
    donkey, 100
    horse, 143
    lion, 88, 127, 130, 146, 151, 173, 186, 199
    lioness, 131, 143
    monkeys, 94
    puppy, 106
    sea fish, 148
    snake, 102, 106, 128, 131, 138, 145–46, 172, 184
Anthropology, 1, 19, 26
Anthropomorphism, 39
Aphek, 95, 121, 150–51, 153
Aqhat Epic, 39
Arad, 186–87, 191, 193, 195, 200
Aramaeans, 197
Architecture, 8, 15, 83, 135, 153
    defensive, 97
    domestic, 91
    Egyptian-style, 137
    maritime, 143
    public, 171
    religious, 35–36, 83, 90, 96, 108–9, 114–15, 170, 176, 202
Ark, 53–56, 69–70, 75, 163, 171
Ashdod, 105, 121, 150–51, 153, 197
Asherah, 52, 146–47, 158, 178, 189, 191, 199

Ashkelon, 101, 105–7, 112, 114, 121, 150, 153, 170
ʿAshtoret, 158
Assyria, 61–62, 67, 77, 123, 166
Astarte, 146, 149–50, 157–58, 178, 184, 198
Avaris, 99. *See also* Tell el-Dabʿa

B

Baal, 39, 58–60, 63, 124, 156, 170, 178, 189, 196
  priests of, 60
  temple of, 92, 123–25
Baal Hadad, 170
Babylon, 138
Balaam, 49, 196
Balaam inscription, 199
Bāmâ, bāmôt, במה, במות, 3–4, 50–51, 54, 56, 58–59, 61, 63, 67, 69, 71, 76–77, 79, 161–68, 171, 183, 191–97, 203
Baqʿah Valley, 140, 154. *See also* Khirbet Umm ad-Danānīr; Tell Ṣafuṭ
Bashan, 155
Bat Yam, 92, 95, 107, 112–14, 117
Beersheba, 47–48, 177, 187, 191, 193
Beit Afula, 197
Beitsaida, 197
Benjaminites, 52
Beth Shean, 98, 104, 107, 119, 135–38, 148–49, 152–54, 157, 170, 179, 181–82, 197
Beth Shean Valley, 135, 180
Beth Shemesh, 54–55, 98. *See also* Givat Sharett
Bethel, 47, 48, 56, 58–59, 62, 67, 69, 76, 164–67, 184, 191, 193, 196–97, 203
Bethlehem, 196
Bible, 1, 8, 10–16, 21, 154, 161, 168, 201. *See also* Hebrew Bible (HB); Tanakh
Biblical archaeology, 2
Birds, 47, 71, 106
  dove, 94
  duck, 148
  pigeon, 148
Bull, 40, 42, 52, 54, 60, 104, 106, 128, 143, 156, 170, 179. *See also* Calf; Cattle; Cow
Bull Site, 170–71, 176, 192, 197
Byblos, 87, 90–94, 96–97, 107–8, 110, 112, 114, 128

C

Calf, 106. *See also* Bull; Cattle; Cow
Canaan, 6–8, 84, 96, 113, 119, 122
Canaanites, 7–8
Carchemish, 117, 127
Cattle, 26, 65, 94, 129, 149, 180. *See also* Bull; Calf; Cow
Central Highlands, 84, 103–4, 116, 121, 140–41, 152, 168, 173, 176
Ceramics, 96–97, 105–6, 115–17, 123, 125, 129–31, 138–43, 145, 147–49, 157, 159, 170–73, 177–79, 181–82, 186, 188, 199. *See also* Pottery
Chemosh, 58, 196
City of David, 54. *See also* Jerusalem
City-state, 6, 8, 17, 105, 108–9, 112, 116, 121–23, 148, 168
Clan, 3–4, 8, 23, 39, 57, 73, 82, 89, 91, 93, 101–2, 105, 109, 111–12, 115, 118, 123, 125, 132, 135–36, 152, 154, 163, 166, 170, 192–93, 196, 202–3
Clergy, 23, 39, 63, 72, 127, 129, 135, 167. *See also* Priesthood

INDEX

Coast
  Mediterranean, 95
  Phoenician, 155
Coastal sites, 84, 90, 96, 102, 117
Courtyard, 88, 90–91, 94, 96,
  99–100, 103–6, 110, 124,
  126–27, 129, 135–36, 138–41,
  143–45, 147–48, 177, 179–82,
  184–88, 198
Cow, 54–55, 129, 173. *See also*
  Bull; Calf; Cattle
Crucible, 96, 145
Cult
  Canaanite, 161
  domestic, 125, 131, 189
  Egypto-Canaanite, 100
  of the dead, 117, 130, 190, 192.
    See also Funerary customs;
    Mortuary practices
  royal, 59, 64, 154, 166–67, 184,
    202
Cult stand, 124–25, 172–73, 179,
  182, 198
Cyprus, 105

D

D (documentary source), 46. *See also* Deuteronomistic writers
Dagan, 39
  temple of, 89, 92, 123–25
Damascus Gate, 151
Dan, 58–59, 62, 76, 92, 94–95, 97,
  110, 112, 118, 162, 165–67,
  172, 176–77, 179, 184–85,
  191–94, 196, 200, 203
Danel, 39
David, 1, 53–56, 58, 68, 75–76,
  164–65, 178, 180–82, 192, 195
  House of, 58, 62
Day of Atonement, 45
Deir el-Balah, 137, 149
Deposit, 95–97, 116. *See also*
  Foundation deposit
Deuteronomistic writers, 44, 46,
  50–52, 57, 62, 65–66, 68–69,
  72, 74, 77–78, 161, 163,
  166–67. *See also* D (documentary source)
Deuteronomistic Historians (DH),
  3, 57–58, 61, 63, 66–68, 72,
  75, 165, 192, 195, 197
Dibon, 196
Divided Monarchy, 45–46, 57, 63,
  165–66, 168, 179, 183,
  186–87, 191–94, 196, 200, 203
Documentary Hypothesis, 46
Dothan, 170

E

E (documentary source), 46, 50–51,
  53, 55, 57, 77. *See also* Elohist
Ebla, 8, 84, 87–89, 92, 97–98,
  107–8, 110, 112, 114, 117, 128
Economic organization, 31, 164
Economy, 16, 26, 30, 43, 98, 123
Edom, 168
Edomites, 197
Egypt, 1, 4, 6–7, 46, 48, 62, 64, 71,
  84, 87, 90–93, 96, 99, 101,
  104–5, 108, 114, 119, 121–23,
  126, 132, 135, 137–40, 146,
  149–53, 155, 157–58
Ein Gedi, 83
El, 39, 158, 170
Elat, 147–48, 150, 158
Elijah, 57, 60, 63, 68, 77
Elisha, 63, 68, 76
Elite class, 4, 36, 83, 87, 89, 97,
  108, 110, 113–15, 133, 152,
  155, 193, 202
Elohist, 3, 45–46, 48–52, 54–55, 74,
  196. *See also* E (documentary source)
'En Gev, 197

Esau, 49
Esdraelon Valley, 198
Ethnography, 15, 17
Expiation, 24, 40–41, 71, 77
Ezekiel, 70–71, 77

F

Faunal remains, 15, 32, 148, 179
Favissa, favissae, 100–101, 103, 105–6, 127, 144, 147–48, 157, 179, 190
Festival, 52–53, 57–59, 63, 66, 73, 75, 202. *See also* Ḥag
Figurine, 11, 90–91, 93–97, 99, 116, 125, 128, 140, 142–43, 145–48, 157, 170, 172–74, 178–79, 181, 184, 186–89, 191, 198–99
First Temple, 4, 57, 67, 75, 78. *See also* Jerusalem Temple; Solomonic Temple
Foundation deposit, 94, 137, 198. *See also* Deposit.
Funerary customs, 89, 100, 133. *See also* Cult of the dead; Mortuary practices

G

Galilee, 98, 118, 172, 198
Gate, 89–91, 103, 106, 126, 132, 136, 185, 187, 190, 199
Gateway shrine, 106, 107
Gaza, 121, 149–50, 153, 158
Geshurites, 197
Gezer, 17, 92, 94, 97, 101, 105, 107, 110, 112, 114, 117–18, 121, 125–26, 152, 194
Gideon, 52, 170
Gift, 20–23, 25, 33, 55, 62, 83, 121, 158
Gilat, 36, 83

Givat Sharett, 97–98, 100, 107, 112, 114. *See also* Beth Shemesh
Goat, 32, 94, 96, 106, 142, 147, 149, 174, 177, 179. *See also* Sheep
Golden Calf, 49, 199

H

Hadad, 129
Ḥag, גח, 49, 59, 68. *See also* Festival
Hama, 84
Hathor, 146, 159
Hatti, 122, 134. *See also* Hittites
Hazael, 61
Hazor, 17, 87, 97–98, 100–102, 107–8, 110, 112, 114–16, 118–19, 122, 126–32, 144, 152–56, 159, 170–72, 176, 189, 191–92, 194, 198
Hebrew Bible (HB), 3–5, 16–17, 22, 37, 39, 44–46, 49–51, 72–74, 77, 143, 154, 162–64, 176, 193, 201. *See also* Bible; Tanakh
Hezekiah, 60–63, 65–67, 77–78, 166–67, 187, 200
High Place, 49, 93–94, 194. *See also* Bāmâ
Hittites, 7, 119, 122–23, 153–54, 157, 159, 174, 178. *See also* Hatti
Ḥorvat Qitmit, 197
Hosea, 57, 64
Household shrine, 134, 190–91
Hyksos, 99

I

Industry, 97, 173, 181, 183. *See also* Workshop
Isaiah, 57, 64, 76, 196

Isis, 151
  temple of, 151
Israel, 1, 6–7, 37, 39–40, 44, 45, 48–52, 56–60, 62–67, 69, 71–74, 77–78, 84, 115, 146, 163–68, 170, 176, 180, 183, 190–94, 196–97, 203
Israelites, 2–3, 10, 17, 24, 28–29, 40, 46–47, 51–52, 56, 58, 63, 66–69, 72, 74, 118, 162, 165, 170–71, 174, 176, 180, 191–92, 195, 197–98, 201

J

J (documentary source), 46–47, 50–51, 54, 71, 74. *See also* Yahwist
Jacob, 48–49
Jaffa, 95, 121–22, 151, 153
JE (documentary source), 78
Jebel el-Rubka, 101, 104, 107, 118
Jehoiada, 61
Jehu, 59
Jeremiah, 57
Jeroboam I, 51, 58–59, 165–66, 184, 193, 196, 199
Jeroboam II, 185, 188
Jerusalem, 1, 12, 51, 54–59, 61–62, 65, 67, 74–77, 150–53, 162–67, 176, 183, 186–87, 190–91, 193, 195, 203. *See also* City of David
Jerusalem Cave 1, 190, 193
Jerusalem Temple, 30, 55, 56, 60, 62–63, 68–69, 72, 77–78, 164–67, 191, 196. *See also* First Temple; Solomonic Temple
Jethro, 49
Jewelry, 30, 43, 91, 94, 97, 104, 135, 138, 140, 142–43, 145, 147, 149, 159, 173

Jezreel Valley, 118, 136, 181
Joash, 60–61
Jordan, 6–7, 84, 154, 168, 175, 197. *See also* Transjordan
Jordan River, 6, 98, 99
Jordan Valley, 8, 96, 113–14, 118–19, 136, 138–40, 154, 157, 179, 181–82, 188, 198
Joshua, 74, 197
Josiah, 60, 62–63, 65, 67, 166–67, 187, 197, 200
Judah, 1, 4, 29, 44, 51, 57–59, 61–64, 66–67, 76–77, 163, 166–68, 183, 190–91, 193, 196

K

Kamid el-Loz, 128
Kedesh, 193
Kfar Rupin, 97, 99–100, 107–8, 110, 112, 114
Kfar Shemaryahu, 92, 95, 107, 112, 113–14
Khirbet Raddana, 173–74, 176
Khirbet Umm ad-Danānīr, 140, 154. *See also* Baqʿah Valley; Tell Ṣafuṭ
Kiln, 96
Kingship, 58, 73, 202. *See also* Monarchy; Royalty
Kirta Epic, 39
Kourbánia, 23–24, 32–33, 37
Kuntillet ʿAjrud, 189, 191, 193

L

Lachish, 22, 119, 121, 126, 134, 136–37, 139, 145–50, 153, 178–79, 182–83, 193
Lebanon, 6–8, 84, 123, 168
Levant, 5, 6, 66, 108, 112, 118, 122
Levites, 56, 65, 165–66, 196
Liver models, 157
Loom weights, 180

M

Makmish, 197
Manasseh, 170
Manoah, 52
Mari, 6, 8, 84, 87, 89, 92, 106, 108, 112, 114
Maṣṣebâ, maṣṣebôt, מצבות, מצבה, 44, 48–50, 64, 78, 82, 91, 96, 103, 105, 110, 115, 117, 141, 162, 170–71, 174, 177, 179, 185, 202. *See also* Obelisk; Standing stone
Mediterranean, 123
Megiddo, 11, 17, 83, 92–97, 100–102, 107–8, 110, 112–14, 117–18, 121, 131, 133–35, 150, 152–53, 156, 172–73, 176–78, 182–83, 188, 192–94, 198, 200
Mekal Stele, 157
Memphis, 151
Meremoth, 200
Merneptah, 121
Merneptah Stele, 6
Mesha, 196
Mesha Stele, 76
Mesopotamia, 6, 84, 87, 111, 118
Metal, 42–43, 75, 90, 94, 96–97, 117, 128, 139, 143, 182, 199
Metalworking, 110, 172–73, 176
Min, 149
Minet el-Beida, 125
Minḥâ, מנחה, 21–22, 27, 47, 52, 60–61, 64, 76
Mitanni, 138
Moab, 60, 77–78, 164–65, 168, 196
Molech, 58
Monarchy, 9, 44, 46, 50, 53, 57, 62, 64, 67, 133, 161, 166–67, 176, 178–79, 182–83, 185, 188, 193, 196

Mortuary practices, 101. *See also* Funerary customs
Moses, 7
Mt. Ebal, 74, 197–98
Mt. Gerizim, 74, 103, 115, 117, 117–18, 158, 197. *See also* Shechem

N

Nahariya, 92–97, 100–101, 107, 110, 112–15, 117, 125–26, 152, 194
Nebuchadnezzar, 76, 187
Necromancy, 192
Negev, 9, 36, 82, 106
Neo-Hittites, 178
New Testament, 1, 12
Noah, 17, 47, 71

O

Obelisk, 90, 96, 110, 117. *See also* Maṣṣebâ; Standing stone
Offerings, 4, 23, 25, 30, 40–45, 60–62, 65–66, 68–69, 71, 73, 76, 90–91, 96–97, 128, 142, 145–46, 150, 170, 174, 179, 185–86, 192, 199. *See also* Sacrifice; Substitution; Votives
ʿolâ, ʿōlōt, עולה, עולת, 26, 42, 47, 49, 51–52, 54–56, 58, 60, 63, 65, 67–68, 73
Old Testament, 1, 12
Olive oil, 184, 199
Omri, 59
Open-air sanctuary, 82, 90, 104, 107, 118, 126, 129, 132, 141, 153, 162–63, 179–80, 192, 197, 202
Ophrah-of-the-Abiezrites, 52

P

P (documentary source), 46, 70–72, 74, 78, 195. *See also* Priestly
Palace, 17, 43, 61–62, 73, 82–83, 89–91, 93, 98, 101–3, 106–7, 111–14, 116–17, 123–25, 131, 133–35, 148, 152–53, 156–57, 177, 195–98, 202
Palestine, 1, 6, 12–13, 17, 84, 119, 121, 155, 195
Palestinian Entity, 7
Papyrus Wilbour, 151
Pella, 101, 104, 107–8, 110, 112, 114, 138, 152, 179
Pharaoh, 47–48
Philistia, 197
Philistines, 54–55, 68, 197. *See also* Sea Peoples
Phoenicia, 73, 197
Phoenicians, 197
Phylakopi, 35
Pilgrimage, 4, 52–54, 57–59, 66, 82–83, 104, 114, 152, 176, 202–3
Pottery, 15, 78, 95–97, 99–100, 102, 104–5, 127, 130–31, 135, 137–43, 145, 147–48, 156–57, 159, 179, 181, 185–86, 190
  Mycenaean, 129–30, 143–44
Priesthood, 30, 41, 44, 56, 59, 60–64, 66, 72, 76, 96, 129, 166–67, 185–86, 192, 203. *See also* Clergy
Priestly, 3, 29–30, 40, 44, 46, 51, 54–55, 57, 66, 69–73, 77–78, 195. *See also* P (documentary source)
Propitiation, 24, 41
Pseudepigrapha, 1
Ptah, 150
Purification, 41–43, 48, 69, 71, 73

Q

Qudshu, 146, 149
Queen Tiy, 151

R

Rameses II, 121, 151, 157, 182
Rameses III, 121, 150, 182, 199
Rameses VI, 135
Rameses VIII, 182
Rehoboam, 196
Reshef, 91, 138, 148–49, 157
Rhyta, 125
Ritual, 3–4, 20, 22–24, 26–27, 30, 33, 35–36, 40–44, 46–49, 51–53, 55–57, 60, 67–69, 72, 162, 179–85, 190–91, 194, 199
Royalty, 3, 37, 39, 60, 62, 92, 98, 102, 123, 154, 183, 203. *See also* Kingship; Monarchy

S

Sacred structure, 3, 81–82, 87–91, 101–2, 107, 109, 112, 114, 116, 123, 129, 131, 135–36, 142, 168, 179, 189
Sacrifice, 3–4, 19, 20–35, 37, 136, 144, 148–49, 163, 179, 194, 199, 201–2. *See also* Offering; Substitution; Votive
  child, 192
Samaria, 59–60, 76, 189, 193
Samaria Locus E 207, 190–91, 193
Sarepta, 197
Scapegoat, 21
Sea Peoples, 119. *See also* Philistines
Seals, 128, 137, 139, 143, 145, 147, 179, 181
Second Temple, 30
Sennacherib, 166
Serabit el-Khadim, 159

Sesostris I, 116–17
Seti I, 126, 137, 182
Sharon Plain, 95
Shechem, 47–48, 59, 76, 101, 103, 104, 107–8, 110, 112, 114, 118, 131, 140–41, 152–54, 156, 159, 175–76, 192, 196–97. *See also* Mt. Gerizim
Sheep, 42, 65, 68, 94, 96, 106, 142, 147, 149, 174, 177, 180. *See also* Goat
Šelēmîm, שלמים, 49, 51–52, 54–55, 58, 61, 64, 67–68, 73
Shephelah, 119, 146
Shiloh, 52–54, 56, 75–78, 101, 104–5, 107, 115, 141–42, 152, 163, 171, 176, 192
Shishak, 183
Sinai, 9, 82, 155, 160
Social science, 13, 16, 20, 36–37, 161, 163, 195, 201
Social structure, 14, 16, 20, 23, 26–27, 33, 36, 81–82, 84, 93, 100–101, 112, 115, 119, 163–64, 201
Socio-economic structure, 31, 108
Socio-political structure, 2–3, 5, 8, 15, 27, 28, 35, 81, 107–8, 111, 116, 118, 122, 133, 152, 154, 161, 166, 201–3
Sociology, 1, 19–20
Solomon, 58, 67, 77, 182, 193, 200
Solomonic Temple, 51, 57, 176, 183. *See also* First Temple; Jerusalem Temple
Standing stone, 82, 90, 162, 175, 194, 199. *See also Maṣṣebâ*; Obelisk
Stele, stelae, 93, 99, 105, 124–25, 128, 130, 132, 136–37, 151, 158, 177, 182, 186, 196, 199

Substitution, 27, 32, 55, 63, 68–69, 74. *See also* sacrifice
Syria, 6–8, 84, 87–92, 128, 138
Syria-Palestine, 6, 7, 14
Syro-Ephraimite War, 77

T

Taʿanach, 178, 182–83, 188, 193, 198
Tabernacle, 45, 70–71, 75, 78, 172
Tanakh, 1. *See also* Hebrew Bible
Tax, 137, 149–50, 153, 158
Tel ʿAmal, 181, 183, 193
Tel el-ʿAjjul, 106
Tel Haror, 101, 106–8, 110, 112, 114, 149
Tel Kedesh, 188
Tel Kittan, 97, 98–101, 107–8, 110, 112, 114–15, 118, 135–36, 152
Tel Masos, 191
Tel Mevorakh, 136, 143–46, 153, 179
Tel Michal, 197
Tel Miqne/Ekron, 197
Tel Mor, 101, 105, 107, 112, 125, 152
Tel Nami, 143, 154
Tel Qasile, 180, 183, 193, 197
Tel Qiri, 174, 176, 192
Tel Reḥov, 170, 179–80, 183, 193
Tel Seraʿ, 106, 149
Tel Sippor, 197
Tel Tayinat, 197
Tell Abū al-Kharaz, 138–39
Tell Abu Hawam, 142–43, 154, 157, 197
Tell Beit Mirsim, 12, 190–91, 193, 200
Tell Deir ʿAlla, 139–40, 157, 181–82, 199
Tell el-Dabʿa, 87, 99–101, 107, 113–14, 118. *See also* Avaris

Tell el-Farʿah (N), 101, 106–7, 112, 116, 149, 159, 191, 199. *See also* Tirzah
Tell el-Ḥammah, 180–81, 183, 193
Tell el-Hayyat, 92, 95–97, 100–101, 107–8, 110, 112–15
Tell el-Mazar Mound A, 181–83, 193, 199
Tell el-ʿUmeiri, 175–76, 192
Tell el-Wawiyat, 173, 176, 192
Tell en-Nasbeh, 190–91, 193, 200
Tell er-Ras, 199
Tell es-Saʿidiyeh, 159, 175–76, 182, 188–89, 191–93
Tell es-Safi, 121
Tell esh-Shariyah, 121
Tell Halif, 191
Tell Irbid, 175–76, 192
Tell Ṣafuṭ, 140, 154. *See also* Baqʿah Valley; Khirbet Umm ad-Danānīr
Temenos, 99, 124, 126, 134, 144, 159, 184–85, 199
Temple
  bipartite, 90, 100–102, 118, 126–27, 132, 175
  coastal, 154
  Egypto-Canaanite, 4, 119, 122, 137, 146, 149–51, 153, 157
  Fortress, 103, 108, 114, 118, 140, 141, 154, 156, 175
  mortuary, 100
  tripartite, 88, 91, 100, 127, 186
Thutmosis III, 121, 133, 135–36, 151
Tiglath-pileser III, 77, 185
Timna, 159
Tirzah, 170. *See also* Tel el-Farʿah (N)
Trade, 87, 97, 99, 100, 123–24, 139–40, 146–47, 152, 193, 202
Transjordan, 6, 9, 58, 82, 142, 158–59, 188, 196. *See also* Jordan
Tribal group, 7–8, 19, 21, 23, 27, 53, 71, 76, 82–83, 97, 109, 111, 113, 158, 164, 202–3
Tribute, 21, 22, 121, 150
Tuleilat Ghassul, 83

U

Ugarit, 3, 5–6, 8, 17, 30, 39, 41–43, 51, 72–73, 87, 92–94, 96–97, 107, 110, 112, 117, 122–26, 128, 131, 148, 155–56, 170, 201
United Monarchy, 7, 45, 75, 164, 166, 168, 176, 178, 180–83, 192–93, 203

V

Vered Jericho, 187–88, 191, 193
Via Maris, 92, 114, 121, 143–44, 151
Votives, 129–30, 145, 148. *See also* Offerings

W

Workshop, 4, 94, 97, 117, 124, 127, 129, 145, 199. *See also* Industry
  jewelry, 91
  metal, 96, 172–73
  pottery, 127, 130, 138, 186
Worship, 4, 10, 21, 34, 36, 39, 44–48, 50–51, 53, 55, 57–59, 61–65, 67, 69–72, 74–77, 81, 83, 90, 96, 100, 103, 107, 109–10, 112–15, 125–27, 129, 131–32, 135, 139, 141, 146–47, 149–50, 152, 155, 157–58, 161, 163–67, 170, 173–76, 178, 180–81, 183,

185, 189, 191–94, 196, 201–3

Y

Yahweh, 39–40, 47–49, 51–60, 63–69, 71–72, 74–78, 118, 165–67, 170, 178, 185, 187, 189, 191, 195–96, 199
Yahwism, 63–64, 162, 168
Yahwist, 3, 45–47, 50–52, 55, 71, 74–75. *See also* J (documentary source)
Yarim-lim, 90

Z

Zebah, zebāḥim, 27, 47, 53
Zuph, 54, 56, 164

OTHER TITLES IN THIS SERIES

1 Larry G. Herr with Warren C. Trenchard
  Published Pottery of Palestine

2 Itamar Singer
  *Muwatalli's Prayer to the Assembly of Gods through the Storm-God of Lightning (*CTH *381)*

3 Tomis Kapitan (ed.)
  Archaeology, History and Culture in Palestine and the Near East: Essays in Memory of Albert E. Glock

4 Stephen L. Cook and S. C. Winter (eds.)
  On the Way to Nineveh: Studies in Honor of George M. Landes

5 Samuel Wolff (ed.)
  Studies in the Archaeology of Israel and Neighboring Lands in Memory of Douglas L. Esse (published jointly with The Oriental Institute of the University of Chicago)

6 Burton MacDonald
  "East of the Jordan": Territories and Sites of the Hebrew Scriptures